CRITICAL THINKING

Dwyer's book is unique and distinctive as it presents and discusses a modern conceptualization of critical thinking – one that is commensurate with the exponential increase in the annual output of knowledge. The abilities of navigating new knowledge outputs, engaging in enquiry and constructively solving problems are not only important in academic contexts, but are also essential life skills. Specifically, the book provides a modern, detailed, accessible and integrative model of critical thinking that accounts for critical thinking sub-skills and real-world applications; and is commensurate with the standards of 21st-century knowledge. The book provides both opportunities to learn and apply these skills through a series of exercises, as well as guidelines on how critical thinking can be developed and practised, in light of existing psychological research, which can be used to enhance the experience of critical thinking training and facilitate gains in critical thinking ability.

Dr Christopher Dwyer is a post-doctoral researcher and lecturer in the School of Psychology at the National University of Ireland, Galway. In addition to critical thinking, he has worked on a wide array of funded research projects in diverse areas, including instructional design, clinical judgment-making and chronic pain. Dr Dwyer has been teaching critical thinking at university level since 2007. Since 2011, he has written more than ten peer-reviewed published manuscripts on the topic of critical thinking.

Critical Thinking

CONCEPTUAL PERSPECTIVES AND PRACTICAL GUIDELINES

Dr Christopher P. Dwyer

School of Psychology
National University of Ireland, Galway

CAMBRIDGE
UNIVERSITY PRESS

CAMBRIDGE
UNIVERSITY PRESS

University Printing House, Cambridge CB2 8BS, United Kingdom

One Liberty Plaza, 20th Floor, New York, NY 10006, USA

477 Williamstown Road, Port Melbourne, VIC 3207, Australia

4843/24, 2nd Floor, Ansari Road, Daryaganj, Delhi – 110002, India

79 Anson Road, #06–04/06, Singapore 079906

Cambridge University Press is part of the University of Cambridge.

It furthers the University's mission by disseminating knowledge in the pursuit of education, learning, and research at the highest international levels of excellence.

www.cambridge.org
Information on this title: www.cambridge.org/9781107142848
DOI: 10.1017/9781316537411

First published 2017

Printed in the United States of America by Sheridan Books, Inc. in 2017

A catalogue record for this publication is available from the British Library.

Library of Congress Cataloging-in-Publication Data
NAMES: Dwyer, Christopher P., author.
TITLE: Critical thinking : conceptual perspectives & practical guidelines / Dr. Christopher P. Dwyer, School of Psychology, National University of Ireland, Galway.
DESCRIPTION: Cambridge, United Kingdom : Cambridge University Press, 2017. | Includes bibliographical references.
IDENTIFIERS: LCCN 2016046827| ISBN 9781107142848 (hbk) | ISBN 9781316509951 (pbk)
SUBJECTS: LCSH: Critical thinking. | Logic. | Reasoning.
CLASSIFICATION: LCC BF441 .D895 2016 | DDC 153.4/2–dc23
LC record available at https://lccn.loc.gov/2016046827

ISBN 978-1-107-14284-8 Hardback
ISBN 978-1-316-50995-1 Paperback

For Lisa

CONTENTS

FIGURES

TABLES

FOREWORD

Diane F. Halpern

Author of Thought and Knowledge: An Introduction to
Critical Thinking (5th ed.) and the Halpern Critical Thinking
Assessment

Moon-landing deniers, who, as you might have guessed, believe that
humans have never landed on the moon; psychic surgery advocates,
who claim that it is possible to remove body parts without making an
incision; and numerology, which is the belief that numbers can have
a significant influence on one's life. There are many beliefs that some
people hold onto despite a wealth of quality evidence that they are false.
Sure, it can be difficult to tell the difference between the science of high-
quality research and evidence and the pseudoscience of low-quality
research and evidence, but in these examples and many others, it is
hard to understand how anyone can maintain these beliefs. They are
not the harmless endorsements of a few weirdos. Someone who does not
believe that humans have ever landed on the moon will not have the
cognitive skills for a career in science or technology. People who have
travelled to distant countries that permit 'psychic surgery' risk serious
health consequences, including death, for eschewing other forms of
empirically supported medicine. If someone believes that numbers hold
the clues to his or her personality and future, this person will not have the
agency to plan for the life she or he may want.

The only way to avoid the harm of wrong beliefs is through the application of critical thinking skills. Everyone can become a better thinker by
using the principles of argument analysis, likelihood and uncertainty,
research evaluation and many others that are included in Chris Dwyer's
new book. Chris has reached his goal of writing a book that presents 'a

modern, detailed description of critical thinking'. In easy-to-read prose, he takes the reader through the history of critical thinking, including its foundations and frameworks, explains why it is so critical in negotiating the complexity of today's world and presents many examples of using the skills of critical thinking to help readers become better thinkers.

Chris makes it clear that critical thinking is not just an educational fad that is likely to have the same fate as the 'new math' or alternative ways of teaching reading. As he documents, critical thinking has a long and rich history, and with hard work, students (and we are all students) can become better thinkers. Of particular note is his emphasis on memory and psychological descriptions of how memory works and a comparison of various models of critical thinking. Thus, his work is grounded in both theory and research.

Readers are taken on a tour of argument analysis – recognizing reasons, conclusions, counterarguments and information that is irrelevant to the argument. The emphasis on argument analysis is consistent with Chris' research on argument mapping, which shows the efficacy of teaching this important critical thinking skill. Chris also explains what does *not* work in critical thinking instruction, specifically 'mind mapping', which bears a surface similarity to argument mapping, but operates at a more superficial level. Thus, readers understand that deep analysis is an essential component of training in critical thinking.

Creative thinking, a topic that is often ignored in critical thinking discourse, is also included. Some scholars deliberately exclude creativity from critical thinking books, arguing that creative thinking is not analytic, but as Chris wisely notes, it is an important component of problem-solving and thus belongs under the critical thinking rubric. Another important distinction that Chris makes well is differentiating formal and informal logic. Formal logic is of very limited use in everyday thinking, whereas people use informal logic in countless situations. How can we decide if global warming poses a real threat to our planet or if aggression is primarily biological in its origin? These are the sorts of questions that people grapple with on a daily basis and the laws of formal logic are usually not helpful with questions like these. However, critical thinking skills can help us think 'our way through' messy real-world problems where the data are often contradictory and the topics are tied to personal belief systems.

I found the section on naturalistic decision-making particularly interesting because Chris explains why expertise may not lead to better decisions. Sometimes, experts are merely doing the same thing over many years rather than learning from their mistakes and successes. Often, experts do not get systematic feedback, so they tend to overestimate their abilities, which can lead to overconfidence. This is an important point to consider when selecting an expert and when deciding if you are an expert in a certain field. As with much in critical thinking, humility is often the best response.

I was pleased to see that the list of critical-thinking applications included argumentation, verbal reasoning, hypothesis testing, likelihood and uncertainty, and problem-solving. I believe that this list could become the defining features of critical thinking because these applications are easy to understand by a lay audience and they are testable. There are ready-made assessments that line up exactly to this list.

Using Chris' structure of argument mapping, I conclude that this is a great book for anyone who wants a better understanding of critical thinking, how it should be taught and its historical origins. There are no 'buts' or 'howevers'.

An Introduction to Critical Thinking

Learning without thought is labour lost; thought without learning is perilous. Study without reflection is a waste of time; reflection without study is dangerous.
~ Confucius (c. 551–479 BC)

'What do you mean, exactly, by *critically evaluate*?' asked one of my final year students, when advised, that in order to achieve an 'A' on their final exam, they would have to critically evaluate the course readings and lecture notes. To be honest, I was shocked that a final year student, who was only months away from being awarded their Bachelor of Arts, found difficulty in the concept of critically evaluating information. I replied that they would have to think critically about the topic they were asked to evaluate by considering the course material in an interrogative manner – analysing and evaluating the information as if they were uncertain of the validity and truth of the claims made, so that they would be able to infer their own conclusions, based on their own reflective judgment of the relevant information gathered. It was at this point, some students began to look worried as they furiously took pen to paper.

Other students in the class, whom I recognized as having participated in my critical thinking lecture series earlier in their university careers, smiled wryly at those who made their confusion explicit. It was these students who understood the importance of critical thinking, especially in the context of preparing for exams. Until this point in my teaching career, I was never more aware of the need for higher-order forms of thought, such as critical thinking, to be cultivated in the classroom for purposes of facilitating both the acquisition and application of knowledge (Folsom-Kovarik et al., 2010; Huffaker & Calvert, 2003; US National Research Council, 2002). This sentiment is further supported by research that indicates that 93% of lecturers and faculty in higher education centres perceive critical thinking as an essential learning outcome of third-level education (Association of American Colleges and Universities, 2005). In addition, a survey of over 11,000 college graduates found that the 'ability to think critically' ranked as the second most important skill (following 'interpersonal skills') used by people on a daily basis (Cooperative Institutional Research Program, 1995).

Based on my observations as a university lecturer, it has become glaringly obvious that too much class and study time is devoted to didactic instruction and the reading of textbooks, while not enough time is devoted to actively analysing and evaluating knowledge as it is acquired and constructed (Hogan, 2006). While traditional means of learning used by students to assimilate knowledge (e.g. rote learning) may be helpful for short-term educational goals, more meaningful learning skills (Good & Brophy, 1986), such as critical thinking, are necessary for deeper comprehension, broader application and comprehensive synthesis of knowledge across domains (Darling-Hammond, 2008; Halpern, 2014; King & Kitchener, 2004; King, Wood, & Mines, 1990; Kuhn, 1991, 1999; Sweller, 1999).

For students to achieve their scholastic requirements, it is often necessary for them to use different cognitive processes to acquire knowledge from a range of sources, including textbooks, didactic instruction, class notes and recommended websites. Indeed, memorization and comprehension strategies are important in this context; however, the development and application are equally, if not more, vital because, in today's world, where there is an exponential increase in the annual output of knowledge, it is not only the ability to draw upon knowledge but also the capacity to engage in enquiry and constructively solve problems (Darling-Hammond, 2008). For example, it is estimated that 500,000 times the volume of information contained in the US Library of Congress print collection was created in 2002 alone; and more amazingly, from the years 1999 to 2002, the amount of new information created equalled the amount of information previously developed throughout the history of the world (Varian & Lyman, 2003). It is further estimated that the creation of new information is doubling every two years (Jukes & McCain, 2002). Arguably, it has become tougher to gauge the actual growth of information in the 15 years since these estimates, particularly in light of Internet-based advancements and social media growth, rather than knowledge growth per se. Nevertheless, it has been suggested that approximately five exabytes (i.e. five quintillion bytes or

1,000,000,000 GB) of data are created each day. However, what is even tougher to decipher is how much of this is simply pictures of cats, videos reporting on conspiracy theories and/or paranormal activities, or simply inaccurate or misinterpreted information. Consequently, successful learning is reliant not only on students' attainment of knowledge, but also on student's ability to adapt both to new information and to new situations. Over the last several decades, educators, employers and organizations around the world have openly expressed concern about student preparedness for a 21st-century world (e.g. Association of American Colleges and Universities, 2010; Bureau of Labor Statistics, 2011; Butler et al., 2012; Halpern, 2010b; Hunt, 1995). As a result,

> nations around the world are reforming their school systems to meet these new demands by revising curriculum, instruction and assessment, in order to support the critical thinking skills necessary in the 21st century – skills needed for framing problems; seeking and organising information and resources; and working strategically with others to manage and address dilemmas and create new products.
>
> *(Darling-Hammond, 2008, p. 2)*

The teaching of critical thinking skills in higher education has been identified as an area that needs to be explored and developed (Association of American Colleges & Universities, 2005; Australian Council for Educational Research, 2002; Higher Education Quality Council, 1996). Such skills are vital in educational settings because they allow students to go beyond simply memorizing information, to actually gaining a more complex understanding of the information being presented to them (Halpern, 2014). Critical thinking skills are important not only in the academic domain but also in social and interpersonal contexts where adequate decision-making and problem-solving are necessary on a daily basis (Ku, 2009). For example, students who critically think about controversial issues in educational settings through group discussions and debates become more informed and more active citizens (Andolina et al., 2003; Barton & McCully, 2007). In addition, good critical thinkers are more likely to get better grades and are often more employable as well (Holmes & Clizbe, 1997; National Academy of Sciences, 2005).

The purpose of this book is to present a modern, detailed description of critical thinking that can be employed in educational settings – one that can be used by *both* educators and students in order to adapt to the new knowledge economy of the 21st century and also to overcome past, potential confusion as to what it is to think critically. Our discussion of critical thinking in this book is more than just a presentation of critical thinking definitions and descriptions of varying conceptualizations – we will also explore historical perspectives on critical thinking and the foundational processes necessary for critical thinking. In addition, practical guidelines for critical thinking assessment and instruction are presented, as are both pedagogical and learning strategies that are likely to enhance critical thinking performance. A number of active learning exercises are presented throughout the book, in order to provide our student readers an opportunity to practise their critical thinking skills and to provide the teacher population of our readers with examples and discussion of the types of critical thinking exercises they should be administering in the classroom.

Critical thinking is a metacognitive process that, through purposeful, self-regulatory reflective judgment, consists of a number of sub-skills and dispositions that, when used appropriately, increases the chances of producing a logical solution to a problem or a valid conclusion to an argument (Dwyer, Hogan, & Stewart, 2012, 2014, 2015). On one hand, the development of critical thinking skills is often endorsed because, as stated before, these skills allow students to transcend lower-order, mem- orization-based learning strategies to gain a more complex understand- ing of the information or problems they encounter (Halpern, 2014; Pollock, Chandler, & Sweller, 2002). On the other hand, in the past century, there has been little agreement on how to define critical think- ing, resulting in the existence of many diverse conceptualizations of critical thinking (e.g. Bensley, 1998; Dewey, 1910, 1933; Ennis, 1987; Glaser, 1941; Halpern, 2014; Paul, 1993). Before discussing these defini- tions and pinpointing exactly what it is we mean by critical thinking, it is necessary to first explore the foundations of thought – in order to gain a deeper perspective on the cognitive processes that both comprise and sustain critical thinking abilities. As a result, the following chapters will present the foundations of critical thinking, in which a number of key cognitive processes that determine the ability to think critically will be discussed, through the consideration of numerous cognitive and educa- tional frameworks.

Specifically, Chapter 1 presents various frameworks of thinking pro- cesses that are necessary for critical thinking (i.e. memory, comprehen- sion, analysis, evaluation, inference and reflective judgment), followed by discussion, in Chapter 2, of memory and comprehension processes, in light of recent theory and empirical research in cognitive psychology. Specifically, Baddeley's model of working memory (1986, 2000) and models of schema construction in long-term memory (e.g. Chi, Glaser, & Rees, 1982; Chase & Simon, 1973; Kotovsky, Hayes, & Simon, 1985) will be discussed. In Chapter 3, historical perspectives on critical thinking are presented, as are brief discussions of the nature and use of falsification, formal logic and informal logic. Once the foundations of critical thinking are laid in Chapters 1–3, our focus will turn in Chapter 4 to the many definitions of critical thinking and to pinpointing exactly what it is we mean by critical thinking through a discussion of metacognition, self-regulatory functions of thinking and the various critical thinking skills. Chapters 5–8 will focus on the description and practical use of the critical thinking skills of analysis, evaluation, inference and reflective judgment, respectively. The focus of Chapter 9 is to investigate the many applications of critical thinking in real-world settings (i.e. argumentation; verbal reasoning; hypothesis testing; judging likelihood and uncertainty; and problem-solving) while the focus of Chapter 10 is to discuss the opposite of reflective judgment – intuitive judgment – and how it affects real-world applications of thinking. Chapters 11 and 12 discuss the nature of critical thinking assessment and instruction; and critical thinking development through pedagogical and learning strategies. Finally, Chapter 13 concludes this book by presenting a general discussion regarding our investigation of critical thinking and summarizes these investigations and conclusions.

PART I

FOUNDATIONS OF CRITICAL THINKING

The only thing I know with reliance is that I know nothing.
~ Socrates (c. 470–399 BC)

1

Frameworks for Thinking

The essence of the independent mind lies not in what it thinks, but in how it thinks.

~ Christopher Hitchens (1949–2011)

This chapter introduces and discusses various frameworks of thinking processes in order to provide an understanding for how we conduct critical thinking skills. That is, the frameworks discussed present a number of cognitive processes that are necessary for critical thinking. These frameworks are important to consider because they organize the processes involved in critical thinking in a manner that makes their relationships with one another explicit.

A framework for thinking is a 'general pool of constructs for understanding a domain' (e.g. cognition and education), 'but is not tightly enough organised to constitute a predictive theory' (Anderson, 1983, pp. 12–13). Simply, a framework for thinking organizes the identified cognitive processes in an effort to explain the structure of thought (Moseley et al., 2005). The identification and description of thinking processes vary from framework to framework, given that the term 'framework' covers a wide variety of structures (Moseley et al., 2005).

More specifically, frameworks differ in complexity, in that some may be very simple (e.g. lists of cognitive processes that students may need to use in different learning situations), while others may be quite complex (e.g. taxonomies that hierarchically structure lower-order to higher-order thinking processes according to complexity or importance). For example, a framework for thinking that is represented as a list may simply present an inventory of thinking processes (e.g. identify, name, describe, construct, order and demonstrate; cf. Gerlach & Sullivan, 1967), which may be helpful given that an inventory can be used to check that a certain cognitive activity has been given attention in the classroom (Moseley et al., 2005). However, a list of thinking processes offers no explicit description of the relationship between thinking processes (e.g. hierarchical relationships among the entries), nor does it rank items on the list according to complexity, importance, sequence or the context in which they might be applied. A more complex thinking framework may be represented as a group, which organizes thinking processes according to shared similarities or interrelationships (e.g. Jonassen & Tessmer, 1996). A group of thinking processes may be subdivided into smaller groups. These groups may stand alone, co-exist alongside other groups or hierarchically subsume other smaller groups (e.g. according to complexity or interdependency), thus creating organized ranks (Moseley et al., 2005).

Hierarchical classification of groups is a common feature of thinking frameworks that are represented as taxonomies. In a taxonomy, groups within groups are created via the classification and organization of thinking processes, which produces an organized hierarchy. Many current frameworks for thinking are taxonomies (e.g. Allen, Feezel, & Kauffeld, 1967; Anderson & Krathwohl, 2001; Bloom, 1956; Ennis, 1998; Marzano, 2001; Romiszowski, 1981). Taxonomies of thinking processes may be developed for a number of specific reasons, for example, to address educational objectives, instructional design, productive thinking or cognitive development. In this context, a number of frameworks are usefully considered in more detail, such as those developed by Bloom (1956), Romiszowski (1981), Anderson and Krathwohl (2001) and Marzano (2001). These frameworks have been chosen for discussion because the cognitive processes they describe as being necessary in educational settings are also necessary for the successful application of critical thinking.

Frameworks will be presented in chronological order, beginning with Bloom's (1956) influential taxonomy, which identifies six core educational objectives (i.e. knowledge, comprehension, application, analysis, synthesis and evaluation). Each of these educational objectives will then be discussed in relation to Romiszowski's (1981) 'skill-cycle', which elaborates upon how the thinking processes identified by Bloom both function and develop in educational settings. Next, Anderson and Krathwohl's (2001) revision of Bloom's taxonomy will be discussed in order to provide a more up-to-date perspective on the kinds of cognitive processes that Bloom had previously identified as important in educational settings. Finally, Marzano's (2001) taxonomy will be discussed in light of his meta-analysis of educational interventions (Marzano, 1998).

BLOOM'S TAXONOMY OF EDUCATIONAL OBJECTIVES

Bloom's taxonomy of educational objectives was developed for the purposes of enhancing education and the manner in which thinking is examined in the classroom via classifying 'mental acts or thinking [resulting from] educational experiences' (Bloom, 1956, p. 12). Bloom's taxonomy, which actually emerged from consensus agreement and work completed by a group of university professors (i.e. B. S. Bloom, M. D. Engelhart, F. J. Furst, W. H. Hill, & D. R. Krathwohl), has been claimed to be 'the most pervasive in curriculum development and provides the clearest definition of educational goals expressed in terms of descriptions of student behaviour' (Reeves, 1990, p. 609). The taxonomy has been a cornerstone of educational practice for many years, as it was one of the first frameworks to characterize thinking as an array of both *lower-order* and *higher-order* thinking processes. Notably, Bloom's concept of higher-order thinking is consistent with many modern conceptualizations of critical thinking.

In the past, Bloom's taxonomy has been used as a pedagogical aid in enhancing writing performance (Granello, 2001), as a basis for performance evaluation in various academic domains (Scott, 2003) and as a guide for planning course curricula and designing instruction (Krathwohl, 2002). Research has also shown that making students aware of Bloom's taxonomy increases their ability to apply the appropriate skills (i.e. knowledge, comprehension, application, analysis, synthesis and evaluation) when critically thinking (Athanassiou, McNett, & Harvey, 2003). More generally, when it comes to designing interventions that seek to cultivate Bloom's lower-order and higher-order thinking processes, there is a vast educational literature that has identified a plethora of educational strategies that are more or less effective (Berkowitz, 1986; Chi, Glaser, & Rees, 1982; Gadzella, Ginther, & Bryant, 1996; Hitchcock, 2004; Reed & Kromrey, 2001; Rimiene, 2002; Robinson & Kiewra, 1995; Solon, 2007; Taylor, 1982; Taylor & Beach, 1984).

Bloom's taxonomy of educational objectives consists of six major categories of thought (see Figure 1.1). The first category pertains to the *knowledge* of specifics (e.g. facts), ways and means of dealing with specifics (e.g. procedures) and the abstract nature of some information (e.g. abstract concepts). This may include knowledge of specific terminology, facts, conventions, patterns, classifications, criteria, methodologies, principles, generalizations, theories and structures; and the ability to *recall* this knowledge upon demand. The second category of thought, *comprehension*, is the ability to understand or grasp the meaning of information. This implies the

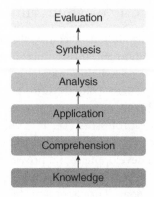

FIGURE 1.1 Bloom's Taxonomy (1956)

ability to interpret and extrapolate information for purposes of developing understanding, and also to translate information from one level of abstraction to another, one symbolic form to another or one verbal form to another (e.g. for purposes of summarizing, paraphrasing or explaining information). The third category, often referred to as the least well-understood category of Bloom's taxonomy (Moseley et al., 2005), is *application*, which is the use of learned information in new and concrete situations. The fourth category, *analysis*, is the ability to break down ideas or arguments into their component parts (e.g. analysing a complex idea by reference to the organizational principles, abstractions and representations expressed by a speaker or author). *Synthesis*, the fifth category, refers to the production of a unique communication or plan (i.e. the ability to put parts of information together to form a new whole). The final category of thought in Bloom's taxonomy is *evaluation*, which is defined as the ability to make judgments in terms of the value of internal evidence and/or external criteria.[1]

The categories of Bloom's taxonomy are hierarchically arranged, starting at the bottom with the lower-order thinking skills of knowledge/ recall and comprehension and proceeding through the progressively higher-order thinking skills of application, analysis, synthesis and evaluation. Even though memory-based knowledge and comprehension are

[1] Despite what seem like clear definitions (Moseley et al., 2005), Wood (1977) found that educators often find it hard to differentiate among the higher-order thinking skills (especially, analysis, synthesis and evaluation). These three processes will be discussed later in detail with regards to both Romiszowski's "skill-cycle" and Facione's (1990b) conceptualization of critical thinking, in order to clarify distinctions among them.

labelled *lower-order* thinking skills, this does not suggest that they are ultimately less important for education than the higher-order thinking skills. For example, the operation of the higher-order processes is dependent upon the existence of knowledge (e.g. comprehending, applying, analysing, synthesizing and evaluating knowledge of specific facts, conventions, patterns and methodologies). More specifically, though Bloom's six categories are organized according to the complexity of each mental act (i.e. from *knowledge* to *evaluation*), this organization is based on a hierarchical interdependence between levels. For example, in order to *evaluate* a theory (level six), one must first be able to *analyse* its propositions (level four) and *synthesize* their interdependence (level five). Furthermore, to be able to *analyse* a theory (level four) one must be able to *comprehend* its propositions (level two) and *remember* them (level one). However, there has been debate over whether Bloom's six categories imply a strict form of hierarchical interdependence or constitute a rigid or interdependent form of hierarchical complexity (e.g. Anderson & Krathwohl, 2001). For example, Kreitzer and Madaus' (1994) review of Bloom's (1956) taxonomy included discussion of research conducted by Kropp, Stoker, and Bashaw (1966), which assessed the performance of students on the thinking processes in Bloom's taxonomy and found no evidence of a difficulty or complexity hierarchy for the higher level skills of evaluation and synthesis. Based on these and other findings, Kreitzer and Madaus (1994) suggest that *evaluation* is not more complex than *synthesis*. In other words, evaluation does not readily subsume synthesis in a higher-order/low-order hierarchical relationship. This issue is further explored in the discussion of Anderson and Krathwohl's (2001) revision of Bloom's taxonomy presented below.

Apart from the influence that Bloom's taxonomy has had on the development of subsequent frameworks (e.g. Anderson & Krathwohl, 2001; Halpern, 2014; Marzano, 2001; Moseley et al., 2005; Romiszowski, 1981), it has prompted the development of practical hierarchical inventories of thinking processes linked to specific learning outcomes in educational settings, as well as operational definitions to facilitate measurement of these learning outcomes. This is particularly useful in the context of educational research, as the translation of operational definitions into specific measurement tools has allowed subsequent research to examine student performance across skills in the hierarchy under different experimental conditions (e.g. Berkowitz, 1986; Butchart et al., 2009; Farrand, Hussain, & Hennessy, 2002; Meyer, Brandt, & Bluth, 1980; Taylor, 1982; van Gelder, Bissett, & Cumming, 2004).

ROMISZOWSKI'S FRAMEWORK FOR KNOWLEDGE
AND SKILLS

Bloom's taxonomy heavily influenced Romiszowski's (1981) investigation of cognitive processes and methods of improving educational instruction. Romiszowski defines instruction as 'a goal-directed teaching process which is more or less pre-planned' (p. 4). According to Romiszowski, the relationship between instruction and learning is described as a three-part sequence, which consists of *input* (i.e. information), the use of a *system* (i.e. a cognitive process – such as those identified by Bloom) and *output* (i.e. performance, application or production of knowledge). During this sequence, one can apply any number of cognitive processes on taught information for the purpose of producing knowledge.[2]

According to Romiszowski, it is often difficult to define or even differentiate systems. Thus, he metaphorically refers to these systems as acting in a *black box*, wherein the contents of the box (i.e. cognitive processes such as those described by Bloom) cannot be viewed directly. The value of a specific instructional method is assessed via a cost–benefit analysis, in which the benefit of training is directly compared with the cost of the training, in terms of time and effort expended by student and/or teacher. If after the training there is a 'deficiency in performance' or the output is not worth the cost, then it may become necessary to 'open the black box' in order to see if the cognitive process (i.e. the system) used was the cause of the deficiency (Romiszowski, 1981, p. 253). Ultimately, Romiszowski provides a *skill-cycle* (see Figure 1.2) to describe not only what processes are 'inside the black box', but also the way in which these processes interact, in the event that the black box 'needs to be opened' (p. 253).

According to Romiszowski's skill-cycle, skill development is dependent on how often the skill is practised and on how well skill development is supported by instructional design and an accommodating learning environment. Skills act upon novel, incoming information as well as pre-existing knowledge. Within this framework are four types of *knowledge*. The first type of knowledge is based on knowing *facts* (e.g. 'knowing objects, events or people', (Romiszowski, 1981, p. 242). The second type of knowledge is based on knowing *procedures* (i.e. 'knowing what to do in given situations', p. 242). The third type of knowledge Romiszowski

---

[2] Romiszowski claims that when designing instruction, it is important that the input, the system and the output are designed or utilized specifically in relation to one another (e.g. if the input is altered, so too will the system and the output). Training must be designed to foster certain skills in order to produce a desired outcome.

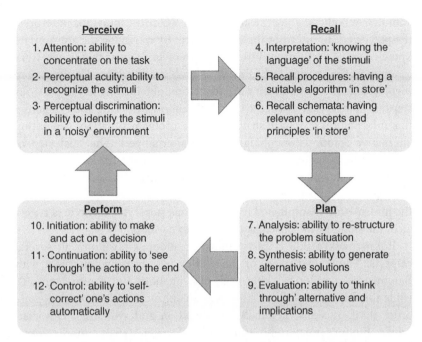

Perceive
1. Attention: ability to concentrate on the task
2. Perceptual acuity: ability to recognize the stimuli
3. Perceptual discrimination: ability to identify the stimuli in a 'noisy' environment

Recall
4. Interpretation: 'knowing the language' of the stimuli
5. Recall procedures: having a suitable algorithm 'in store'
6. Recall schemata: having relevant concepts and principles 'in store'

Perform
10. Initiation: ability to make and act on a decision
11. Continuation: ability to 'see through' the action to the end
12. Control: ability to 'self-correct' one's actions automatically

Plan
7. Analysis: ability to re-structure the problem situation
8. Synthesis: ability to generate alternative solutions
9. Evaluation: ability to 'think through' alternative and implications

FIGURE 1.2   Romiszowski's (1981) Skill-Cycle (Adapted from Moseley et al., 2005)

describes is knowledge based around *concepts* (i.e. 'knowing specific concepts or groups of concepts, such as being able to give or recognise instances of a given phenomena', p. 243). The final type of knowledge is based on knowing *principles* (i.e. 'principles which link certain concepts or facts in a specific way, such as being able to explain or predict phenomena', p. 243). The distinctions Romiszowski makes between different types of knowledge resonate with other theories, including Tulving's (1984) distinction among semantic memory (e.g. memory for meanings and concepts), episodic memory (e.g. memory for events) and procedural memory (e.g. memory for how to do things). Consistent with Bloom's scheme, the four types of knowledge laid out by Romiszowski can be recalled and understood via the processes of 'memory' and 'comprehension'. They can also be used in different ways to plan and perform educational tasks.

During the skill-cycle, an individual *perceives* information, *recalls* information, makes *plans* and *performs* based on that information. According to Romiszowski, when perceiving information, the individual concentrates on a task or problem, recognizes the relevant stimuli (e.g. visual stimuli, verbal stimuli or an integration of both) and is able to discriminate those stimuli from others. The next step, recall, is where the individual interprets the perceived stimuli from the environment by retrieving the appropriate knowledge (i.e. facts, procedures, concepts or principles) that is necessary to apply in the specific task context or problem-situation. The third step involves making plans based on information obtained from the previous steps (i.e. perception and recall), by analysing, synthesizing and evaluating this information (i.e. by restructuring the problem-situation, generating alternative solutions and judging these alternatives). The final step in Romiszowski's skill-cycle is performance: in accordance with the plan just devised, the individual makes and acts on a decision, sees that decision through and is able to correct or self-regulate their own actions, based on the information manipulated in the previous steps. As this cycle is reiterated, the skill(s) which is engaged is able to develop.[3]

Romiszowski's skill-cycle is similar to Bloom's taxonomy in several respects. The second phase of the skill-cycle is broadly congruent with Bloom's lower-order thinking skills (i.e. memory and comprehension), while the third phase of the skill-cycle is congruent with Bloom's higher-order thinking skills (i.e. analysis, evaluation and synthesis). However, unlike Bloom's taxonomy, Romiszowski's skill-cycle is more closely aligned with cognitive architecture (Anderson, 1990) and neuroscientific accounts of the perception–action cycle (Fuster, 2000), and the two phases of Romiszowski's skill-cycle not directly elaborated upon by Bloom are those of perception and performance. With respect to perception, it may be taken for granted by Bloom that any 'stimuli' subject to thought first requires attention (i.e. in order to think about some specific educational task, one must perceive a stimulus). Furthermore, in relation to performance, it may be that this final phase of Romiszowski's skill-cycle is congruent with Bloom's category of application, given that both 'application' and 'performance' refer to utilization of knowledge. However, Romiszowski's concept of performance is also distinct from Bloom's

[3] Romiszowski's theory resonates with Piaget's (1952) *Theory of Cognitive Development* and Fischer's (1980) *Dynamic Skill Theory*, in that knowledge can be conceptualized by the individual as concrete (i.e. facts and procedures) or abstract (i.e. concepts and principles). Fischer's theory and empirical work highlights the fact that skill development is often domain specific (i.e. skills develop independent of one another and at different rates). Different skills draw upon different knowledge. Furthermore, Fischer argues that skills develop through the hierarchical coordination of lower level action systems into higher-order structures, with abstractions and principles derived from the coordination and mapping of actions and representations. Fischer's conceptualization of skill development is important, as it is central to the development of reflective judgment, as discussed in Chapter 8.

notion of application in important ways. For example, while Bloom refers to application in terms of particular uses of knowledge (e.g. applying a theory to a social problem), Romiszowski's concept of performance is much more akin to cognitive notions of executive control (Fuster, 2000) and metacognitive, self-regulatory processes (Boekaerts & Simons, 1993; Marzano, 2001; Pintrich, 2000; see also Chapter 4), specifically, with its focus on the ability to initiate, persevere and control actions.

The development of a skill through Romiszowski's cycle involves the planned operation of that skill on some item of knowledge for a particular purpose. According to Romiszowski, the amount of planning required to perform each skill dictates whether that skill is either *reproductive* or *productive* in practice. A *reproductive skill* refers to 'skills that are more or less reflexive in nature, that are repetitive and that show little variation in execution from one instance to another' (Romiszowski, 1981, p. 250). Romiszowski's description of reproductive thinking is somewhat consistent with Bloom's conceptualization of 'knowledge'. For example, a student may draw upon knowledge of a specific fact, convention, pattern, classification, criteria, methodology, principle or theory in a reflexive manner without much by way of planning, for example, in response to a question posed by a teacher in a classroom setting. Conversely, a *productive skill* refers to 'a skilled behaviour that requires a certain amount of planning, that involves the use of some strategy for decision-making and shows substantial variations in execution from one instance to another' (Romiszowski, 1981, p. 251).[4]

An example of how reproductive and productive thinking is applied is provided by Romiszowski in terms of painting and decorating a home. Romiszowski (1981) suggests that a painter requires little knowledge in order to paint a wall, apart from mixing paint and laying it on the wall without leaving brush marks. This is considered analogous to reproductive thinking because all the painter needs to do is to reproduce a procedure. On the other hand, a decorator who is applying wallpaper and seeking to plan out and configure an ideal living space needs knowledge of not only the *procedure* for measuring the room, cutting the paper and mixing/applying paste but also the aesthetic *principles* of obtaining a high quality

---

[4] Romiszowski's concept of productive thinking is akin to the description of metacognitive processes provided by others (e.g. Boekaerts & Simons, 1993; Brown, 1987; Ku & Ho, 2010b; Marzano, 1998, 2001), which is characterized by both the dispositional/self-regulatory functions of thinking; and the strategic planning and application of high-order thinking skills (i.e. analysis, evaluation and inference) when thinking about thinking (Brown, 1987; Flavell, 1979; Ku & Ho, 2010b).

of finish (in order to visualize the finished product), concerning, for example, the positioning of patterns and joints in the wallpaper, the balance of the patterns in the wallpaper around doors and windows and accentuating or conversely hiding certain features of the wallpaper, in order to produce a pleasing effect. These principles are derived from a much larger knowledge base and combined into a more complex set of decision-making strategies that enables the decorator not only to know how to complete each task but also to know why it is being done.

Previous research suggests that both reproductive and productive components of thinking can be measured and enhanced. For example, past research conducted on verbal recall performance (i.e. a type of reproductive thinking) suggests that recall can be improved by reading from and constructing organizational representations of text-based information (e.g. Berkowitz, 1986; Dwyer, Hogan, & Stewart, 2011; Farrand, Hussain, & Hennessy, 2002; Taylor, 1982; Taylor & Beach, 1984). Past research also suggests that critical thinking (i.e. a type of productive thinking; Ennis, 1998; Halpern, 2014; Moseley et al., 2005) can be enhanced through critical-thinking-focused training interventions (e.g. Abrami et al., 2008; Alvarez-Ortiz, 2007; Dwyer, Hogan, & Stewart, 2012; Hitchcock, 2004; Reed & Kromrey, 2001; van Gelder, 2001; van Gelder, Bissett, & Cumming, 2004).

The importance of Romiszowski's framework is that it positions many of the thinking processes identified by Bloom as acting in a cycle (e.g. recall processes, analysis, synthesis and evaluation), describing how and when they are to be utilized in educational settings. In addition to Romiszowski's framework, more recent efforts have been made to build upon Bloom's taxonomy of educational objectives (e.g. Anderson & Krathwohl, 2001; Marzano, 2001). Anderson and Krathwohl's (2001) taxonomy follows Romiszowski's general path of development (i.e. which placed an action-oriented focus on each thinking process as working in a skill-cycle) by, first, transforming Bloom's hierarchical thinking processes from noun form to verb form (i.e. naming actions instead of 'things') and, second, by placing acts of 'creation' as the pinnacle process in the hierarchy.

ANDERSON AND KRATHWOHL'S REVISION OF BLOOM'S TAXONOMY

To reiterate, Anderson and Krathwohl's (2001) revised taxonomy made a number of changes to Bloom's taxonomy, including the ordering of the processes (i.e. the process of evaluation and synthesis [now creating] were exchanged) and the presentation of each process in verb form as opposed

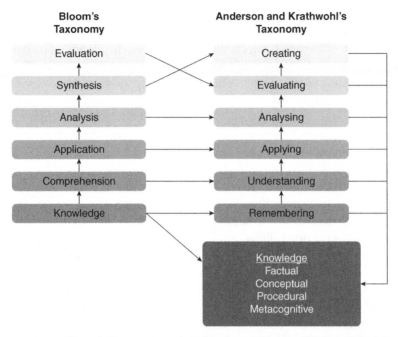

FIGURE 1.3 Bloom's Taxonomy and Anderson and Krathwohl's (2001) Revision

to noun form (see Figure 1.3). Another change was that Anderson and Krathwohl (2001) were explicit in proposing that the listed categories of cognitive processes no longer form a unified cumulative hierarchy. That is, one does not need to master lower levels of the taxonomy in order to ascend to higher levels (e.g. working at level six [*creating*] does not require mastery of level five [*evaluating*]). However, Anderson and Krathwohl claim that a cumulative, hierarchical interdependence exists between the activities of *understanding, applying* and *analysing* (i.e. located in the mid-section of the framework; again, see Figure 1.3) and that all processes are dependent upon *knowledge* as it is not possible for one to use thinking processes (located on the subsequent rungs of the taxonomy) if one does not know, or cannot remember, the information one is supposedly thinking about (Krathwohl, 2002). This is an important issue to consider, given that it has been argued by researchers in the field of critical thinking that the ability to think critically about specific information (i.e. analyse, evaluate and infer) is directly affected by one's ability to recall and understand (i.e. lower-order thinking skills) the information one is required to think about (Halpern, 2014; Maybery, Bain, & Halford, 1986).

The implied dependence of the various cognitive processes upon knowledge/remembering in the revised taxonomy results from another important difference between these taxonomies. In Bloom's taxonomy, a single, hierarchical arrangement of cognitive processes was explicated (i.e. consisting of knowledge, comprehension, application, analysis, synthesis and evaluation), whereas in Anderson and Krathwohl's (2001) revised taxonomy, two dimensions are described – a knowledge dimension and a cognitive process dimension. Specifically, in Bloom's taxonomy, 'knowledge' encompassed both *knowledge* of different forms of facts, procedures and abstractions, as well the ability to *remember* facts, procedures and abstractions (Krathwohl, 2002). In the revised taxonomy, knowledge is described as a separate dimension (Krathwohl, 2002; Moseley et al., 2005), whereas the ability to remember is described as one of the thinking processes in the other dimension.

Anderson and Krathwohl made this decision to highlight their belief that each of the six processes acted upon knowledge in their own right (i.e. remembering, understanding, applying, evaluating and creating knowledge).

Furthermore, the addition of this new dimension of knowledge is an important feature of Anderson and Krathwohl's (2001) revised taxonomy because it also includes an additional knowledge component not included in Bloom's original taxonomy: *metacognitive knowledge*, which in this context refers to strategic knowledge, knowledge about cognitive processes and tasks, and self-knowledge (Anderson & Krathwohl, 2001). However, the presentation of this additional feature in Anderson and Krathwohl's revised taxonomy is not to suggest that Bloom's original taxonomy did not take metacognitive processes into account. In fact, Bloom's higher-order thinking skills can be viewed as metacognitive processes. That is, when 'thinking about thinking' (i.e. metacognition; Hofer, 2004), the processes of analysis, synthesis and evaluation, along with self-regulation, can aid strategic planning (Brown, 1987; Flavell, 1979; Ku & Ho, 2010b). For example, an individual may use metacognition to think about thinking in the context of *analysing, synthesizing* and *evaluating* their own thinking and/or the thinking of others.

Notwithstanding the fact that Romiszowski's framework also captures these metacognitive processes in his skill-cycle steps of *planning* and *performing*, Anderson and Krathwohl's development of Bloom's taxonomy is important to consider because it is the first framework discussed which *explicitly* includes reference to a distinct metacognitive component within the thinking processes. Anderson and Krathwohl's taxonomy is further important to consider because it presents knowledge and remembering knowledge as separate functions of information storage and recall, respectively, as opposed to a collation of processes under one heading (as in Bloom's taxonomy). Another recent taxonomy which includes a separate knowledge construct, as well as a metacognitive component, is Marzano's (2001) taxonomy of educational objectives, which is heavily informed by a large-scale meta-analysis of educational interventions designed to facilitate a broad range of different learning outcomes (Marzano, 1998).

MARZANO'S NEW TAXONOMY OF EDUCATIONAL OBJECTIVES

Similar to Anderson and Krathwohl (2001), Marzano (2001) also developed a taxonomy of educational objectives (see Figure 1.4) based on Bloom's taxonomy. The importance of Marzano's taxonomy is that it is also based on very specific empirical research – summarized in Marzano's (1998) meta-analysis – which examined the effect of various instructional techniques on academic achievement. Marzano utilized over 4,000 effect sizes involving roughly 1.237 million subjects. Broadly speaking, the results of the meta-analysis revealed that instructional techniques that focused directly on the *knowledge domain* had an average effect size of .60. Interventions that focused on the *cognitive system* had an average effect size of .75. Interventions that focused on the *metacognitive system* had an average effect size of .55, and interventions that focused on the *self-system* had an average effect size of .74.

Though the structure of Marzano's taxonomy differs from those developed by Bloom (1956), Romiszowski (1981) and Anderson and Krathwohl

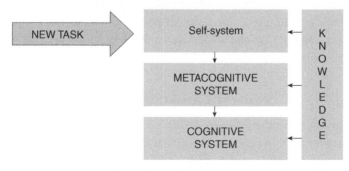

FIGURE 1.4 Marzano's (2001) 'New' Taxonomy of Educational Objectives

(2001), it remains similar to all three in that it includes (under the broad category of the *cognitive system*) the processes of *knowledge retrieval* (i.e. memory/recall), *comprehension* (i.e. knowledge representation), *analysis* (i.e. classifying, identifying errors, generalizing, matching and specifying) and *knowledge utilization* (i.e. decision-making, problem-solving, investigation and experimental enquiry). In addition, Marzano's (2001) taxonomy is also similar to Anderson and Krathwohl's taxonomy in that it explicitly includes a metacognitive component of thought. In Marzano's taxonomy, the *metacognitive system* acts as an executive control of all processes; more specifically, a self-regulatory process with a focus on goal and process specification, as well as process and disposition monitoring (Marzano, 1998). Marzano's taxonomy also presents a *self-system* in which goals are produced (to be executed by the metacognitive system) as a result of motivation, attention, beliefs and the interaction of such processes (Marzano, 1998; Moseley et al., 2005). Specifically, it is the self-system that determines whether or not any given task will be undertaken. These three systems (i.e. the cognitive, metacognitive and self-systems) all act upon retrieved content from an individual's *knowledge domain*, the fourth component of Marzano's taxonomy, which consists of stored information as well as knowledge of mental and psychomotor procedures. According to Moseley et al. (2005), this knowledge can be represented verbally, non-verbally or in an affective manner.

In light of the broader meta-analytical findings, Marzano (1998, p. 121) proposes that when the metacognitive and cognitive systems function together, they can enhance learning, as they 'provide individuals with an awareness of the manner in which their minds work' and 'requires them to monitor their mental activity'. Marzano (2001) further suggests that recognition by educators of the influence of both the self-system and the metacognitive system on the cognitive system and the development of knowledge is of utmost importance in educational settings. Marzano's work represents an important advance upon past frameworks as it provides empirical support for the inclusion of self-regulatory and monitoring processes within frameworks for thinking.

SUMMARY AND CONCLUSION

In summary, a number of frameworks have identified cognitive processes necessary for thinking in educational settings. Broadly speaking, two major components of thinking are often distinguished, variously described as lower-order thinking skills and higher-order thinking skills (Bloom, 1956);

reproductive and productive thinking skills (Romiszowski, 1981); and a cognitive process dimension and knowledge dimension (Anderson & Krathwohl, 2001; Marzano, 2001). Similarly, for the remainder of this book, lower- and higher-order thinking skills will be referred to as functioning in a cognitive system (i.e. thinking processes such as memory and comprehension) and a metacognitive system (i.e. both regulatory and strategic thinking processes used when 'thinking about thinking'), respectively.[5]

Though the frameworks presented above are adequately descriptive in terms of identifying thinking processes and the links among them, it is also important to consider the empirical cognitive psychology research which has investigated these processes. In addition, a possible weakness of the frameworks discussed above is that they do not elaborate on the manner in which one *applies* higher-order thinking processes. Bloom (1956) himself admitted that the process of *application* (i.e. the ability to use learned material in new and concrete situations) is the least well elaborated skill presented in his taxonomy. Though Anderson and Krathwohl did elaborate upon application by describing it as involving 'carrying out or using a procedure in a given situation [through] execution or implementation' (Krathwohl, 2002, p. 215), the concept remains incompletely revealed. Application may instead be reconsidered as a distinct, conjoint process (Moseley et al., 2005), similar to that described by Romiszowski (1981) as *perform* in his model of the skill-cycle, which implies that one must perform (i.e. initiate, continue and control) thinking processes based on the knowledge gained through the preceding processes (e.g. one may apply what was comprehended, what was analysed or what was evaluated). One feature of *application* that is pertinent in the context of this book is the *reflective judgment* an individual brings to bear in the application of knowledge. Reflective judgment, which is the ability to *apply* critical thinking skills of analysis, evaluation and inference whilst acknowledging uncertainties and limitations within one's knowledge (King & Kitchener,

---

[5] The conceptualization of higher-order thinking skills in Bloom's taxonomy and Anderson and Krathwohl's revision are analogous to the concept of critical thinking used in this book, as it consists of the skills of analysis, evaluation and synthesis. Though Bloom uses the term *synthesis*, his description of it is akin to *inference* as described by others in the field of critical thinking (i.e. the gathering of information to develop a conclusion based on previous evaluation and analysis; Facione, 1990b). Notably, Reeves (1990, p. 6) has amalgamated levels 3 (i.e. application) through 6 (i.e. evaluation) of Bloom's taxonomy and relabelled the resulting collection of processes as *critical thinking*. Thus, the metacognitive process of critical thinking referred to here is analogous to Bloom's higher-order thinking skills. Furthermore, the term synthesis will no longer be used in its more colloquial sense of creative synthesis, but will be referred to from here on as inference.

1994), will be discussed in Chapter 8 and elaborated upon as a key feature of higher-order thinking processes that can be the focus of educational interventions.

Based on the discussion of thinking frameworks and the identification of the thinking processes necessary for critical thinking (i.e. memory, comprehension, analysis, evaluation, inference and reflective judgment), it is important to examine these thinking processes in more detail and by reference to research from the field of cognitive psychology. Thus, the following chapter presents an empirical outlook on the foundational thinking processes discussed in this chapter, namely memory and comprehension. To reiterate, such discussion is important given that the ability to think critically is directly affected by one's ability to recall and understand the information in question.

EXERCISE 1.1

Based on our discussion of frameworks for thinking and cognitive processes that are involved in, or necessary for, critical thinking, please develop your own framework of thinking processes. Please include the processes and skills that you think are the most important for critical thinking and

1 Explain why you included them.
2 Explain the relationships shared among the processes in your framework.
3 Explain why you may have decided to exclude certain processes.

2

Memory and Comprehension

An investment in knowledge always pays the best interest.
~ Benjamin Franklin (1706–1790)

Though the frameworks presented in the previous chapter provide a descriptive representation of the thinking processes necessary for critical thinking, as well as links and shared relationships among them, it is also important to consider empirical cognitive and educational psychology research that has investigated these processes. Thus, this chapter presents an empirical outlook on the foundational thinking processes discussed in the previous chapter. Specifically, memory and comprehension are discussed in detail by reference to research from the fields of cognitive and educational psychology.

For an individual to remember information, a number of processes must first take place, such as active processing, encoding, storage and retrieval of information. More specifically, one must first attend to the information and then organize it in a meaningful way, for the purposes of successful recall. For example, when reading for the purpose of learning, people actively process information. Broadbent (1958) proposed that information is held in limited capacity short-term storage after it is actively attended to or processed; and through manipulation of that information within short-term storage, it can be transferred into permanent storage, where it is presumably represented as a form of knowledge (Atkinson & Shiffrin, 1968; Baddeley, 2000; Baddeley & Hitch, 1974; Broadbent, 1958; Craik & Tulving, 1975). The effective transfer of information from short-term storage to long-term memory (LTM) dictates what will be remembered. A number of multi-storage models of memory have been developed since Broadbent's proposal more than half a century ago, and the distinction between short-term storage, working memory and LTM remains prominent in cognitive psychology literature (Atkinson & Shiffrin, 1968; Baddeley, 2000; Baddeley & Hitch, 1974; Cowan, 2000, 2008; Ericsson & Kintsch, 1995).

WORKING MEMORY

Early studies referred to the storage of newly acquired information for brief periods of time as short-term memory. A large body of empirical research conducted by Alan Baddeley and colleagues (e.g. Baddeley, 1986, 2000, 2002; Baddeley, Eldridge, & Lewis, 1981; Baddeley & Hitch, 1974; Baddeley & Wilson, 2002), spanning the course of thirty plus years, suggests that this short-term memory storage is better described as a multiple component working memory system. Baddeley and Hitch (1974) argued that short-term memory was in fact a number of cognitive processes that work together to aid the encoding, storage and retrieval of information within brief periods of time (i.e. working memory; Baddeley, 1986, 2000). Baddeley and Hitch (1974) also distinguished working memory from LTM, by stating that, unlike the latter, working memory does not involve cognitive processes associated with the construction of mental representational frameworks and the enablement of relatively permanent storage.

Baddeley and Hitch (1974) suggested that working memory is a multi-component system which includes two slave systems, referred to as the phonological loop and the visuospatial sketchpad, and, more recently, a storage centre known as the episodic buffer (Baddeley, 2000, 2002). These components of working memory are governed by a central executive,[1] which integrates the information from the slave systems by

---

[1] Alternative models describe LTM as the governing component of working memory, that is, LTM acts as the *central executive* within working memory (Sweller, 2005). To clarify, this is not to claim that a central executive does not exist, but instead that what has previously been accepted as a central executive (e.g. Baddeley, 1986, 2000, 2002; Baddeley & Hitch, 1974) is actually an additional function of LTM (Sweller, 2005). According to Sweller, schemas (as discussed in a later section) govern the way in which information is processed in working memory for the simple reason that they are organized representations of previously encoded information, which directly aid the processing of novel information in working memory. This view is consistent with Baddeley's (2000, 2002) model of how the episodic buffer functions to support working memory. Sweller disputes Baddeley's conception of the central executive because it is 'not feasible for any conception of a central executive apart from a *learned* (i.e. schema-based) central executive to function' (Sweller, 2005, p. 25). For example, Sweller argues, 'If schemas are not available, as occurs when dealing with new information, there is no alternative central executive to call upon' (Sweller, 2005, p. 25). Another alternative view of the central executive is that of *executive functioning*, which is discussed in Chapter 4.

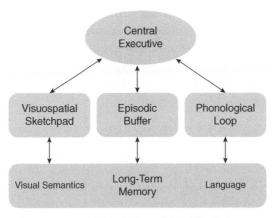

FIGURE 2.1 Baddeley's (2000) Model of Memory

acting as a limited capacity attentional system (Baddeley, 2002; see Figure 2.1). Though Baddeley (2012) admits that the central executive is the least understood aspect of working memory, it is not dissimilar to Norman and Shallice's (1986, 2000) concept of a *supervisory activating system*, which acts as an attentional processor responsible for the organization, coordination and monitoring of incoming information through the use of existing schemas. The phonological loop encodes phonological, speech-based information (i.e. what is heard and read). The visuospatial sketchpad deals specifically with visual and spatial information (i.e. what is seen).

The Slave Systems

Baddeley and Hitch (1974) proposed that both working memory slave systems are critical for the ability to recall information. The phonological loop, which processes auditory and verbal information (Baddeley, 2002), is crucially involved in the memorization of information (e.g. while generating a sub-vocal representation of words). The phonological loop can be broken down into two components: a *phonological store* (i.e. used for the storage of information that is heard or read) and *articulatory rehearsal* (i.e. used for the processing and rehearsal of what is heard or read). At the same time, it is proposed that the visuospatial sketchpad is also crucially involved in the memorizing of information because it provides one with a workspace, or *sketchpad*, in which to manipulate visual stimuli that have been attended to within working memory, and briefly stores this information based on its various visual and spatial characteristics (e.g. colour, shape, orientation and location). Based on research by Logie (1995), the visuospatial sketchpad has also been identi-fied as having two components: a *visual cache* (i.e. used for storing visual information) and an *inner scribe* (i.e. used for processing and rehearsing spatial information).

Having access to two slave systems – a visuospatial sketchpad and a phonological system – provides two routes to potential LTM storage and increases the overall capacity base of working memory. Consistent with the model of working memory proposed by Baddeley and Hitch, research conducted by Paivio (1971, 1986) suggests that visual information and verbal (i.e. phonological) information are processed differently, and as a result, separate representations of the information are created. According to Dual-Coding Theory, memory for verbal information can be enhanced if a relevant visual aid is simultaneously presented or is imagined (Paivio, 1971, 1986). Likewise, memory for visual information can be enhanced when paired with a relevant verbal or phonological aid.

Building upon Paivio's assertions that separate representations of the same information are created from both coding processes and that their simultaneous use aids memory, Mayer (1997) suggests that not only do separate visual spatial and verbal information processing systems exist in working memory, but the simultaneous use of these systems aids learning. In the context of instructional design, Mayer (2005) refers to the explicit use of these systems for educational purposes as multimedia learning. Specifically, Mayer (1997) proposed that learning is optimized when lear-ners select, organize and integrate verbal and visual information presented to them, and then construct a new internal representation from that information, which integrates verbally based and visually based models (see Figure 2.2). According to Mayer (1997), for integration to take place, both the visual and the verbal information must be held in working memory at the same time. However, due to the limited capacity of working memory (discussed later), integration can sometimes be difficult (Chandler & Sweller, 1991; Sweller et al., 1990).

Nevertheless, in a series of eight experiments, Mayer and colleagues (Mayer, 1989; Mayer & Anderson, 1991, 1992; Mayer & Gallini, 1990) highlighted the potential benefits of offering students integrated study materials to work with (i.e. study materials that integrate visual and verbal information into one representation). They compared the problem-solving transfer performance of students who learned about the mechanics of tyre

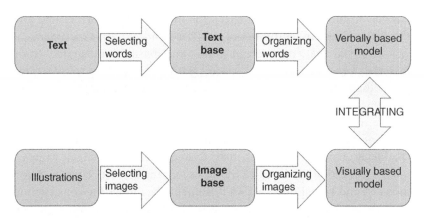

FIGURE 2.2 Mayer's (1997) Model of the Integration of Visual and Verbal Information

pumps and braking systems from *integrated* visual and verbal study materials with those who learned from verbal materials *only*. Specifically, these study materials presented students with step-by-step procedures for how tyre pumps and braking systems work. Problem-solving transfer questions used in this series of studies were, for example, 'What can be done to make a pump more reliable, that is, to make sure it would not fail?' and 'Suppose you push down and pull up the handle of a tyre pump several times but no air comes out. What could have gone wrong?'

Three of these experiments compared study materials with narration (i.e. verbal) integrated with animation (i.e. visual) and study materials using narration alone (Mayer & Anderson, 1991, 1992), and five experiments compared text integrated with illustrations versus text alone (Mayer, 1989; Mayer & Gallini, 1990). In all experiments, participants were instructed to study their allocated materials on mechanics and then generate as many solutions as possible to a series of transfer problems. Based on these eight experiments, overall, those who received integrated verbal and visual study materials produced more than 75% more creative solutions to the transfer problems than those who received the learning materials in verbal form only (Mayer, 1997).

Similarly, Mayer and colleagues (Mayer, 1989; Mayer & Anderson, 1991, 1992; Mayer & Sims, 1994; Mayer et al., 1995) conducted a series of ten experiments comparing the problem-solving transfer performance of students who studied from *integrated* study materials with those who studied the same information from verbal and visual materials *at separate times*. The topics of study were mechanics principles (similar to those described earlier), the human respiratory system and the development of lightning storms. Based on these ten experiments, it was observed that, on average, those who received integrated study materials produced over 50% more creative solutions to transfer problems than those who learned from verbal and visual materials at separate times (Mayer, 1997).

The combined use of both verbal and visual systems of representation to improve learning is supported by numerous research studies (Baddeley, Eldridge, & Lewis, 1981; Chandler & Sweller, 1991; Murray, 1968). In addition to Mayer's hypothesis that the combined presentation of visual and verbal information to students facilitates the construction of 'integrated internal representations of information', it has also been proposed that presenting both visual and verbal forms of information to students can help to reduce cognitive load (i.e. demands placed upon an individual in using and distributing working memory resources during cognitive activities; Chandler & Sweller, 1991; discussed in greater detail later).

The Episodic Buffer

Baddeley (2000) expanded his initial model of working memory to include the episodic buffer. The newly conceptualized episodic buffer is the temporary storage system within working memory, capable of storing information from the visuospatial sketchpad, the phonological loop or integrated information from both slave systems (Baddeley, 2002). This component is episodic because it is assumed to bind information into a unitary episodic representation (e.g. the chronological organization of events in a narrative, 'whereby this information is integrated across (storage) space and potentially extended across time' (i.e. information held in the episodic buffer can be subject to manipulation from LTM; Baddeley, 2000, p. 421). Essentially, the episodic buffer is much like the traditional view of short-term memory, as it acts as a limited capacity storage unit for information manipulated by the slave systems.

The episodic buffer also builds upon Ericsson and Kintsch's (1995) conceptualization of long-term working memory (LTWM), which is similar to the episodic buffer in that LTWM integrates novel information processed in short-term, working memory with that from long-term storage. Ericsson and Kintsch claim that the existence of LTWM explains remarkably rapid and accurate processing of novel information even when there is a considerable amount of information and/or it is highly complex. They suggest that this accuracy and speed result from the aid of LTM in processing novel information. For example, based on the work of Chase and Simon (1973) and de Groot (1965), Ericsson and Kintsch (1995) speculated that some form of established knowledge and expertise (which is represented in LTM) must aid chess masters when assessing an opponent's move, as the limited capacity of working memory cannot simultaneously store and process all the information necessary to complete the often-complex game assessments that expert chess players engage in.

Baddeley's theory on the episodic buffer is based on empirical research conducted by Wilson and Baddeley (1988) and Baddeley and Wilson (2002), which revealed that amnesiac patients who were not able to encode new information from working memory into long-term storage were nevertheless able to recall more novel information than what can be stored in short-term storage (Baddeley & Wilson, 2002). This finding suggests that working memory must be in some way aided by information or schemas (discussed later) in long-term storage, encoded prior to the onset of amnesia. Baddeley (2000, p. 419) further clarifies these results via the following example: 'if asked to recall a sequence of unrelated words, subjects typically begin to make errors once the number of words exceeds 5 or 6. However, if the words comprise a meaningful sentence, then a span of 16 or more is possible'. According to Baddeley, given that an individual possesses some level of expertise in literacy (i.e. the sentence is meaningful as a result of pre-existing knowledge stored in LTM), this 'chunking' of words (Chase & Simon, 1973; Gobet & Clarkson, 2004) is facilitated by LTM and aids in the retention of more information in the episodic buffer.[2] Nevertheless, in attempting to *permanently* store information, efforts must be made to transfer information from working memory to LTM.

LONG-TERM MEMORY

Whereas working memory can store a limited amount of information for a limited amount of time, LTM is a region of memory that enables relatively permanent storage of information, for example, facts in *semantic*

---

[2] Based on Baddeley's research, the episodic buffer may potentially be considered the workspace where higher-order cognitive skills (i.e. critical thinking) engage novel information and draw from pre-existing knowledge in order to draw conclusions, judge situations or solve problems.

LTM, events in *episodic* LTM and procedures in *procedural* LTM (Tulving, 1984). The transfer of information from working memory to LTM depends crucially on the manner in which the information is encoded (Tulving, 1984; Tulving & Thompson, 1973). Encoding refers to the efforts made to organize information in working memory, for example, through rehearsal (Craik & Watkins, 1973) and/or schema construction (Craik, 1983) for purposes of storage in LTM and potential retrieval. The success of encoding depends on the amount, or depth, of information processing in working memory. For example, research suggests that more successful encoding results from deep, semantic processing of information, whereas shallow processing of information (e.g. a focus on the colour, as opposed to the meaning of words) may result in poor subsequent recall (Craik, 1983). Furthermore, the likelihood of information being stored in LTM is increased when it is encoded into one's existing schemata/schemas (i.e. representations of knowledge that have been assembled from previous experience, which function as a plan or a set of expectations that guide subsequent information processing).

Schemas

Though there is no single definition of the concept of a schema, various descriptions have been offered. Bartlett (1932) described a schema as an active organization of past reactions or experiences. Another definition is provided by Sweller (1999, p. 10), who describes a schema as:

> a cognitive construct that permits people to treat multiple elements of information as a single element categorised according to the manner in which it will be used.

In the context of memory research and theory, cognitive psychologists often assume that schemas are large cognitive structures within LTM (Neisser, 1976), which can be used to facilitate the assimilation of new information. Schemas can also be used to build knowledge structures by organizing elements of information. For example, smaller, specific schemas (i.e. lower-order schemas) can be reconstructed into a larger, more comprehensive and complex schema (i.e. a higher-order schema).

The role of schemata in memory is complex. Information that is the focus of active processing in working memory can be processed and organized in many different ways, depending on the manner in which items of information are classified and arranged into systems of representation. These active, ongoing systems of representation may be transformed not only by new incoming information from the environment but also by pre-existing schemas in LTM. For example, to determine the criteria people use for inclusion of information into certain categories and the method of categorization they use, Chi, Glaser and Rees (1982) asked two groups with different levels of expertise (novice and expert) to categorize twenty-four physics problems based on their similarities. Though both groups identified approximately the same number of categories, qualitative analysis revealed that novices (i.e. those with insufficient, relevant schemata) categorized the problems according to either the objects referred to in the problem (e.g. a spring), the keywords that have meaning in physics (e.g. friction), or the interaction or configuration of various objects (e.g. a block on an inclined plane). Conversely, it was found that experts (i.e. those with sufficient, relevant schemata) categorized the problems according to the law of physics that governed each problem (i.e. the solution method).

The authors argued that such expert solution methods are *higher-order schemas* because they are coordinated in the context of mathematical formulae and computational systems of relations between abstract and concrete features of the problem. The authors also argued that these solutions were more advanced and abstract than the *lower-order schemas* possessed by the novices, which largely focused on concrete aspects of the problem. Thus, consistent with many developmental accounts that focus on knowledge growth and the levels of complexity and integration of concrete and abstract forms of representation (e.g. Fischer, 1980; Piaget, 1952), schema theories of memory often assume that schemas can have subordinate schemata embedded in them (e.g. a system of concrete representations embedded in a lower-order schema) and can also be embedded in superordinate schemata (e.g. a system of abstractions embedded in a higher-order schema; see Figure 2.3).

As part of LTM, schemas aid working memory by providing a system of representations that facilitate the encoding, storage and retrieval of information. When novel information is processed within working memory, any number of schemas can be used to provide relevant knowledge to assist the processing of the novel information. In Baddeley's model, schemas may act upon information in the episodic buffer and thus facilitate the reconfiguration and transfer of information into LTM. In this way, novel information can be integrated into existing schemas in LTM, thus

FIGURE 2.3 Expert Schema for Principles of Mechanics (Chi, Glaser, & Rees, 1982)

freeing up space within working memory. The role of the schema, in this context, is very important as processing space within working memory is limited.

The findings of Chi, Glaser and Rees (1982) as well as similar research by Chase and Simon (1973) and Kotovsky, Hayes and Simon (1985) suggest that once information is adequately encoded into a schema, it is treated as stored knowledge (Sweller, 1999). To elaborate, in order to create knowledge, schemas must be constructed in a meaningful way; that is, specifically linked with the context in which they are to be used, in order for them to be retrieved or to aid in the encoding of new information at a later time. For schemas to be constructed in a meaningful way, the information subject to schema construction must be understood, or comprehended (Sweller, 2005, 2010).

Comprehension as LTM

In addition to the recall of knowledge, comprehension also shares interdependency with schema construction, given that schema construction, according to some theorists, is essentially the same as building understanding, or comprehension (Pollock, Chandler, & Sweller, 2002; Sweller, 2005). According to Bloom (1956), comprehension is the ability to understand or grasp the meaning of information, which implies the ability to translate information from one level of abstraction to another, one symbolic form to another, or one verbal form to another. Bloom's taxonomy further describes comprehension as the confirmation of knowledge, in the sense that knowledge can be confirmed via explaining, summarizing, paraphrasing, or illustrating information based on prior learning (Huitt, 2011).

A more recent conceptualization of comprehension is the view developed by Sweller (2005). Broadly speaking, Sweller (2005, p. 21) describes comprehension as 'changes in LTM, along with the effect of those changes on working memory. Without changes in LTM, nothing has been understood'. The nature of *changes* in LTM that Sweller speaks of refers specifically to schema construction. Sweller further describes comprehension, or understanding, as the ability to integrate schemas from LTM with novel information simultaneously in working memory. See Figure 2.4 for a diagram of the relationships among working memory,

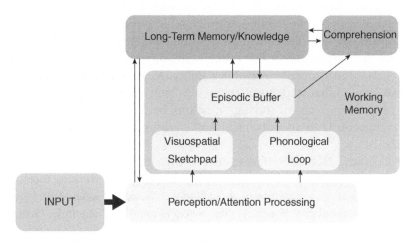

FIGURE 2.4 Working Memory as a Buffer between Informational Input and Storage in LTM as Knowledge

LTM and comprehension in this context. Sweller (1994) also claims that the acquisition of knowledge (i.e. in LTM) is dependent upon schema construction, because it is only once a schema (i.e. knowledge) has been constructed that information can be understood or comprehended. Sweller (1999) further simplifies his conceptualization of comprehension by describing it as the ability to make required connections between novel items of information and/or schemas.

Given the importance of the foundational processes necessary for critical thinking discussed earlier (i.e. memory and comprehension), it becomes important to also explore some of the factors that may negatively impact these processes (and likewise, the subsequent application of critical thinking skills), namely, cognitive load. Cognitive load refers to the cognitive demands put upon an individual in using and distributing working memory resources during cognitive activities such as learning and problem-solving (Sweller, 1999). The following discussion of cognitive load as an impediment to learning will pave the way for a closer analysis of the historical perspectives of critical thinking and the ways in which we apply critical thinking skills in the chapters that follow.

COGNITIVE LOAD

Based on the earlier review of working memory and frameworks for thinking, excess demands placed on working memory resources during cognitive activities are speculated to impede performance of all higher-order thinking processes, given that subsequent thinking processes are dependent upon one's ability to process and remember individual propositions and interdependent proposition sets (Halpern, 2014; Maybery, Bain, & Halford, 1986). For example, in support of the link between memory and deductive reasoning ability, Maybery, Bain and Halford (1986) found that students often have difficulty in inferring conclusions in deductive problem-solving situations because of the necessity to simultaneously recall and consider all elements in a premise or a set of premises.

Cognitive load also refers in part to the amount of information that needs to be processed within an already limited capacity working memory (Baddeley, 2000, 2002; Cowan, 2000; Gobet & Clarkson, 2004; Miller, 1956; Pollock, Chandler, & Sweller, 2002; Sweller, 1999). For example, George Miller (1956) postulated that only seven (plus or minus two) items of information can be processed in short-term working memory at any given time. More recent research disputes Miller's 'magical number' of seven items, or chunks[3], that can be processed, claiming that the number is actually closer to four items of information (Cowan, 2000), or possibly less (Gobet & Clarkson, 2004). According to Sweller (1994), there are two types of cognitive load that constrict working memory capacity, impede learning and together determine total cognitive load – *intrinsic* and *extraneous* cognitive load.

Intrinsic Cognitive Load

Intrinsic cognitive load refers to the cognitive demands 'imposed by the basic characteristics of information' (Sweller, 1994, p. 6). The amount of intrinsic cognitive load placed on an individual during a cognitive task depends on the element interactivity, which refers to the number of elements, or items of information that must be simultaneously processed in working memory in order to learn and understand the information. 'All of the learning elements interact and unless all are considered simultaneously in working memory, the problem and its solution will not be understood' (Sweller, 2010, p. 41). Simply, intrinsic cognitive load is caused by the necessity to simultaneously assimilate a relatively high number of elements, and their interactivity, in order to solve a problem.

For example, Pollock, Chandler and Sweller (2002) found that working memory capacity is often at its peak when trying to assimilate complex, or too much, information (i.e. where there are many elements of information to assimilate and high levels of element interactivity). In their research, twenty-two first-year industrial trade students were asked to study materials designed to facilitate learning of electrical tests. Two study formats were available to students. One group of students studied from an *interacting elements* format and the other group studied from what the authors called an *isolated-interacting elements* format. The interacting elements group were provided with a diagram of 'the insulation resistance test' and 'the Earth continuity test' along with a set of instructions that explained the theory behind the steps they were to follow. Those asked to learn in this condition had to simultaneously consider multiple elements, such as the

---

[3] This limited capacity can be increased by *chunking*, or organizing items of information together into *chunks*, each of which possesses its own discrete meaning and acts as a new, higher-order (i.e. more complex) item of information. Since it is not necessarily five to nine discrete items of information that a person can recall, but five to nine *chunks*, chunking allows one to increase the amount of information that can be encoded, stored and retrieved in working memory.

aim of the test, the required setting of the voltmeter, the required setting of the appliance switch, the location of the earth lead and the line lead during both phases of the test, and the criteria by which to judge if the voltmeter readings were safe. Interacting elements are 'characterised by the inclusion of all elements required for understanding but at the cost of an impossibly high working memory load' (Pollock, Chandler, & Sweller, 2002, p. 66). Those in the isolated-interacting elements group were provided the same diagrams as the other group and only brief instructions of exactly what to do for each step. As these isolated elements required less integrated understanding, but rather sequential understanding and application of rules, they also placed less of a load on working memory.

Participants were asked to rate the mental effort needed to study and were then tested for their knowledge based on their study materials. Forty-eight hours later, both groups were again asked to study, but this time both groups received the interacting elements format. Results revealed that those who had initially studied isolated-interacting elements performed significantly better on subsequent high-element interactivity questions and better, on average, on practical tests than those in the interacting elements group. Those in the isolated-interacting elements group also found their learning condition to be significantly less demanding than those in the interacting elements group.

Furthermore, in a follow-up experiment by Pollock, Chandler and Sweller (2002), no differences in learning and self-reported difficulty of learning conditions were found between novices who studied via the isolated-interacting elements approach and experts who studied via the interacting elements approach. According to the authors, findings indicated that expertise can also reduce intrinsic cognitive load on working memory and allows for less stressful learning (i.e. in terms of perceived difficulty), due to the experts already possessing the schemas necessary to learn and succeed on the tests. Thus, the authors proposed that complex information cannot be simultaneously processed for purposes of understanding and memorization unless the information has been previously organized into a schema. The authors further proposed that the promotion of schema construction would lead to an increase in the learner's understanding, which in turn would facilitate subsequent memorization (Pollock, Chandler, & Sweller, 2002, p. 82).

In summary, Pollock, Chandler and Sweller (2002) argue that a high level of element interactivity can cause cognitive load and that readers perform better when they learn by first processing information in an organized, sequential manner, possibly by integrating this new information into existing schemas or by building new schemas via sequential addition of elements; and then by re-reading the text, in order to commit the information to memory. That is, read first to understand and read a second time to remember. Notably, an individual's level of expertise or prior knowledge of a subject area may influence the experience of intrinsic cognitive load (Sweller, 1999, 2010). That is, even if information possesses a high level of element interactivity, individuals with relevant, pre-existing knowledge may not experience as much intrinsic cognitive load as those with less knowledge (Chi, Glaser, & Rees, 1982; Kotovsky, Hayes, & Simon, 1985; Larkin et al., 1980).

As such, although intrinsic cognitive load is fixed by virtue of the number of elements that need to be coordinated to solve a problem, if working memory has access to established schemas from LTM, then the demand associated with element interactivity in working memory may be decreased as a result of schema-driven chunking, thus reducing overall cognitive load. Though intrinsic load cannot be reduced by the format of instructional materials (i.e. regardless of format, a fixed body of information contains a fixed number of elements; Moreno & Park, 2010; Paas, Renkl, & Sweller, 2003), research suggests that efforts to promote schema construction through training can aid in the reduction of intrinsic load (Pollock, Chandler, & Sweller, 2002; van Merriënboer, Kirschner, & Kester, 2003). Those who are trained in a specific domain are provided the opportunity to develop expertise in that domain through the construction of relevant schemas during training (Chi, Glaser, & Rees, 1982; Kotovsky, Hayes, & Simon, 1985) and, thus, are better equipped to assimilate information with high element interactivity than are those who do not possess the relevant pre-existing knowledge (Pollock, Chandler, & Sweller, 2002; Sweller, 2010). Notably, a vast body of research (e.g. Gadzella, Ginther, & Bryant, 1996; Hitchcock, 2004; Reed & Kromrey, 2001; Rimiene, 2002; Solon, 2007) indicates that training in critical thinking yields better critical thinking performance than performance prior to training. These findings suggest that critical thinking, which may be applied to problematic situations with high levels of element interactivity, can be trained. Subsequently, it is possible that schemas for critical thinking strategies can reduce the cognitive load associated with high element interactivity by offering the critical thinker a set of cognitive, or metacognitive, strategies that allow them to navigate problematic situations and infer reasonable solutions to problems. Furthermore, critical thinking implies a deeper level of understanding, which aids in overcoming intrinsic cognitive load – provided it is conducted in preparation for remembering, or rehearsal. Though domain-specific knowledge training and the training of critical thinking may facilitate schema construction, which may in turn aid in overcoming intrinsic cognitive load, there still remains the issue of overcoming extraneous cognitive load.

Extraneous Cognitive Load

Extraneous cognitive load refers to the cognitive demands imposed by instructional design (van Merriënboer & Ayres, 2005) and can be caused by a number of features of instructional materials that impose different demands on working memory. Sweller and colleagues have argued that extraneous cognitive load is caused by the demands placed on working memory associated with, for example, the need to switch attention during the assimilation of information and assimilating redundant information (Ayres & Sweller, 2005; Chandler & Sweller, 1991; Sweller et al., 1990; Sweller, 1999; Tindall-Ford, Chandler, & Sweller, 1997). In the context of extraneous cognitive load, redundancy refers to the presence of information that does not contribute to schema acquisition or interferes with learning (e.g. irrelevant information and information presented more than once; Sweller, 1999, 2010). Attention-switching demands refer to the demands placed on working memory by switching between multiple sources of information that are unintelligible in isolation and result in less learning than if the multiple sources were presented in an integrated format (Sweller, 1999, 2010).

While intrinsic cognitive load is fixed by virtue of the number of elements one must coordinate to solve a problem or assimilate new knowledge, extraneous cognitive load can be reduced via the manipulation of instructional materials. For example, Chandler and Sweller (1991) conducted multiple experiments and found that when two sources of study information are integrated (e.g. a diagram and text), students recall more information than when asked to study from separated texts and diagrams. In one of their experiments, Chandler and Sweller (1991) compared two groups of students who studied an electrical wiring installation procedure from either conventional study materials (i.e. separate diagram and text) or integrated study materials (i.e. text appropriately placed within the diagram). Those in the integrated group spent significantly less time processing the electrical wiring installation material than those in the conventional group. In addition, those in the integrated group scored significantly higher than the conventional group on subsequent tests of their knowledge for electrical wiring installation. These results suggested that switching attention from one source of information to another, while studying the conventional materials, was a source of cognitive load that impeded learning. Similar results were reported by Sweller et al. (1990) and Tindall-Ford, Chandler, and Sweller (1997).

Like Chandler and Sweller (1991), Tindall-Ford, Chandler, and Sweller (1997) also found that learning is impeded when instructional materials require a high degree of attention switching. Their research examined participants' ability to recall a list of instructions for an electrical test. Two groups were examined: a group that was given a diagram with the instructions integrated into the diagram and a group that was given the instructions separate from the diagram. The group that used integrated diagrams and instructions performed significantly better than the group with separate diagram and instructions on a test of transfer knowledge (i.e. the ability to apply the principles of electrical testing, which the group studied, to other electrical systems). Tindall-Ford, Chandler, and Sweller (1997) concluded, in conjunction with research by Sweller et al. (1990) and Chandler and Sweller (1991), that encoding environments that increase the cognitive load placed on the learner (e.g. via attention switching) tend not only to slow the learning process but also reduce overall levels of learning (Sweller et al., 1990; Sweller & Chandler, 1991; Tindall-Ford, Chandler, & Sweller, 1997). Extraneous cognitive load will be revisited in discussion of facilitating the application of critical thinking in Chapters 11 and 12.

SUMMARY AND CONCLUSION

This chapter elaborated upon the foundational processes necessary for critical thinking, by presenting memory and comprehension in light of empirical research, and also investigated cognitive load as a potential impediment to these processes. Specifically, working memory is a multi-component system for the processing, encoding, and retrieval of information within brief periods of time; and through manipulation of that information within short-term storage, it can be transferred into LTM (i.e. a region of memory that enables relatively permanent storage of information), where it is presumably represented as a form of knowledge. According to Sweller (1994), the acquisition of knowledge is dependent upon schema construction, because it is only once a schema (i.e. knowledge) has been constructed that information can be comprehended.

Research suggests that memory and comprehension are interconnected processes (Sweller, 1994, 1999, 2005) that are necessary for the application of critical thinking skills (e.g. Halpern, 2014; Maybery, Bain, & Halford, 1986). Furthermore, research indicates that in order to improve learning and avoid cognitive load, efforts should be made to assimilate information multiple times – first, to understand the information and again in order to remember the information (Pollock, Chandler, & Sweller, 2002). Through investigation of the foundational processes necessary for critical thinking in both Chapters 1 and 2, we may now progress to discussion of the historical perspectives of critical thinking.

EXERCISE 2.1

Please conduct your own investigation of empirical research on working memory, long-term memory and comprehension. Compare the research found in your own investigation with the research cited in this chapter with respect to both the findings and the methods in which the research was conducted. What can you conclude about the nature of working memory, long-term memory, and comprehension?

3

Historical Perspectives

The trouble with the world is that the stupid are cocksure and the intelligent are full of doubt.
~ Bertrand Russell (1872–1970)

Cogito ergo sum, or *I think, therefore I am,* is the widely recognizable phrase penned by Rene Descartes in the 17th century. To Descartes, this concept proved his existence, as up until this realization, he entertained the notion that perhaps his existence was nothing more than an elaborate deception. However, through realizing that he had the ability to entertain the potential for this deception and subsequently doubt his existence, he concluded that he must exist as a result of his *ability to think and reason about* the possibility of this deception and the nature of his own existence. Though this is certainly a very abstract line of thinking, and to some extent circular, this phrase, *I think, therefore, I am,* is largely inspirational in the field of logic and indeed critical thinking as it exhibits our very existence as dependent on our ability to think.

Descartes was by no means the first to grapple with the concept of cognition. The study of the nature of thought and reasoning arguably began alongside the birth of Western philosophy in ancient Greece. Greek philosophers such as Parmenides, Socrates, Democritus, Plato and Aristotle, all played a large role in the development of our understanding of the nature of thought and reasoning. For example, according to Democritus, there are two types of knowing: *bastard knowledge* and *legitimate knowledge.* 'Bastard' knowledge refers to knowledge gained through perception (i.e. observation through the five senses), which is subjective and, thus, insufficient for purposes of making generalizations. The attainment of 'legitimate' knowledge is achieved through applying logical reasoning to the perceived sensory data (i.e. bastard knowledge). Essentially, Democritus' process of developing of legitimate knowledge is one of the first examples of scientific thinking and, likewise, inductive reasoning (see Chapter 9), as attaining legitimate knowledge involves the gathering of sensory-based bastard knowledge (i.e. separate parts) and the examination and reasoning about these parts in order to generate a conclusion (i.e. the whole).

FALSIFICATION

Though no written legacy of Socrates exists, his student Plato avidly relates his mentor's teachings throughout his works; and it is from this that we are provided with the *Socratic Method*. At the core of the Socratic Method, according to Plato's account of Socrates, is the *elenchus*. The elenchus refers to the procedural refutation of a claim based on in-depth examination and consists of four major steps. This procedure begins with (1) the refutation of a central claim, or thesis statement, through the (2) identification of further related propositions that are either true or agreed upon. These additional propositions are then used to (3) indicate the falsity of the central claim (i.e. these propositions are used to contradict the central claim, acting as the refutation). The acceptance of these propositions and their subsequent contradiction of the central claim (4) reveal that the original, central claim is false and the initial refutation (i.e. negation) is true. Generally, the falsification of a claim through elenctic examination leads to the realization that the original claim requires refinement to make it true. This may be as simple as the addition or removal of a single word (e.g. 'Rex is a brown dog' becomes either 'Rex is a dog' or 'Rex is a black dog'), or the complete overhaul of the claim's meaning (e.g. 'Rex is a cat' becomes 'Rex is not a cat' or 'Rex is a dog').

Though debate exists over whether the Socratic Method actually leads to the attainment of knowledge or is used simply to make another's argument look foolish (i.e. the negation of false knowledge), from a scientific perspective, it must be regarded as the former. That is, through the falsification of a claim (which may have been previously accepted as true; e.g. 'X is Y'), new knowledge is created (e.g. 'Actually, X is *not* Y'). For example, the acknowledgement of the fact that the Earth is not flat was just as important as the discovery that the Earth is round. Simply, a finding that indicates the truth of a null hypothesis is still a valuable finding and is in itself new knowledge.

Over two millennia later, the use of the Socratic Method and its associated mantra of falsification remains an integral function of critical thinking. According to the 20th-century logician and philosopher of science,

Karl Popper, we cannot prove things true – only false. Essentially, we live in a world where lasting certainty does not exist and the best we can do is simply improve upon old theories. According to Popper (1934/1959, 1999), knowledge is theoretical. That is not to say that there may or may not be something that is knowledge, but rather, what we think we know may or may not be the case. Essentially, all that we hold as true is not fact, but simply the best working model for how things are – they are theories and not laws.

For example, prior to the Enlightenment, it was widely believed that the Earth was flat. Though it may seem to us preposterous that this was actually believed, generations from now, people might view one of our near-and-dear beliefs equally silly. The manner in which beliefs, such as these, change is through falsification. According to Popper, no amount of consistently occurring outcomes can prove a theory – it simply suggests, at best, that the theory is likely not to be false. On the other hand, in order to falsify or disprove a theory, it only takes one occurrence of an outcome that contradicts the theory to prove it false. For example, in the case of problem-solving, we use strategies that have worked for us or others we know in the past. If the problem-solving strategy fails us, we discard it and develop a new one.

From Popper's perspective, scientific knowledge (and knowledge in general) develops based on a process characterized by the formula:

$$PS \text{ (problem-situation)}_1 \rightarrow TT \text{ (tentative theories)}_1 \rightarrow$$
$$EE \text{ (error elimination)}_1 \rightarrow PS_2$$

According to this formula, theories are developed and tested in light of a given problem and those that are falsified, or proven incorrect, are eliminated, thus leaving those that have not yet been falsified. After this process, there may be only one or even several that are still open to falsification. This does not mean that one of these theories is true but instead better fit the problem-situation it was designed to solve. Again, just because a theory is consistently tested does not make it true, nor does it save it from falsification in the future. According to Popper, the manner in which theories develop and adapt is what we perceive as our improved understanding of the universe; and as a result, the problem-situations we face also adapt, develop and become more complex, in line with our theories.

Popper's philosophy owes a great deal to Socrates' elenchus and, more generally, the Socratic Method. Essentially, the Socratic Method is a form of investigative inquiry and debate, conducted between individuals with opposing views regarding a given subject, in which each individual attempts to falsify or refute the claims of their opponent. Within the debate, the opposing views are questioned by each individual and subsequently require justification. The manner in which one justifies their thinking can be completed in one of two ways – through formal or informal logic.

Perhaps the most important classical thinker in the fields of reasoning, argumentation and indeed critical thinking was Plato's protégé, Aristotle. Aristotle is credited with giving birth to the study of logic, which is the study of valid reasoning with respect to argumentation and is exhibited in his compiled works, the *Organon*. Specifically, Aristotelian logic, or formal logic, is the study of deriving inferences from propositions based, not on the subject matter, but on the form or structure of the propositions that comprise the argument. The foundations of formal logic were laid out by Aristotle in the 4th century BC, through his work with syllogistic reasoning (i.e. the ability to infer the validity of an argument in which a conclusion follows from two premises). Whereas classical Aristotelian logic has a long history, symbolic logic, which is a development of concepts and techniques that were implicit in the work of Aristotle, has a relatively short history, though the difference between them is only that of different stages of development (Basson & O'Connor, 1968). Prior to the 17th century, logic seemed to most of Aristotle's successors to be a finished science, due largely to both their failure to make significant contributions to the subject in light of the thoroughness of Aristotle's achievement and the undeveloped state of the mathematical sciences. Since then, however, it has been realized that Aristotle's treatment of logic covered only a small, though important, branch of its study. Thus, formal logic can be considered as consisting of both classical Aristotelian logic and the more modern symbolic logic, in which the latter is treated as an extension of Aristotle's classical logic. In order to understand the process of syllogistic reasoning and indeed the nature of formal logic, it is necessary to consider both symbolic logic and Aristotelian logic.

According to Lewis (1918), there are three main characteristics of symbolic logic: (1) the use of *ideograms* (i.e. symbols), which stand directly for concepts; (2) the use of the *deductive method* (i.e. from a small number of statements, an indefinite number of other statements can be generated through the application of a limited number of rules; or inferring from the general to the specific); and (3) the use of *variables* (i.e. having a definite range of significance). The main function of symbolic logic is to provide methods of testing the validity of arguments, which is accomplished by separating the logical form from the subject matter of the argument. In this context, logicians are interested in the logical form only and dispense with the words that refer to the subject matter by replacing them with variables (e.g. p and q), given that the validity of an argument depends exclusively on its logical form. This is interesting to consider, given that one might perceive the purpose of reasoning and debating as being able to arrive at conclusions that are *true* with respect to the subject(s) one is reasoning or debating, rather than *validity*. However, upon reflection, the two conditions (i.e. truth and validity) are necessary to guarantee the conclusions of any piece of reasoning. First, the propositional evidence, from which deductions are made, must be true. Second, the deductions themselves must be valid. However, formal logic can only guarantee the latter. Thus, the truth must be established as a secondary goal (if desired), outside the scope of formal logic. The method of establishing the truth of an argument, as best one can, is known as informal logic. Though we now turn our focus to discussion of informal logic, we will return to a deeper review of formal logic and its implications in our discussion of the critical thinking skill of inference in Chapter 7.

INFORMAL LOGIC

According to Johnson and Blair (1987), informal logic is the analysis, interpretation, evaluation, criticism and construction of argumentation through the development of non-formal standards and criteria. Noting the important relationship between informal logic and argumentation, van Eemeren (2009) further differentiates informal and formal logic by stating that the former is a study of reasoning that is closer related to argumentation theory than the latter. According to van Eemeren et al. (1996, p. 5), argumentation is 'a verbal and social activity of reason aimed at increasing (or decreasing) the acceptability of a controversial standpoint ... by putting forward a constellation of propositions intended to justify (or refute) the standpoint'. In argumentation, like formal logic, one must work with some form of representation of the argument, in order to identify, analyse and evaluate the logical relationships among propositions within the argument (Walton, 2006). However, instead of focusing exclusively on the form, or structure, of the argument, additional consideration must be paid to the argument's subject matter. By taking into account both the structure of reasoning and the subject matter of that reasoning, we are able to begin to think critically about that subject.

Continuing with this notion of the interrelatedness of informal logic and argumentation, notably, both are inextricably linked with the manner in which we conduct and apply critical thinking (Alvarez-Ortiz, 2007; Daly, 2001; Kuhn, Katz, & Dean, 2004; Twardy, 2004). For example, according to Davies (2008), argumentation is the embodiment of being able to make sound inferences and evaluate them objectively. Sanders, Wiseman and Gass (1994) further support this link by making the point that the only method in which to adequately differentiate weak and strong arguments is through critical thinking.

The common usage of informal logic began in the 1950s, marked by the work of Monroe Beardsley and, to a larger extent, Stephen Toulmin. In his influential book, *The Uses of Argument* (1958), Toulmin argued against traditional, formal logic (e.g. syllogistic reasoning) as the sole strategy of inference, as he believed reasoning should not be concerned solely with inferential relationships, but also with the justificatory function of argumentation (i.e. establishing a claim and then supporting it by a statement of justification). Given our discussion of formal logic, a number of limitations may have become apparent; for example, it does not take into account the *truth* regarding the subject matter of an argument. In this sense, formal logic is not always practical, especially in real-world settings. This is due largely to the fact that though it ensures validity, it does not ensure truth. For example, though the syllogism, *All things with four legs are dangerous* and *cats are not dangerous; therefore, cats do not have four legs*, is valid, it does not reflect truth. Perhaps some cats (i.e. with four legs) are not dangerous; perhaps, some are dangerous; and most certainly, most cats do have four legs.

Furthermore, formal logic does not adequately take into account the justificatory function of argumentation when used to infer conclusions. Although common in scientific thinking, the provision of justification for propositions was used less by philosophers when building arguments using traditional strategies, which tended to emphasize training in the use of syllogisms – the core of formal logic. Toulmin argued in favour of informal logic, which operates at the heart of scientific thinking. He found that this type of logic required a grounded, practical strategy which stressed the provision of justification for every reason and objection related to a core claim.

FIGURE 3.1 An Example of Toulmin's Model of Mapping

According to Toulmin's approach, each claim within an argument must be supported by a satisfactory warrant (i.e. a generally accepted belief or value which is taken for granted by both the writer and the reader), which either explicitly or implicitly bridges both datum and conclusion. Through his investigation of argumentation, Toulmin derived what many perceive as the first example of modern argument mapping. Please see Figure 3.1 for an example of Toulmin's mapping strategy and Figure 3.2 for an example of a more recent strategy of argument mapping, created using Rationale (van Gelder, 2007). Thus, argument mapping is grounded in informal logic, where the strength of any claim presented is dependent solely on the strength of its justification, in terms of logical strength (i.e. the strength of the relationship among propositions used in order to infer a conclusion), credibility (i.e. trustworthiness or reliability of the information's source) and relevance (i.e. the pertinence or applicability of one proposition to another). Argument mapping is a method of visually representing an argument for the purposes of easing cognitive load; maintaining the integrity of logical reasoning; facilitating enhanced assimilation and subsequent critical thinking. Though argument mapping is discussed in greater detail in Chapter 12, with respect to presentation of pedagogical and learning strategies used to enhance critical thinking ability, the concept is introduced here in order to briefly exemplify how it can used in situations where critical thinking is necessary. This is also important to consider given that later description and discussion of critical thinking and its associated skills, in Chapters 4–8, will be presented, in large part, through the utilization of argument maps.

Informal logic is a useful strategy of deliberation for when relevant information to support or refute a claim is scarce, when an argument is open-ended or when a problem to which the argument pertains is ill-structured (Means & Voss, 1996), in which case, multiple, alternative,

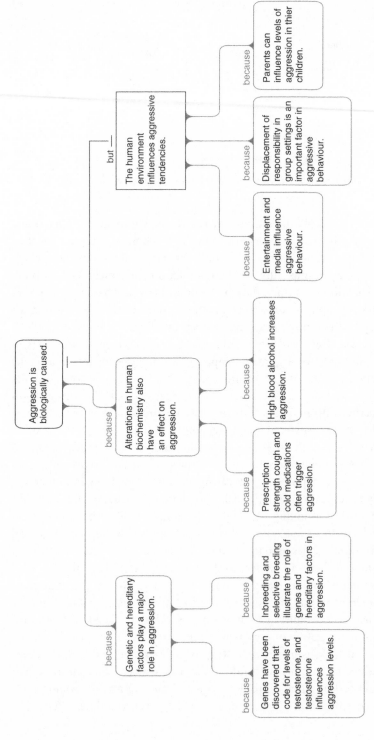

FIGURE 3.2 An Example of an Argument Map using Rationale™ (van Gelder, 2007)

solution methods can be (and often are) constructed to attempt to solve the problem. Ill-structured problems often refer to everyday, real-world dilemmas where there is conflicting information and where those involved in the argument disagree about the potential solutions to the problem. While training in formal logic is invaluable in many situations (e.g. for philosophical deliberation, following or constructing a line of deductive reasoning, identifying logical fallacies and rhetorical strategies in political discourse), informal logic is essential because it is very often necessary to provide justification for propositions, claims or decisions when grappling with every day, real-world, ill-structured problems. This applies to both local and personal problems and questions (e.g. 'Is social networking technology a waste of my time or a useful time investment?'), as well as more complex, global problems and questions (e.g. 'How can global warming be stopped?').

On the other hand, many well-structured problems, such as physics and mathematics problems, are open to resolution using formal or mathematical logic and may have singular solutions that are either right or wrong. For example, when presented with the question 'If a car has been travelling at 60 mph for 6 hours, how far has the car travelled?', mathematical computation implies that the only correct answer is 360 miles, and all other solutions are incorrect. However, the problem with relying exclusively on formal logic for the purpose of problem-solving is that for many real-world problems, arriving at solutions – in terms of simply being 'right-or-wrong' solutions – is not always necessarily feasible.

As arguments can possess a variety of claims, supports and objections, it becomes increasingly important to be certain of the linkage among propositions within the argument, especially in terms of evaluating their relevance to one another and their logical strength of interdependence. However, in the context of reading, writing or deliberation, this 'interlinking', or integration, of propositions within an argument can be difficult and may lead to a cohesion deficit (Duchastel, 1990). For example, when faced with reading about a newly encountered topic, a student may experience a cohesion deficit if they are unable to integrate arguments within the text itself, or link these novel arguments with knowledge they may have previously assimilated. Thus, the relations among propositions in an argument must be made clear to the reader; otherwise, the argument may appear incoherent and may cause a cohesion deficit in the mind of the reader. In terms of the structure of the argument on the page, any potential incoherence in the logical interdependencies between propositions may require that the reader engage in additional cognitive processing such that they can coherently tie the arguments together – thus increasing cognitive load and potentially having a negative impact on ongoing memory, comprehension and critical thinking processes. In addition, a lack of cohesion between or among propositions in the learning context can increase the likelihood of a student failing to achieve their goal of constructing a good, logical argument under examination (Duchastel, 1990; Fox, Grunst, & Quast, 1994).

Historically, Dewey's (1933, p. 8) conceptualization of reflective thought as 'active, persistent, and careful consideration of any belief or supposed form of knowledge in the light of the grounds that support it and the further conclusions to which it tends' helped give birth to the concept of *critical*[1] thinking (Moseley at el., 2005; Paul, Elder, & Bartell, 1997), which was coined by Edward Glaser eight years later. According to Glaser (1941), critical thinking is a cognitive skill that possesses three characteristics: (1) a positive attitude towards the thoughtful consideration of problems that people experience, (2) knowledge of logical reasoning strategies and (3) the ability to apply the fore-mentioned attitudes and strategies. Recognition of the importance of critical thinking in education soon followed and gained further momentum due to the growth of interest in informal logic initiated in part by the work of Stephen Toulmin in the late 1950s (Allen, Feezel, & Kauffeld, 1967; Toulmin, 1958). To reiterate, informal logic is a type of logic that emphasizes the justificatory function of argumentation, namely that a good argument requires sufficient support (e.g. reliable and valid empirical evidence). Deliberations in relation to critical thinking skills grew in part from the notion of informal logic, in that, claims could only be made (and justified) after a sufficient amount of analysis and evaluation had been conducted on propositions and their logical interdependencies.

SUMMARY AND CONCLUSION

Critical thinking has a long and rich history, dating back 2,400 plus years to the time of Socrates. The work conducted by Aristotle on what we know as classical, formal logic alongside more recent endeavours in informal logic and argumentation has also largely contributed to what we know as critical

---

[1] Notably, students often inappropriately associate critical thinking with *critiquing*, for example, an argument, idea or point of view. Though critiquing arguments, ideas and points of view is an important aspect of critical thinking, the type of thinking in question is *critical* with respect to the word's origin, which refers to the Greek word *kritikos*, meaning 'able to make judgments'.

thinking. That is, by being able to assess the logical structure of an argument and the subject matter of that reasoning, we are able to begin to think critically about that subject. Furthermore, recognition of the important links among critical thinking, logic and argumentation; and subsequent work in these fields have provided us with a means of visually representing our thinking in a graphical manner – argument mapping. Though we will continue our discussion of argument mapping and its relationship with critical thinking in Chapter 12, it is important that we first come to consider what exactly is meant by critical thinking, with respect to clearly identifying both a definition and a description of the skills involved.

EXERCISE 3.1

Please investigate other uses of argument mapping or other methods of using boxes and arrows to represent one's thinking. Do you think the method of visually representing the argument/reasoning in this instance was helpful? Why or why not? What could have made it more helpful in representing the reasoning behind the argument?

PART II

CRITICAL THINKING SKILLS
AND DISPOSITIONS

After much effort, as names, definitions, sights, and other data of sense are brought into contact and friction one with another, in the course of scrutiny and kindly testing by men who proceed by question and answer without ill will, with a sudden flash there shines forth understanding about every problem, and an intelligence whose efforts reach the furthest limits of human powers.

~ Plato (427–347 BC)

4

What Is Critical Thinking?
Definitions and Conceptualizations

Critical thinking is thinking about your thinking while you're thinking
in order to make your thinking better.
~ Richard Paul (1940–2015)

In the previous chapter, we discussed in detail the work of Stephen
Toulmin and the contributions he made to the fields of both informal
logic and argumentation. However, such contributions would not have
been possible without the influential work conducted by Edward Glaser –
the man who coined the term 'critical thinking'. According to Glaser (1941),
critical thinking (CT) is a cognitive skill that possesses three characteristics:
(1) a positive attitude towards the thoughtful consideration of problems
that people experience; (2) knowledge of logical reasoning strategies; and
(3) the ability to apply the fore-mentioned attitudes and strategies.
As discussed in Chapter 1, a more modern description of CT (yet commensurate to a large extent with Glaser's definition) is as being a metacognitive process that consists of a number of sub-skills (i.e. analysis,
evaluation and inference) that, when used appropriately, increase the
chances of producing a logical solution to a problem or a valid conclusion
to an argument. In order to understand what this process entails and,
likewise, what the comprising sub-skills refer to, we must first come to
understand the nature of metacognition.

METACOGNITION

Making the necessary connections between novel information and pre-
existing knowledge is important in educational settings because it allows
students to understand new information, develop new levels of comprehension and add to an existing cache of knowledge. Subsequently, such

understanding and knowledge are applied by students to answer questions, draw conclusions and solve problems. In order to develop a reasonable answer, conclusion or solution, students must reflect upon their own thinking processes and often the thinking of others as well. A large body of research suggests that the ability to apply knowledge and understanding successfully depends on an individual's metacognitive abilities (Anderson & Krathwohl, 2001; Dwyer, Hogan, & Stewart, 2012; Ennis, 1998; Halpern, 2006; Ku & Ho, 2010b; Marzano, 2001).

As discussed in Chapter 1, though the term *metacognition* was not used by Bloom, many modern conceptualizations of metacognition are similar to what he described as higher-order thinking processes. For example, Wegerif (2002, p. 6) has described metacognition as being 'another term often used as a synonym for thinking skills or higher-order thinking', which 'originates in an information processing model of the mind as something like a computer running both low-level software, to do the basic cognitive processes and high-level software, to monitor and correct the low-level software'. Metacognition was first described by Flavell (1976, p. 232) as 'knowledge concerning one's own cognitive processes and products or anything related to them; and the active monitoring, consequent regulation and orchestration of these processes'. According to Boekaerts and Simons (1993), Brown (1987), and Ku and Ho (2010b), individuals think metacognitively in two ways: first, individuals must be aware of their own cognitive processes (e.g. through self-monitoring or self-regulation); second, individuals must be able to apply available cognitive processes for purposes of learning or devising solutions to problems (e.g. using CT or reflective judgment – a component of CT discussed in Chapter 8). These concepts are also reflected in other definitions of *metacognition*:

- The higher-order control processing used in executive planning and decision-making (Sternberg, 1985, p. 226).
- The higher-order cognitions that supervise a person's thoughts, knowledge and actions (Weinert, 1987).
- The awareness of one's own knowledge and the ability to understand, control and manipulate individual cognitive processes (Osman & Hannafin, 1992, p. 83).
- One's ability to consciously think about thinking as a self-regulatory function, that is, the monitoring of one's own cognitive activities, as well as the results of those activities (Demetriou, 2000).
- Thinking about thinking, usually conceptualised as an interrelated set of competencies for learning and thinking, and include many of the

skills required for active learning, critical thinking, reflective judgment, problem-solving and decision-making (Dawson, 2008, p. 4).
• Knowing one's cognitive processes and the strategies one applies to
control these processes (Ku & Ho, 2010b, p. 263).

Another perspective on metacognition is that of Deanna Kuhn (1999,
2000), who defines *metacognition* by reference to three types of knowing,
which differ in terms of their declarative, procedural and epistemological
focus. First, *metacognitive knowing* is a type of declarative knowledge – the
knowledge a person may possess in relation to cognition. The second form
of metacognition, *metastrategic knowing*, involves procedural knowledge –
a person's knowledge about cognitive processes and of their impact on
performance. Metastrategic knowledge comes in two forms, according to
Kuhn, meta-task knowledge about task goals and metastrategic knowledge
about the strategies one has available to address these goals. Metastrategic
knowledge is seen as a fundamental driver of cognitive development in
Kuhn's scheme, as thinking skills cannot develop in the absence of
awareness and control over goals and strategies. Finally, the third form of
metacognition, *epistemological knowing*, refers to an individual's understanding of what knowledge and knowing are in general, and how one
comes to know. Kuhn and colleagues have argued that these metacognitive
skills are the 'intellectual skills most closely associated with critical thinking', given that it is 'through such coordination processes that knowledge is
acquired' (Kuhn & Weinstock, 2002, p. 18).

Consistent with King and Kitchener's (1981, 1994) model of reflective
judgment (see Chapter 8), Kuhn's perspective on metacognition is developmental in nature, in that 'thought' and its associated processes can
gradually become more and more open to self-awareness as one develops
and, subsequently, more easily self-regulated. Notably, as metacognition
develops, a critical thinker can select and monitor the cognitive strategies
they plan to apply and, according to Kuhn (1999, p. 18), 'to be competent
and motivated to "know how you know" puts one in charge of one's own
knowing, of deciding what to believe and why and of updating and revising
those beliefs as one deems warranted'. Notably, albeit structurally distinct,
Kuhn's model is largely commensurate with other metacognitive frameworks in that it reflects both self-regulatory and skills-based approaches
(Hogan et al., 2014).

Though Marzano (2001) distinguishes the self-regulatory functions
of thinking from dispositional factors, as acting in distinct systems (i.e. a
metacognitive system and a *self-system*, respectively; see Chapter 1),

consistent with definitions of *metacognition* that have been developed in the literature (e.g. Boekaerts & Simons, 1993; Demetriou, 2000; Ku & Ho, 2010b), the conceptualization of metacognition used in this book is characterized by the self-regulatory functions of thinking, as well as the strategical planning and application of higher-order thinking processes or CT skills (i.e. analysis, evaluation and inference) when thinking about thinking (e.g. Brown, 1987; Flavell, 1979; Ku & Ho, 2010b; Kuhn, 1999, 2000).

SELF-REGULATORY FUNCTIONS OF METACOGNITION

A key underlying feature of metacognitive skill is the development of self-regulation. During childhood, changes in self-regulation primarily encompass changes in controlling emotions, attention and behaviour, including self-monitoring and response inhibition (Gestsdottir & Lerner, 2008). In order to self-regulate our thinking, we must be consciously *willing* to engage, regulate and monitor our own cognitive and metacognitive processes (e.g. CT), with respect to the extent to which we are disposed, inclined and motivated to perform such activities (Dwyer, 2011; Pintrich, 2000). According to Zimmerman (1989, p. 4), self-regulated thinkers are 'metacognitively, motivationally and behaviourally active participants in their own learning process'. Self-regulated thinkers are more inclined to set reasonable goals, maintain motivation and take responsibility for their thinking and learning (Heikkila & Lonka, 2006; Phan, 2010). Though we may possess the cognitive skills necessary to conduct CT, our tendency and willingness to apply these skills ultimately dictates how well they are performed. The tendency and willingness to self-regulate may refer to our dispositions towards thinking, our motivation towards thinking and learning, our perceived need to conduct cognitive processes, our executive control and our mindfulness (Hogan et al., 2014).

Critical Thinking Dispositions

Disposition towards thinking refers to the extent to which an individual is *disposed*, or inclined, to perform a given thinking skill (Norris, 1992; Valenzuela, Nieto, & Saiz, 2011) and is essential for understanding how we think and how we can make our thinking better, in both academic settings and everyday circumstances (Siegel, 1999). Past research has demonstrated a significant relationship between CT dispositions and CT ability (Colucciello, 1997; Facione, 2000; Facione, Facione, & Sanchez, 1994; Profeto-McGrath, 2003), as well as significant increases in both CT dispositions and CT ability as a result of CT training (Rimiene, 2002). For example, Colucciello (1997) examined the relationship between dispositions towards thinking and CT ability in a sample of nursing students of varying academic levels (i.e. sophomore, juniors and seniors) and found that CT performance was significantly correlated with truth-seeking, open-mindedness, analyticity, systematicity, confidence, inquisitiveness and maturity, as measured by the California Critical Thinking Dispositions Inventory (Facione & Facione, 1992). Research by Dwyer (2011) also found a significant correlation between CT and a number of dispositions towards thinking, including the dispositions towards truth-seeking, analyticity, confidence and inquisitiveness. Profeto-McGrath (2003) similarly found a significant correlation between overall CT ability and self-reported positive dispositions towards thinking. The relationship between CT skills and dispositions was further corroborated in research studies by Facione (2000) and Facione, Facione and Sanchez (1994).

A number of researchers in the field of CT have developed conceptualizations of disposition towards thinking, with some simply providing descriptions of such tendencies (see Table 4.1) and others listing

TABLE 4.1 *List of Dispositions Identified in CT Research*

Delphi Report (Facione, 1990b)	
Approaches to life and living in general:	Inquisitiveness
	Concern to be well-informed
	Alertness to opportunities to use CT
	Trust in the processes of reasoned inquiry
	Self-confidence in one's own ability to reason
	Open-mindedness
	Consideration of alternatives and opinions
	Understanding of the opinions of other people
	Fair-mindedness in appraising reasoning
	Honesty in facing one's own biases, prejudices, stereotypes, and egocentric or sociocentric tendencies
	Prudence in suspending, making or altering judgments
	Willingness to reconsider and revise views where honest reflection suggests that change is warranted
Approaches to specific issues, questions or problems:	Clarity in stating the question or concern
	Orderliness in working with complexity
	Diligence in seeking relevant information

TABLE 4.1 *(continued)*

Delphi Report (Facione, 1990b)	
	Reasonableness in selecting and applying criteria
	Care in focusing attention on the concern at hand
	Persistence through difficulties that are encountered
	Precision to the degree permitted by the subject and the circumstance

Ennis (1987, 1991, 2013)	
Ideal critical thinkers are disposed to:	Seek alternative hypotheses, explanations, conclusions, plans, sources, etc.; and be open to them
	Consider seriously other points of view than their own
	Try to be well informed
	Endorse a position to the extent that, but only to the extent that, it is justified by the information that is available
	Use their critical thinking abilities
	Discover and listen to others' view and reasons
	Be clear about the intended meaning of what is said, written or otherwise communicated, seeking as much precision as the situation requires
	Determine, and maintain focus on, the conclusion or question
	Seek and offer reasons
	Take into account the total situation
	Be reflectively aware of their own basic beliefs
	Take into account the feelings and thoughts of other people

Halpern (2014)	
Disposition	*Description*
Willingness to plan	Check impulsivity, plan response and prevent habitual responses
Flexibility	To consider new ideas or multiple options, review evidence, reconsider old problems and see things from another's point of view
Persistence	Willingness to start or engage and ability to keep at a task
Self-correction	Acknowledge and learn from mistakes, avoid self-justification
Being mindful	Direct attention to the processes and products of one's thoughts, avoiding mindless or routinized way of thinking
Consensus-seeking	Allowing others to accept what is good about an alternative position, allowing doubts while working towards a solution
Transfer of training	Recognize when CT is needed; identify and use the most appropriate skills
Metacognitive monitoring	Monitor one's thinking process, check on progress, ensure accuracy; make decisions about use of time and mental effort

Paul and Elder (2008)	
Disposition	*Description*
Fair-mindedness	Treat all viewpoints alike, without reference to our own feelings or vested interests or the feelings or vested interests of our friends, community, nation, etc.
Intellectual humility	Distinguish what one knows from what one does not know
Intellectual courage	Willingness to challenge popular beliefs
Intellectual empathy	Sympathetically enter into points of view that differ from one's own and articulate those views in an intelligent and insightful way
Intellectual integrity	Hold oneself to the same standards they expect others to meet
Intellectual perseverance	Work through complexities and frustration inherent in an intellectual task without giving up
Confidence in reason	Recognize that good reasoning is the key to living a rational life and to creating a more fair and just world
Intellectual autonomy	Take responsibility for one's own thinking, beliefs and values

dispositions they believe are necessary for CT, for example, disposition towards inquisitiveness, open-mindedness, systematicity, analyticity, truth-seeking, CT self-confidence and maturity (Facione & Facione, 1992). Though Facione and Facione's (1992) conceptualization is based on a consensus agreement of forty-six CT experts that proposed a set of nineteen core CT dispositions (i.e. the Delphi Report; Facione, 1990b; see below for more detailed discussion), these differ somewhat from the seven traits identified in Facione and Facione's (1992) framework and it is unclear what method was used to arrive at the revised set of seven traits. Also, while 83% of the Delphi committee agreed that critical thinkers can be characterized as exhibiting the set of nineteen dispositions, only 61% regarded these dispositions as a core part of the conceptualization of CT.

Ennis (1987, 1991, 1996) proposed that in order to teach and develop CT in students, there must be a clear definition of the skills and dispositions necessary for CT. Ennis also emphasized the importance of this clarity to better assess students' level of CT, provide feedback, motivate students to develop as critical thinkers and carry out research about CT instruction. Notably, Ennis highlighted a number of CT dispositions as important. While the list includes a number of dispositions that are similar to those proposed by Facione (1990b), the list also includes a number of unique dispositions including focus, carefulness and reflective awareness.

Likewise, according to Halpern (2014), CT is more than using a particular skill in an appropriate context – it is both the ability to recognize when a skill is needed and the willingness to apply it. Halpern highlights the importance of teaching learners how to use their CT skills; specifically, CT requires the right knowledge, thinking skills and the right attitude. She proposes that developing the attitude, or dispositions, of a critical thinker is an essential component of CT and that many errors occur because people do not think critically, not because they are not able to do so but because they are not disposed to doing so. Halpern highlights a range of important CT dispositions, including a unique focus on planning, mindfulness and metacognitive monitoring.

According to Paul and Elder (2008), when students are intellectually engaged, they take ownership of content through actively thinking it through – they value questions more than answers, they seek understanding over rote memorization and, importantly, they 'learn how to learn'. The aim of their disposition framework was to provide academics with a checklist of ideal CT traits in order to aid the design of CT instruction, as well as assignments and tests in CT. Another important aim of Paul and Elder was to help students develop CT independently.

Consistent with Paul and Elder's approach, the idea of 'negotiating the curriculum' has been proposed as having significant advantages over traditional means of curriculum development (Boomer 1992). Negotiating the curriculum refers to 'deliberately planning to invite students to contribute to, and to modify, the educational program, so that they will have a real investment both in the learning journey and in the outcomes' (Boomer, 1992, p. 13).

Following this line of thinking, Dwyer et al. (2016) investigated how both students and educators conceptualize CT using a collective intelligence methodology, *interactive management*. The study highlighted the value of consulting with both students and educators in the development of consensus-based models regarding CT dispositions. While it may be useful for educators to begin with expert definitions of CT, these definitions may be perceived by educators as rather diverse and complex, and they may not align with what either students or a broader array of educators consider important. This research identified and structured a range of dispositions, which fit into the categories of self-efficacy, inquisitiveness, open-mindedness, intrinsic goal orientation, perseverance, attentiveness, truth-seeking, organization, reflection, scepticism, creativity and resourcefulness (see Table 4.2). Results revealed that the critical drivers (i.e. most influential) of CT disposition were

TABLE 4.2 *Disposition towards Critical Thinking Categories (Adapted from Dwyer et al., 2016)*

Disposition Category	Description
Reflection	An inclination to reflect on one's behaviour, attitudes and opinions, as well as the motivations behind these; to distinguish what is known and what is not, as well as limited knowledge or uncertainty; to approach decision-making with a sense that some problems are necessarily ill-structured, some situations permit more than one plausible conclusion or solution and judgments must often be made based on analysis and evaluation, as well as feasibility, standards, contexts and evidence that preclude certainty.
Open-mindedness	An inclination to be cognitively flexible and avoid rigidity in thinking; tolerate divergent or conflicting views and treat all viewpoints alike, prior to subsequent analysis and evaluation; to detach from one's own beliefs and consider, seriously, points of view other to one's own without bias or self-interest; to be open to feedback by accepting positive feedback and to not reject criticism or constructive feedback without thoughtful consideration; amend existing knowledge in light of new ideas and experiences; and to explore such new, alternative or 'unusual' ideas.
Self-efficacy	The tendency to be confident and trust in one's own *reasoned* judgments; to acknowledging one's sense of self while considering problems and arguments (i.e. life experiences, knowledge, heuristics, biases, culture and environment); to be confident and believe in one's ability to receive and internalize resulting feedback positively and constructively; to be self-efficacious in leading others in the rational resolution of problems; and recognize that good reasoning is the key to living a rational life and to creating a more just world.
Truth-seeking	To have a desire for knowledge; to seek and offer both reasons and objections in an effort to inform and to be well-informed; a willingness to challenge popular beliefs and social norms by asking questions (of oneself and others); to be honest and objective about pursuing the truth even if the findings do not support one's self-interest or pre-conceived beliefs or opinions; and to change one's mind about an idea as a result of the desire for truth.
Organization	An inclination to be orderly, systematic and diligent with information, resources and time when determining and maintaining focus on the task, conclusion, problem or question, while simultaneously considering the total situation and being able to present the resulting information in a fashion likewise, for purposes of achieving some desired end.

TABLE 4.2 *(continued)*

Disposition Category	Description
Resourcefulness	The willingness to utilize existing internal resources to resolve problems; search for additional external resources in order to apply analogies and resolve problems; to switch between solution processes and/or knowledge to seek new ways/information to solve a problem; to make the best of the resources available; to adapt and/or improve if something goes wrong; and to think about how and why it went wrong.
Scepticism	Inclination to challenge ideas; to withhold judgment before engaging all the evidence or when the evidence and reasons are insufficient; to take a position and be able to change position when the evidence and reasons are sufficient; and to look at findings from various perspectives.
Perseverance	To be resilient and to be motivated to persist at working through complex tasks and the associated frustration and difficulty inherent in such tasks, without giving up; motivation to get the job done correctly; a desire to progress.
Inquisitiveness	An inclination to be curious; desire to fully understand something, discover the answer to a problem and accept that the full answer may not yet be known; to make sure to understand a task and its associated requirements, available options and limits.
Intrinsic goal orientation	Inclined to be positive, competitive and enthusiastic towards a goal task, topic of focus and, if not the topic itself, enthusiasm for the process of learning new things; to search for answers as a result of internal motivation, rather than an external, extrinsic reward system.
Attentiveness	Willingness to focus and concentrate; to be aware of surroundings, context, consequences and potential obstacles; to have the 'full picture'.
Creativity	A tendency to visualize and generate ideas; and to 'think outside the box' (i.e. think differently than usual).

inquisitiveness, open-mindedness and self-efficacy, whereas the CT dispositions most enhanced by other dispositions were reflection and resourcefulness (see Figure 4.1).

Despite the differences among extant conceptualizations of CT dispositions, they all share the same foundation – good critical thinkers have particular tendencies towards applying CT skills. According to Facione

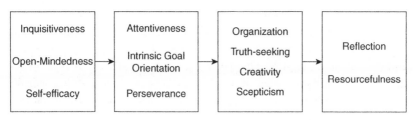

FIGURE 4.1   Influence Model of CT Dispositions (Dwyer et al., 2016)

(1990b), good critical thinkers possess positive dispositions towards think-ing. In addition, it has been argued that the *disposition* to think critically is as important to CT as is the ability to perform CT *skills* (Ennis, 1996; Halpern, 2014; Perkins & Ritchhart, 2004). Notably, there is an important distinction between dispositions and skills. Whereas dispositions are con-ceptualized as inclinations, the use of skills can be thought of as a particular behaviour. The interaction between the two is that dispositions are the inclinations or tendencies to engage in a behaviour (i.e. in this context utilizing a CT skill). For example, though an individual may be aware of which CT skills to use in a given context and may have the capacity to perform well when using these skills, they may not be disposed to use them. Conversely, an individual may be prepared and willing to use CT skills, but may not know how to do so. In both contexts, it is unlikely that CT will be applied well (Valenzuela, Nieto, & Saiz, 2011). Siegel (1999, p. 213) similarly exemplifies this distinction:

> If Mary has the disposition to challenge authority, we can predict that if she is confronted by an authority, other things being equal, Mary will challenge it. This is not a behaviour; Mary has the disposition even when she is alone, asleep and there is no authority in sight.

Furthermore, along with the ability to engage CT skills, 'a critical thinker must also have a strong intention to recognise the importance of good thinking and have the initiative to seek better judgment' (Ku, 2009, p. 71). In other words, the combination of the ability to use CT skills and possessing the disposition to apply these skills together determines a person's actual thinking performance (Ennis, 1998; Facione et al., 2002; Halpern, 2006, 2014; Ku & Ho, 2010a). Ku's (2009) recommendation also alludes to two other aspects of disposition towards thinking that require consideration: dispositions' strength and engagement. First, dispositions may be strong or weak. For example, you may have the dispositions of open-mindedness and scepticism. However, though you might be inclined to be open-minded, this might be weak; and on the other hand, you may have a strong tendency to be sceptical. Thus, in certain contexts, you may be more inclined to behave in a way that seems more sceptical than open-minded. Even in a context where one, the other or both dispositions might appropriately influence a behaviour, there is no guarantee that they will, for example, due to fatigue or perhaps a lack of motivation at a given point in time (Siegel, 1999).

Second, the concept of engagement must be considered. Though a large body of research indicates that CT can be taught (see Chapter 11), this sentiment might be better described more specifically; that is, CT *skills* can be taught – the development of CT *dispositions* is perhaps a little trickier. CT dispositions are not reducible to skills, behaviours and rules or steps in a process - the fostering of such dispositions and self-regulatory aspects of CT may require a focus on the development and enhancement of student sensitivity to occasions in which CT skills and dispositions are *engaged* (Dwyer, Hogan, & Stewart, 2015; Perkins, Jay, & Tishman, 1993; Siegel, 1999). Similar to the earlier example concerning Mary, Siegel (1999, p. 210) presents another example:

> Sugar is disposed to dissolve in liquid. This disposition is manifested countless times every day, as people prepare their coffee, tea and other beverages: when put in liquid, the sugar actually dissolves. But consider the sugar in Joe's sugar bowl. Joe does not take sugar in his coffee. He keeps a filled sugar bowl in his cupboard, just in case company should call, but in fact Joe hardly ever has visitors, and when the rare visits take place, the visitors either do not have coffee or do not take sugar in theirs. So his sugar bowl sits, unused, year in and year out ... (though) the sugar in Joe's sugar bowl has the disposition to dissolve, even though it never actually dissolves ... had it been placed in liquid, it would have dissolved. This is true even in cases in which the sugar is never, in fact, so placed, and so never has the opportunity actually to dissolve, or engage in the behaviour, and so never actually dissolves. Having the disposition is independent of the behaviour actually being manifested.

Thus, for dispositions to develop, opportunities for them to influence a behaviour (i.e. the application of a CT skill) need to be engaged often over time.

Motivation to Think Critically

According to Valenzuela, Nieto and Saiz (2011), while many conceptualizations of CT focus on the attitudinal and intellectual habits of thinking (e.g. disposition towards thinking), others emphasize the importance of motivational features associated with a positive disposition towards CT (e.g. external/extrinsic motivation). That is, these motivation-focused conceptualizations emphasize the importance of motivation as a process used to activate the cognitive and metacognitive resources necessary to conduct good CT (Ennis, 1996; Norris, 1994; Perkins, Jay, & Tishman, 1993; Valenzuela, Nieto, & Saiz, 2011). Furthermore, motivational factors may have important impacts on the way cognitive processes are applied; for example, motivation may predict the level of one's impulsivity in decision-making (Strack & Deutsch, 2004). Motivation towards thinking and learning includes, for example, the motivation to regulate effort, thinking processes and learning beliefs (Pintrich et al., 1991).

Though few empirical studies have examined the motivational aspects of CT dispositions, research by Valenzuela, Nieto and Saiz (2011) revealed that motivation, or drive, to think critically is a stronger correlate of CT ability ($r = .50$) than is a general, positive disposition towards CT ($r = .20$). Research by Garcia, Pintrich and Paul (1992) found a significant, positive correlation between CT ability and motivation towards intrinsic goal orientation, elaboration and metacognitive self-regulation – three sub-scales of the Motivated Strategies towards Learning Questionnaire (Pintrich et al., 1991). Similarly, research by Dwyer, Hogan and Stewart (2012) found positive correlations between CT ability and motivation towards intrinsic goal orientation, controlling one's beliefs about learning, metacognitive self-regulation, elaboration and, importantly, motivation towards CT. In addition, research has also shown that motivation to learn positively influences CT and learning in general (Hattie, Biggs, & Purdie, 1996; Robbins et al., 2004).

Need for Cognition

Furthermore, our perceived need to conduct cognitive processes, or *need for cognition*, refers to the willingness to explore and engage in relatively complex cognitive activities (Cacioppo, Petty, & Kao, 1984). Research suggests that, in addition to dispositions and motivations to think and learn, need for cognition is also significantly correlated with CT performance. For example, research by Halpern (2006), as well as by Dwyer, Hogan and Stewart (2012), found that performance by a group of college students on the Halpern Critical Thinking Assessment was positively, significantly correlated (i.e. $r = .35$, $r = .47$, respectively) with scores on the

Need for Cognition Scale (Cacioppo, Petty, & Kao, 1984). In addition, research by Jensen (1998) found a significant, positive correlation between need for cognition and reflective judgment of first-year college students, and also that the higher an individual's need for cognition, the more likely they were to generate solutions to ill-structured problems that reflected an understanding of the uncertainty of knowledge – thus demonstrating better reflective judgment (King & Kitchener, 2002). Furthermore, research by Toplak and Stanovich (2002) found that those with high levels of need for cognition are more likely to use disjunctive reasoning (i.e. reasoning strategies similar to CT 'that require the exhaustive consideration of all of the possible states of the world'; p. 197) during problem-solving and are also more likely to demonstrate better reasoning ability. Arguably, need for cognition *is* disposition towards thinking (Dwyer, 2011), but may be more generalized given its one-factor assessment (Cacioppo, Petty, & Kao, 1984), as opposed to consisting of an inventory of dispositions towards thinking.

Executive Function

In addition to disposition, motivation and perceived need for cognition, the development of executive functioning[1] is essential for the metacognitive processes involved in self-regulatory functioning, strategic planning and application of higher-order thinking, such as CT. Although many models of executive functioning have been developed (Baddeley & Hitch, 1974; Cowan, 2008; Duff et al., 2005; Miyake et al., 2000; Norman & Shallice, 1986, 2000), there is an emerging consensus that executive functioning involves three basic processes: updating, inhibition and shifting (Hogan et al., 2014). *Updating* refers to the active revision and maintenance of information processed in working memory; *shifting* refers to switching between tasks or mental sets; and *inhibition* refers to the active, deliberate suppression of thoughts or responses and the maintenance of attention on goal-relevant information (Miyake et al., 2000). These basic processes have been shown to interact differentially to control higher-order problem-solving (Burton et al., 2006) and decision-making (Del Missier, Mäntylä, & Bruine de Bruin, 2010). For example, Del Missier and colleagues (2010) found that, in a task where the application of decision strategies became

---

[1] In the context of this discussion, executive functioning can be considered as commensurate with Baddeley's (1986, 2000) conceptualization of the *central executive* as the governing body of information processing within working memory, as discussed in Chapter 2.

increasingly complex, inhibition was the most crucial process observed, as attention must be directed away from no longer relevant information, while in a separate task where participants were asked to assess the probability of risky events, shifting was identified as a key process observed, as attention must be switched between varying judgment contexts.

Executive functioning skills are particularly important in situations or tasks which are novel, where automatic, intuitive or learned automatic responses are not adaptive or where a conflict between goals and the situation has been detected; and thus, additional control is required (Hofmann, Schmeichel, & Baddeley, 2012). Hofmann, Schmeichel and Baddeley (2012) have outlined how integral executive functioning is to self-regulation by arguing that executive functions allow us to organize our thoughts in a goal-directed manner and are essential for success in education, work and everyday living. The updating and maintenance of working memory is vital for the accurate active representation of goals and goal-related information in situations where self-regulatory routines have not been automatized (Hofmann, Schmeichel, & Baddeley, 2012). Furthermore, greater working memory capacity protects goal representations from thought intrusions and decreases mind-wandering – often referred to as goal shielding (Brewin & Smart, 2005).

Mindfulness

This notion of decreasing mind-wandering is important for CT because it implies that an important metacognitive construct is that of being *mindful* (Bishop et al., 2004; Holas & Jankowski, 2012). Though conceptualizations of mindfulness vary, all highlight its role in enhanced self-regulation of thought and behavior, as well as emotional and physiological reactivity; and all contrast mindful information processing with automatic, habitual or heuristic information processing (see Chapter 10), often referred to as mindlessness (Brown, Ryan, & Creswell, 2007; Hart, Ivtzan, & Hart, 2013). More specifically, mindfulness is often operationalized as a two-component process. The first component involves the deployment of attention to both internal and external experience in the present moment (Bishop et al., 2004). This component has been associated with greater sensitivity to perceptual cues and facilitates conflict monitoring (Anicha et al., 2011; Teper & Inzlicht, 2013; Teper, Segal, & Inzlicht, 2013) and executive control skills, particularly switching between and updating the contents of working memory (Bishop et al., 2004; Moore & Malinowski, 2009). The second component of mindfulness is characterized by non-

judgmental acceptance of emotions and thoughts. This too involves executive control to inhibit elaboration and/or suppression of affective cues and
allows for the early engagement of emotion regulation before intense
emotional reactivity to the attended thoughts, feelings and sensations can
occur (Teper, Segal, & Inzlicht, 2013). This operationalization of mindfulness implies both monitoring and control skills, which are inherently
metacognitive (Bishop et al., 2004). Though studies investigating the
mechanisms and outcomes of mindfulness often involve either brief meditation inductions or more long-term meditation interventions, it is also
possible to take a dispositional approach where measures of trait mindfulness are associated with specific outcome variables (Chiesa, Calati, &
Serretti, 2011). For example, evidence for improved self-regulation of
thoughts and emotions comes from the extensive literature on the clinical
benefits of mindfulness (cf. Hofmann et al., 2010).

Notably, both components of mindfulness involve executive control
(Bishop et al., 2004; Teper & Inzlicht, 2013). The sustained attention to
current experience developed through mindfulness practise requires the
ability to switch attention between stimuli in current experience and back
to current experience when the mind wanders, updating the contents of
working memory and inhibiting elaborative processing (Holas &
Jankowski, 2012). Research also suggests that it is through the enhancement
of executive functioning that mindfulness facilitates successful self-
regulation and that these effects may extend to higher-order thinking skills,
including problem-solving, decision-making and both divergent and con-
vergent thinking, and social cognitive skills (Chiesa, Calati, & Serretti, 2011;
Glomb et al., 2011; Ostafin & Kassman, 2012; Shapiro, Jazaieri, & Goldin,
2012). Though the self-regulatory functions of thinking (i.e. disposition,
motivation, need for cognition, executive function and mindfulness) are
important to consider as part of any effort to understand how an individual
applies their cognitive and metacognitive skills (see Chapter 9), the following discussion now turns to past conceptualizations of CT and CT skills
(i.e. analysis, evaluation and inference).

CRITICAL THINKING DEFINED

On one hand, the development of CT *skills* in educational settings is often
endorsed because it is believed that these skills allow students to transcend
lower-order, memorization-based learning strategies to gain a more complex understanding of the information or problems they encounter
(Halpern, 2014; Pollock, Chandler, & Sweller, 2002). It is important to

TABLE 4.3 *Past Definitions and Descriptions of Critical Thinking*

Author	Definition/Description
Glaser (1941)	CT is an attitude of being disposed to consider, in a thoughtful way, problems and subjects that come within the range of one's experience, knowledge of the methods of logical enquiry and reasoning and some skills in applying those methods. CT calls for a persistent effort to examine any belief or supposed form of knowledge in the light of the evidence that supports it and the further conclusions to which it tends.
Ennis (1987)	CT is reasonable, reflective thinking focused on deciding what to believe or do.
Paul (1993)	A unique kind of purposeful thinking, in which the thinker systematically and habitually imposes criteria and intellectual standards upon thinking, taking charge of the construction of thinking, guiding the construction of the thinking according to the standards and assessing the effectiveness of the thinking according to the purpose, the criteria and the standards.
Bensley (1998)	CT is reflective thinking in which a person evaluates relevant evidence and works to draw a sound or good conclusion.
Halpern (2014)	CT is purposeful, reasoned and goal-directed thinking – the kind of thinking involved in solving problems, formulating inferences, calculating likelihoods and making decisions.
Dwyer, Hogan and Stewart (2014)	CT is a metacognitive process that, through purposeful, self-regulatory reflective judgment and application of a number of sub-skills (i.e. analysis, evaluation and inference), when used appropriately, increases the chances of producing a logical solution to a problem or a valid conclusion to an argument.

note that there is a large body of research that suggests that this endeavour is a feasible one, given that such research indicates that CT can be developed through instruction (Butler et al., 2012; Dwyer, Hogan, & Stewart, 2011, 2012; Halpern, 2014; Marin & Halpern, 2011; Moseley et al., 2005). On the other hand, in the past century, there has been little agreement on how to define CT, resulting in the existence of many diverse conceptualizations of CT (e.g. Bensley, 1998; Dewey, 1910, 1933; Ennis, 1987; Glaser, 1941; Halpern, 2014; Paul, 1993; see Table 4.3). Interestingly, this may also be another reason why some of my students failed to comprehend the phrase 'critically evaluate', as discussed in the Introduction.

According to Gabbenesch (2006), the identification of one, consistently used, well-defined consensus conceptualization of CT is necessary because the value of CT (and its related research) may be weakening due to 'terminological disarray'. Though the value of CT, as a concept, may be diminishing, most educators desire and often require it of their students; however, they themselves have problems conceptualizing and measuring it. For example, though 92%of academics surveyed indicated that it was important for students to be able to think and learn in a manner that stimulates a change in their perspectives, 54% of students surveyed indicated that they felt as though "they have not yet been provided the opportunity to do so" (UWA, 2007). According to one university lecturer interviewed in Lloyd and Bahr's (2010, p. 13) qualitative research, 'we expect students to do it [think critically], but now you are questioning me on my understanding of it, I wonder if I actually understand it myself'. Lloyd and Bahr's research further revealed that while 37% of academics instructing or assessing CT in university courses at least acknowledge the dispositional and self-regulatory aspects of CT, only 47% described CT in terms of involving processes or skills.

Though debate is ongoing over the definition of CT and the core skills necessary to think critically, one definition and list of skills stand out as a reasonable consensus conceptualization of CT. In 1988, a committee of forty-six experts in the field of CT gathered to discuss both a definition and the skills necessary to think critically. The report of the findings of this meeting, known as the Delphi Report, defined *CT* as:

> purposeful, self-regulatory judgment which results in interpretation, analysis, evaluation, and inference, as well as explanation of the eviden-tial, conceptual, methodological, criteriological, or contextual consid-erations upon which that judgment is based.   *(Facione, 1990b, p. 3)*

Furthermore, the Delphi panel overwhelmingly agreed (i.e. 95% consensus) that *analysis, evaluation* and *inference* were the core skills necessary for CT (Facione, 1990b; see Table 4.4 for the description of each skill provided by the Delphi Report). The relationships among these skills has been noted in more recent research, as analysis and evaluation ($r = .40$, $p < .001$), analysis and inference ($r = .36$, $p < .001$) and evaluation and inference ($r = .48$, $p < .001$) were all significantly, positively correlated (Dwyer, Hogan, & Stewart, 2011).

However, it can be argued that the Delphi Report fails to acknowledge that the ability to apply these skills implies a reflective sensibility and the capacity for reflective judgment (Dwyer, Hogan, & Stewart, 2014, 2015; King & Kitchener, 1994), which is an important component of CT – one that will be discussed in greater detail in Chapter 8. Indeed, given the need for CT in adapting to the new knowledge economy, it is necessary that this

TABLE 4.4 *Core CT Skills according to the Delphi Report*
(Adapted from Facione, 1990b)

Skill	Description
Analysis	To identify the intended and actual inferential relationships among statements, questions, concepts, descriptions or other forms of representation intended to express beliefs, judgments, experiences, reasons, information or opinions.
	Examining ideas: to determine the role various expressions play or are intended to play in the context of argument, reasoning or persuasion; to compare or contrast ideas, concepts or statements; to identify issues or problems and determine their component parts; and also to identify the conceptual relationships of those parts to each other and to the whole.
	Detecting arguments given a set of statements or other forms of representation, to determine whether or not the set expresses, or is intended to express, a reason or reasons in support of or contesting some claim, opinion or point of view.
	Analysing arguments: given the expression of a reason or reasons intended to support or contest some claim, opinion or point of view, to identify and differentiate: (1) the intended main conclusion; (2) the premises and reasons advanced in support of the main conclusion; (3) further premises and reasons advanced as backup or support for those premises and reasons intended as supporting the main conclusion; (4) additional unexpressed elements of that reasoning, such as intermediary conclusions, non-stated assumptions or presuppositions; (5) the overall structure of the argument or intended chain of reasoning; and (6) any items contained in the body of expressions being examined which are not intended to be taken as part of the reasoning being expressed or its intended background.
Evaluation	To assess the credibility of statements or other representations, which are accounts or descriptions of a person's perception, experience, situation, judgment, belief or opinion; and to assess the logical strength of the actual or intended inferential relationships among statements, descriptions, questions or other forms of representation.
	Assessing claims: to recognize the factors relevant to assessing the degree of credibility to ascribe to a source of information or opinion; to assess the contextual relevance of questions, information, principles, rules or procedural directions; to assess the acceptability, the level of confidence to place in the probability or truth of any given representation of an experience, situation, judgment, belief or opinion.
	Assessing arguments: to judge whether the assumed acceptability of the premises of an argument justify one's accepting as true (deductively certain), or very probably true (inductively justified), the expressed conclusion of that argument; to anticipate or to raise questions or

What Is Critical Thinking?

TABLE 4.4 *(continued)*

Skill	Description
	objections, and to assess whether these point to significant weakness in the argument being evaluated; to determine whether an argument relies on false or doubtful assumptions or presuppositions and then to determine how crucially these affect its strength; to judge between reasonable and fallacious inferences; to judge the probative strength of an argument's premises and assumptions with a view towards determining the acceptability of the argument; to determine and judge the probative strength of an argument's intended or unintended consequences with a view towards judging the acceptability of the argument; to determine the extent to which possible additional information might strengthen or weaken an argument.
Inference	To identify and secure elements needed to draw reasonable conclusions; to form conjectures and hypotheses; to consider relevant information; and to deduce the consequences flowing from data, statements, principles, evidence, judgments, beliefs, opinions, concepts, descriptions, questions or other forms of representation.
	Querying evidence: to recognize premises which require support and to formulate a strategy for seeking and gathering information which might supply that support; in general, to judge that information relevant to deciding the acceptability, plausibility or relative merits of a given alternative, question, issue, theory, hypothesis or statement is required, and to determine plausible investigatory strategies for acquiring that information.
	Conjecturing alternatives: to formulate multiple alternatives for resolving a problem, to postulate a series of suppositions regarding a question, to project alternative hypotheses regarding an event, to develop a variety of different plans to achieve some goal; to draw out presuppositions and project the range of possible consequences of decisions, positions, policies, theories or beliefs.
	Drawing conclusions: to apply appropriate modes of inference in determining what position, opinion or point of view one should take on a given matter or issue; given a set of statements, descriptions, questions or other forms of representation, to educe, with the proper level of logical strength, their inferential relationships and the consequences or the presuppositions which they support, warrant, imply or entail; to employ successfully various sub-species of reasoning, as for example to reason analogically, arithmetically, dialectically, scientifically, etc.; to determine which of several possible conclusions is most strongly warranted or supported by the evidence at hand or which should be rejected or regarded as less plausible by the information given.

conceptualization of CT is re-evaluated, consistent with a more recent outlook, such as being a metacognitive process that, through purposeful, self-regulatory reflective judgment and application of a number of sub-skills (i.e. analysis, evaluation and inference), when used appropriately, increases the chances of producing a logical solution to a problem or a valid conclusion to an argument (Dwyer, Hogan, & Stewart, 2014). Nevertheless, now that we have a working understanding of what CT is and, subsequently, what it entails, we are able to explore various situations that we may choose to or, inevitably, need to use it. Following this discussion, we will progress by delving deeper into the various CT sub-skills in the following chapters.

CRITICAL THINKING IN THE REAL WORLD

We all think and we do so for different reasons – sometimes we have a clear goal in mind and sometimes we let imagination take over and carry us away in a creative, fantasy world. Sometimes we strive to be logical and to reason carefully. Sometimes we care less for logic. Careful reasoning is necessary whenever we care about the implications of our thinking (e.g. deciding on the best course of action, deciding whether or not to accept a belief as true, or believe someone who communicates this belief to us). Taking these possibilities into account, it can be said that we think:

1. in order to decide what to do;
2. in order to decide what to believe;
3. for fun (such as stories and jokes).

The great thing about stories, jokes and other types of creative thinking is that they generally allow for the free play of imagination. Stories and jokes have a structure, naturally, but we do not necessarily have to be very logical when telling a story or a joke. That is, we are not necessarily trying to convince people that what we are saying is true and reasonable. However, if our goal is to decide what to do or what to believe; and if we genuinely care about the outcome of our decision-making process, thinking about what to do or what to believe tends to activate the careful, logical, reasonable part of our mind – a part of our mind that is important for quality CT. Quality CT is not a prerequisite for thinking for fun (e.g. stories and jokes). In educational settings, the core of learning is an emphasis on this careful, logical, reasonable type of thinking – the kind of thinking that we use in order to decide what to believe and in order to decide what to do.

DECIDING ON WHAT TO DO

Not only scientists think carefully and logically. We all tend to think carefully and logically when we care about our decisions, as best as we can. Consider the following dilemma: *You wish to buy a dog because you like dogs. However, you don't want to leap to a decision too quickly.* Given this dilemma, you decide first that you want to think carefully about your decision for a while. Perhaps, you might consider three important questions in this context:

1. What things might you think about to persuade yourself that buying a dog is a good idea? For example:

   - *Because*, I have had dogs in the past and I love them.
   - *Because*, dogs are *man's best friend*.
   - *Because*, I can go out walking every evening, keep fit and meet other people with similar interests, for example, dogs.

2. What things might you think about to dissuade yourself from buying a dog. That is, what would make you think that this is not a good idea right now?

   - *But*, walking my dog every evening will mean I cannot pursue my new hobby.
   - *But*, I will feel guilty if I am forced to leave my dog alone in the house all day.
   - *But*, a new dog would be expensive and I am short of money right now.

3. How do you arrive at a final decision in this context?

The third and final question is critical. We will return to it again later. The simple answer for now is that we arrive at our final decision by reference to the way we 'weigh up' each of the reasons (e.g. *Because*, dogs are *man's best friend*) and objections (e.g. *But*, a new dog would be expensive and I'm really short of money right now). Which is more important to you: having your best friend by your side or money in your pocket? We weigh up our own arguments and we make a decision one way or the other. Our ultimate decision about what to do very often hinges upon our decision about what we *believe*. For example, what would make you believe the statement: *Dogs are man's best friend*? Please consider a few reasons that would make you believe this claim.

DECIDING ON WHAT TO BELIEVE

How do we ultimately decide what to believe in this context? Deciding on what to believe involves much the same process as before: we 'weigh up' the arguments. We consider each of the reasons and decide if they point to the core belief that *Dogs are man's best friend*. When dealing with our own arguments, we simply weigh up our own arguments and make a decision one way or the other. Now, consider the reasons provided next:

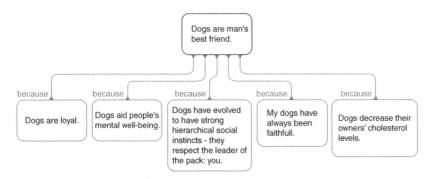

It seems that these are five pretty good reasons that suggest that, yes, *Dogs are man's best friend*. However, what do you notice about the *structure* of this argument? Unlike our previous example, where we were thinking through whether or not to buy a dog, in this example, there are no *buts*, only *becauses*. In this argument, no objections are raised in relation to the core belief that *Dogs are man's best friend*, or in relation to any of the specific reasons provided, for example, *Dogs aid people's mental well-being*.

When deciding what to believe, we need to be careful not to focus only on reasons for accepting our beliefs; and avoid simply working to confirm our beliefs, which leads to a confirmation bias (i.e. the inclination to promote or favour information that corroborates one's own pre-existing beliefs). As a result, not only must we decide on what to believe; but also, we must question these beliefs in turn. For example, are dogs *really* man's best friend? We also need to question the reasons we provide as a *basis* for our beliefs, such as whether dogs *really* aid people's mental well-being? We need to be sceptical and ask ourselves not only what makes us believe these claims; but also, what would make us disbelieve them.

Consider the belief: *People should only work a 35-hour week.* In the
following argument map, please add an objection to the claim in the box
marked *but*. Then, on the bottom level of the argument map, add an
objection to the two reasons provided (i.e. the two *becauses*) and add
a reason to support your initial objection to the belief that people should
only work a 35-hour week on the second row.

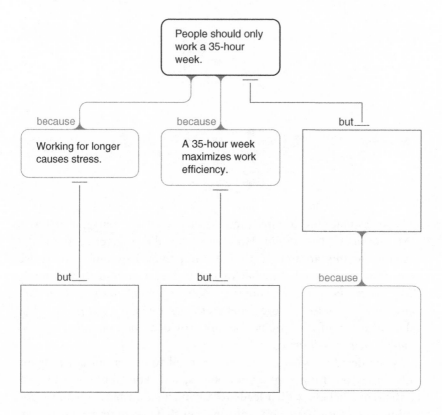

In Exercise 4.1, we had three levels that were hierarchically arranged:

Level 1: A core belief expressed in a simple proposition: *People
should only work a 35-hour week*
Level 2: A set of propositions that either support or refute this
core belief
Level 3: Another set of propositions that either support or refute
the first set of propositions (i.e. on Level 2).

SUMMARY AND CONCLUSION

In the past, there have been a number of varying definitions and conceptualizations of CT. However, this chapter may shed some light on what CT is, through elucidating the common agreement of CT as a metacognitive process consisting of a number of sub-skills (i.e. analysis, evaluation and inference) and dispositions, that through purposeful, self-regulatory reflective judgment, increases the chances of producing a logical conclusion to an argument or solution to a problem. We use this conceptualization of CT and its associated skills when we care about what to do and believe. When we want to decide what to do or what to believe, we can choose to think in a careful, logical, reasonable way. We weigh up our own reasons and objections when deciding what to do, and our decisions about what to do very often hinge upon what we believe. We can question our beliefs and the arguments that support our beliefs. This sceptical mode of thinking is a core part of what we call CT. Furthermore, arguments are hierarchical structures. Whether we are trying to decide what to do or what to believe, an argument of sorts ensues, in which we have a core idea/belief, a set of propositions (i.e. reasons and/or objections) that either support or refute the core idea/belief and, if we like, additional sets of propositions that support these reasons and objections and in turn add to the complexity of our argument.

EXERCISE 4.2

Please add two objections to the two supporting propositions (i.e. the *becauses*).

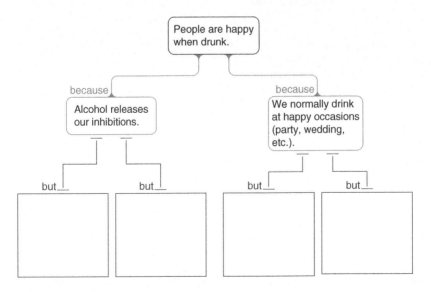

Arguments are hierarchical structures and we can continue to add more levels to arguments if we so choose. Taking the argument in Exercises 4.1 and 4.2, for example, we can offer a *rebuttal* to one of the *buts* and construct a four-level propositional structure. In this exercise, please add two rebuttals to the two objections in order to complete this four-level argument structure. Essentially, you are asked to object to the objections.

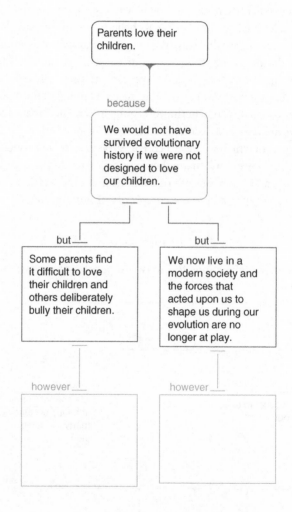

Understanding the hierarchy of an argument is vital to CT. This importance will be discussed in greater detail in the following chapter. But before moving forward, please complete the four-level argument map, by including *becauses, buts* and *howevers*.

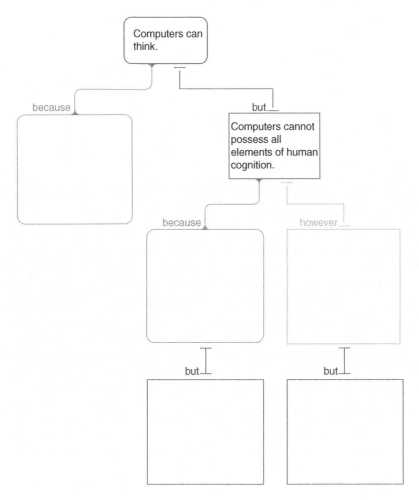

5

Analysis

Read not to contradict and confute; nor to believe and take for granted;
nor to find talk and discourse; but to weigh and consider.
~ Sir Francis Bacon (1561–1626)

In real-world settings, people often convey ideas and beliefs to others
without providing basis for their beliefs. As a result, we must often ask
people why they believe what they believe. When people *do* provide an
explanation, we can unpack the basis of their belief (i.e. the structure of
their argument) and subsequently analyse their reasoning. The Delphi
Report, as discussed in Chapter 4, describes *analysis* as a critical thinking
skill that is used in the context of argumentation to detect, examine and
identify the propositions within an argument and the role they play; for
example, the main conclusion, the premises and reasons provided to
support the conclusion, objections to the conclusion and inferential relationships among propositions (Facione, 1990b). To reiterate, the Delphi
Report outlines a number of sub-skills involved in analysis including the
following:

- The ability to identify the intended and actual inferential relationships
  among statements, questions, concepts, descriptions or other forms of
  representation intended to express beliefs, judgments, experiences,
  reasons, information or opinions.
- The ability to determine the role various expressions play or are
  intended to play in the context of argument, reasoning or persuasion;
  to compare or contrast ideas, concepts or statements; to identify issues
  or problems and determine their component parts; and also to identify
  the conceptual relationships of those parts to each other and to the
  whole.

- The ability to detect arguments given a set of statements or other forms of representation to determine whether or not the set expresses, or is intended to express, a reason or reasons in support of or contesting some claim, opinion or point of view.
- The ability to identify and differentiate: (1) the intended main conclusion; (2) the premises and reasons advanced in support of the main conclusion; (3) further premises and reasons advanced as backup or support for those premises and reasons intended as supporting the main conclusion; (4) additional unexpressed elements of that reasoning, such as intermediary conclusions, non-stated assumptions or presuppositions; (5) the overall structure of the argument or intended chain of reasoning; and (6) any items contained in the body of expressions being examined, which are not intended to be taken as part of the reasoning being expressed or its intended background.

ANALYSING THE STRUCTURE OF AN ARGUMENT

At the core of the Delphi definition of analysis is the ability of an individual to analyse the structure of an argument, which depends not only on their knowledge and skill as a reader/listener, but also on the way in which the author of the argument uses relational cues, or signals, that guide the reader/listener (Meyer, Brandt, & Bluth, 1980). For example, words like *but, because* and *however* can be used by the author to indicate that propositions that follow are *objections, reasons* or *rebuttals* of propositions that have come before. Consider the following dialogue:

PERSON A: *I think emotions make thinking irrational.*

PERSON B: *Why?*

PERSON A: *Because in order to be rational one needs to be impartial. Positive emotions make one too agreeable and inclined to making risky decisions. Negative emotions make one too sceptical and inclined to reject all forms of evidence.*

PERSON B: *But is not scepticism a critical part of good critical thinking?*

PERSON A: *Yes, however, rejecting all forms of evidence means one must also reject every belief, and that's not rational.*

We can see, in the argument map on the following page, that this dialogue forms a four-tiered argument structure, much like one of the arguments we considered in the previous chapter. Please take a moment to analyse this argument map. Based on the use of relational cues used in the dialogue, does the structure of the argument map resemble the structure you had in your head?

In the context of reading, translating a written, prose-based argument into an argument map involves a process similar to that of translating a dialogue. That is, relational cues shape the organization of paragraphs within an argument, as well as the various paths of reasoning an argument may take based on the evidence presented. For example, an author may decide to present all their reasons in support of a particular claim in the first few paragraphs of the argument and follow this with a series of paragraphs presenting all the objections in relation to a particular claim, followed by justification for these objections and/or rebuttals. Alternatively, an author may choose to mix reasons, objections and rebuttals throughout all of these paragraphs; and thus, sequence and organize their argument in different ways.

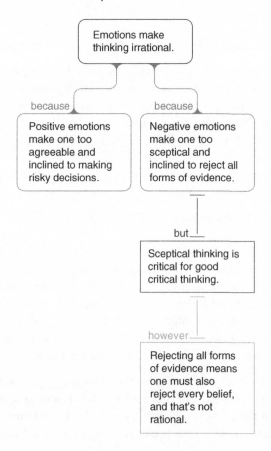

The organization and identification of propositions within an argument is critical for the reader, as the structure of propositions has been found to affect the reader's ability to comprehend the information within the argument (e.g. Meyer, Brandt, & Bluth, 1980; Munch, Boller, & Swasy, 1993; Myers, 1974). Consider arguments that reject the claim that 'Emotions make thinking irrational':

> *A commonly held belief is that emotions make thinking irrational. However, some people argue that neither emotion nor mood necessarily interferes with rational thought. For example, it has been found that low levels of positive emotion often maintain behaviour, not disrupt it. Thus, if a behaviour, such as reasoning, is associated with a pleasant, positive feeling, the behaviour is likely to continue.*
>
> *Emotion can enhance forms of cognition other than reasoning. For example, emotion can increase expressive communication. Also, a positive mood may actually help a person on creative kinds of tasks. However, these forms of cognition are not necessarily forms of rationality.*

Notably, a good piece of prose puts related arguments into one paragraph and other related arguments into a separate paragraph. This rule, *one paragraph = one idea unit*, helps the reader to see and extract the structure of the argument. A paragraph can be long or short and can contain many or few propositions. The main thing is that it holds together as a single idea unit.

Now, consider the same argument in argument map form:

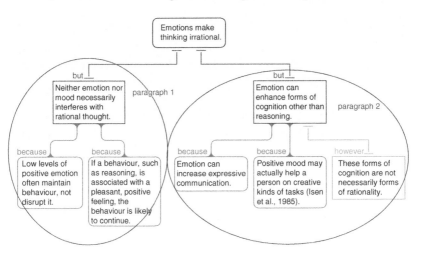

There are two major objections to the central claim, both of which pertain to a separate paragraph, both of which are supported by sub-claims and one of which has a rebuttal. To reiterate, a good piece of prose puts related arguments into the one paragraph. It is important to keep this rule in mind, not only when reading and analysing the structure of an argument, but also when it comes to planning out our own writing. When writing we ask the following question of ourselves: What is the main idea/ what is the central claim? For example, we might be presented the task of writing an essay with the title: 'We are happy when we are good'. We might ask ourselves: What set of arguments either support or refute the central claim/main idea? How are each of these arguments supported and can any of them be refuted? Now, we must write; we must decide what information, from the set of propositions generated, will be included in our essay.

EXERCISE 5.1

Extract the argument structure contained in the following dialogue (Note: there are five propositions presented). Next, fill in each empty box of the argument map on the next page with the correct proposition from the preceding dialogue (Note: one box is already filled in – the central claim, so you will only have to fill in four propositions).

PERSON A: I think our country should adopt a more rigorous procedure for controlling immigration.

PERSON B: Why?

PERSON A: Because in order to maintain stability one needs to monitor and regulate immigration. Unregulated immigration places a burden on schools and unstable pressures in the housing sector. Unregulated immigration also makes it difficult to ensure quality social integration and good relations between people.

PERSON B: But shouldn't we simply be building more schools and welcoming immigrants with open arms. Are they not adding to the wealth of the nation?

PERSON A: Yes, however, without knowing how many immigrants are due to arrive next year, who they are, where they're from, what their needs are, etc., we have no way of planning for the future.

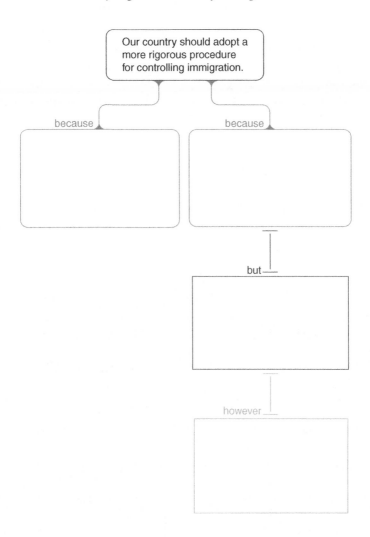

Similar to Exercise 5.1, extract the argument from the following text and transfer the correct propositions into the appropriate boxes in the argument map on the following page.

Positive psychology is a field of study that examines positive emotions, positive personality traits and positive institutions. Central to positive psychology is the claim that we are happy when we are good. Positive psychologists draw upon a number of sources of evidence to support this claim.

Positive psychology research has found that happy people evaluate life experiences as more pleasant than do their less happy peers – they rate hypothetical situations more positively, and they rate strangers more positively, too - expressing a stronger interest in becoming friends with the stranger. Happy people are less vulnerable to social comparisons – they do not seem to mind when other people do better than them on performance tasks; and, unlike unhappy people, they do not experience more positive emotion when others do worse than them. When asked to choose from a range of desserts, happy people tend to be more satisfied with all of their available options. But what does all of this mean?

One cannot argue that evaluating desserts as more positive makes one a good person. Likewise, one cannot argue that evaluating situations and

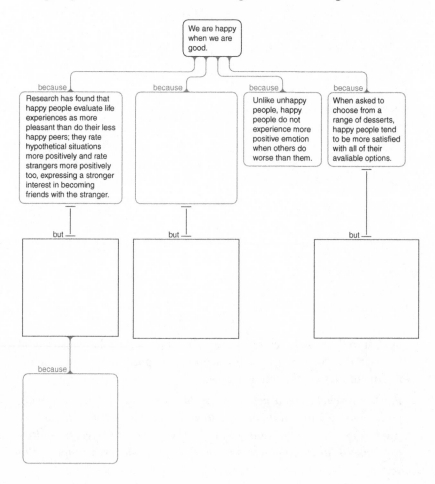

people as more positive makes one a good, or better, person either. Sometimes it helps to be able to identify whether or not strangers are dangerous or psychotic. Also, there might be situations where it is important to care about whether or not someone performs better than you, for example, if by beating you in some contest a person achieves a position that allows them to do harm to others.

ANALYSING THE SOURCES OF ARGUMENTS AND CLAIMS

Just as people do not always tell us the basis of their beliefs (i.e. people do not always tell you the reasons for what they do or believe), even if we get them to present the basis for their beliefs (i.e. which we can use to unpack the structure of the argument), quite often they will not tell you what *types* of arguments they are using or the sources of these arguments and claims. However, once you become familiar with the different sources arguments come from, you will come to know what type of arguments another person is using. The ability to identify the sources and types of arguments people use helps us to better evaluate their arguments, given that not all argument types are equal – some are better than others. Consider the example we used in the previous chapter, that *Dogs are people's best friend.*

What can we believe about this argument, given the types, or sources, of each proposition? Consider the first proposition. *Dogs are loyal.* This is a common belief. But, the problem with common beliefs, and likewise, common sense, is that it is not always correct. For example, it is also commonly believed that *opposites attract,* that we come to like and love people who are different, or opposite, in some way. But, research in social psychology suggests that we tend to like people who are similar to us and dislike people who are different (e.g. *birds of a feather flock together*). In other words, scientific research findings are sometimes at odds with common beliefs. Also, different examples of 'common sense' can be at odds with one another. For example, we noted in the last chapter that another common sense position in relation to dogs is that, without sufficient training, dogs can wander off and fail to obey their owners. In this sense, they are not always loyal.

Consider the second proposition – *Dogs aid people's mental well-being.* Though this proposition is derived from empirical research, which is a strong source of information, it may be that this specific research was limited in some respect; for example, it may be that the design of the studies in this area of research is of poor quality. Suppose we simply compare

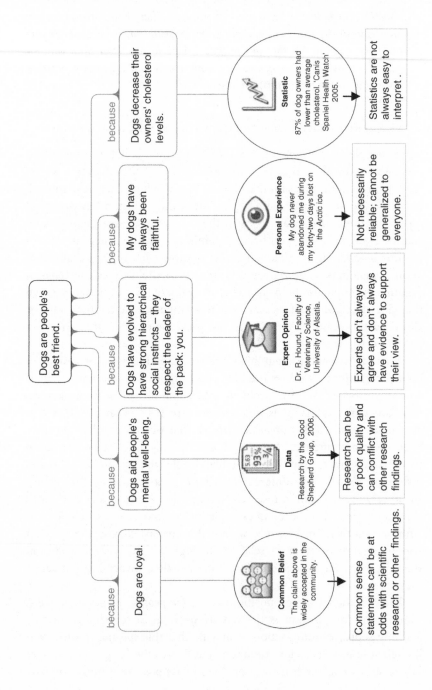

Dogs are people's best friend.

because — Dogs are loyal.

Common Belief
The claim above is widely accepted in the community.

Common sense statements can be at odds with scientific research or other findings.

because — Dogs aid people's mental well-being.

Data
Research by the Good Shepherd Group, 2006.

Research can be of poor quality and can conflict with other research findings.

because — Dogs have evolved to have strong hierarchical social instincts – they respect the leader of the pack: you.

Expert Opinion
Dr. R. Hound, Faculty of Veterinary Science, University of Alsatia.

Experts don't always agree and don't always have evidence to support their view.

because — My dogs have always been faithful.

Personal Experience
My dog never abandoned me during my forty-two days lost on the Arctic ice.

Not necessarily reliable; cannot be generalized to everyone.

because — Dogs decrease their owners' cholesterol levels.

Statistic
87% of dog owners had lower than average cholesterol. 'Canis Spaniel Health Watch' 2005.

Statistics are not always easy to interpret.

people who have dogs with people who do not have dogs with respect to the owners' mental well-being. Suppose also that we find that people with dogs report higher mental well-being. Can we conclude that *Dogs aid people's mental well-being*? Why, or why not?

Perhaps, the dog owners were already scoring very high on mental well-being, prior to owning dogs. Alternatively, this hypothetical finding could result from something other than owning a dog. For example, in this context, it could be that caring for another living thing and the nurturing emotions this fosters are what aids people's mental well-being. Thus, the same effect on mental well-being may be observed in people who care for cats, plants, other people's dogs or other people's children.

With respect to the third proposition, if an expert tells us that *dogs have evolved to have strong hierarchical social instincts*, we might be inclined to believe them, especially if they have relevant qualifications in the field in which they are commenting. Like data, or information from research, expert opinions are a strong source of information (i.e. a strong type of proposition), given that these opinions are often based on empirical evidence. However, experts often argue with one another and do not always agree when it comes to evaluating the scientific evidence. Sometimes, an expert makes a bold statement that lacks credibility because it lacks supportive evidence. For example, Freud argued, in the absence of scientific evidence, that everything we do is motivated by sexual desire. We often see experts disagree in the law courts, for example, when arguing over whether or not someone they have assessed was likely to be clinically insane; and thus, incapable of clear thought when committing a crime.

Consider the fourth proposition, *My dogs have always been faithful*, which is derived from personal experience. The problem with personal experience is that all it amounts to is anecdotal evidence. Simply, an anecdote is a story. We often tell others a story, or describe a personal experience, when trying to convince them of our point of view. These anecdotes can be a very powerful tool of persuasion, but anecdotal evidence is a weak source for an argument as it is not necessarily reliable. For example, I could be lying about my dogs having always been faithful. Maybe one of my dogs was very disobedient and that's why we sent him away. However, you do not hear that story – you only hear the story that supports the argument of which I am trying to convince you. The other problem with anecdotal evidence is that we cannot generalize one person's experience to the population at large. Other people may have had very different experiences with dogs. Their dogs may have been terribly unfaithful. As a result, what we need is some quality research that surveys a representative sample of the population. For example, we can ask 1,000 people who own, or have owned, dogs to tell you about their experience. In this way, we might be able to make *some* generalizations about the population.

The fifth and final proposition is derived from statistical findings. Statistics are one type of output we get from doing research. The problem with a statistic like '87% of dog owners had lower than average cholesterol' is that it might not actually support the claim that *Dogs decrease their owners' cholesterol.* Questions we might wish to ask are: 'How was the average cholesterol level of the population calculated?' 'Were the dog owners representative of the population at large (or were they much younger or older, richer or poorer, etc., than the population used to calculate average cholesterol)?' Without measuring cholesterol levels in a sample of non–dog owners who are similar in every other important aspect to dog owners (other than the fact they do not own a dog), it is difficult to know the true meaning of this statistic. Furthermore, it is difficult to conduct a study that actually measures two groups who are very similar to one other, other than the fact that in one group everyone owns a dog and in the other group no one owns a dog.

In addition to identifying the sources of each of these propositions, you may have also noticed that this example changed slightly from the last chapter. Where it was presented as *Dogs are man's best friend*, it became *Dogs are people's best friend.* This change is subtle, but makes an important point about CT. I used to teach this example as *Dogs are man's best friend*, but in one class, upon asking a question about the argument, a student raised her hand immediately. I called on her to answer, but instead she complained about the adage, claiming that it was wrong of me to suggest such a thing - dogs could just as easily be woman's best friend. I explained that I didn't have a problem with that, but 'woman' would be inclusive in this context, as 'man' is referring to 'mankind' as opposed to specifically males. The student responded that she didn't care what was intended or implied, that it was sexist against women and should be amended at once, perhaps to *Dogs are people's best friend.* I have since done as she asked, by amending my class exercises; however, not for the reason she gave, but rather, as a reminder. Likewise, I have presented the argument *Dogs are people's best friend* here as the same reminder – that being, if we want to be able to think critically, we must remove our emotions from our thinking. You will see an argument presented in Chapter 5 that *Emotions make thinking irrational.* Even though the example provided is a simple argument, with respect to size and rationale, its message rings true throughout the book. Sometimes the arguments we are required to think critically about may be controversial, they may evoke feelings, challenge beliefs and may sometimes make you or others feel uncomfortable. The point is that, regardless of how an argument or its topic makes you feel, it is of utmost importance that you remain objective in your thinking and not to let feelings or unjustified beliefs cloud the thinking around your judgments and decisions. We will return to the subject of emotion's effect on thinking in Chapter 10, with respect to the *affect heuristic*.

EXERCISE 5.3

In the following argument map, all of the *buts* are arguments against the claim that we are happy when drunk. However, each of these propositions is different with respect to the source from which it is derived; and thus, some might persuade you more than others. Consider what source each proposition is derived from:

Common belief

Research evidence/data

Expert opinion

Personal experience

Statistics

Identify each in the corresponding rebuttal box beneath and also provide a rebuttal. In this sense, we are doing more than simply identifying what types of arguments we are dealing with – we are doing something more important – thinking about how each argument type might influence our ultimate conclusion, *People are happy when drunk*.

SUMMARY AND CONCLUSION

In summary, analysis is a critical thinking skill that is used to detect, examine and identify the propositions within an argument, their sources (e.g. research, common beliefs, personal experience) and the role they play (e.g. the main conclusion, the premises and reasons provided to support the conclusion, objections to the conclusion), as well as the inferential relationships among propositions. When it comes to analysing the basis for a person's belief, we can extract the structure of their argument for analysis (from dialogue and prose) by looking for arguments that support or refute the belief, by looking for arguments that support this first level (or tier) of arguments and so on. What we see as a result is a hierarchical structure, in

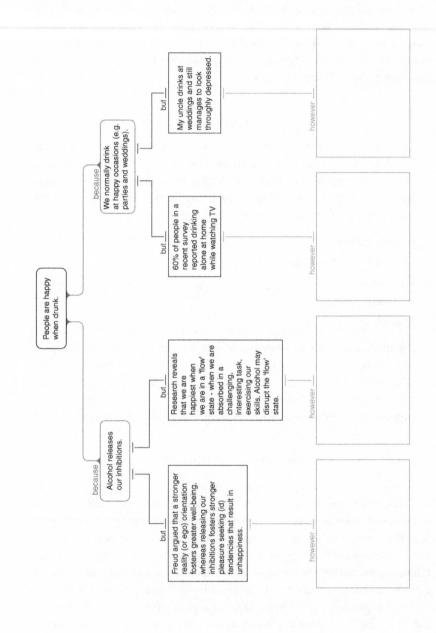

People are happy when drunk.

because Alcohol releases our inhibitions.

but Freud argued that a stronger reality (or ego) orientation fosters greater well-being, whereas releasing our inhibitions fosters stronger pleasure seeking (id) tendencies that result in unhappiness.

however [ ]

but Research reveals that we are happiest when we are in a 'flow' state - when we are absorbed in a challenging, interesting task, exercising our skills. Alcohol may disrupt the 'flow' state.

however [ ]

because We normally drink at happy occasions (e.g. parties and weddings).

but 60% of people in a recent survey reported drinking alone at home while watching TV

however [ ]

but My uncle drinks at weddings and still manages to look throughly depressed.

however [ ]

which we can analyse each independent proposition by identifying what types of arguments others are using when trying to persuade us to share their point of view. Being able to analyse the structure of an argument and the types, or sources, of propositions used within an argument allows us to begin *evaluating* the argument by examining: the credibility of the propositions used in the argument; the relevance of the propositions used in the argument; the logical strength among propositions in the argument; and potential omissions, bias and imbalance in the argument.

EXERCISE 5.4

Step 1

Read the argument, *Critical thinking is necessary for establishing the truth*. Analyse the argument structure. Take notes or highlight the passage in any way you wish.

I believe that critical thinking is necessary for establishing the truth, because no truths are established without thinking, and critical thinking includes all the essential thinking processes necessary for arriving at the truth. Why? Because, arriving at the truth implies a thorough examination of the basis of our beliefs. Critical thinking involves careful analysis and evaluation of the reasons and objections that either support or refute our beliefs, and further careful analysis and evaluation of the arguments that support these primary reasons and objections. It is only by using this careful, logical, strategy of analysis and evaluation that we can infer whether or not our beliefs are true.

Nevertheless, some people argue that even with critical thinking, we can never arrive at the truth, because every argument is limited in some respect. For example, arguments based on personal experience are potentially biased and unreliable. Common sense statements can be at odds with scientific research or other common sense statements. Research can be of poor quality and can conflict with other research findings. Experts/ authorities do not always agree and do not always have evidence to support their view. However, when we have multiple sources of evidence (different types of arguments), the majority of which are deemed to be reliable and valid, then we can make very good quality inferences that approach the truth.

Step 2

Analyse the structure of the argument in more explicit detail by filling in the missing propositions in the argument map.

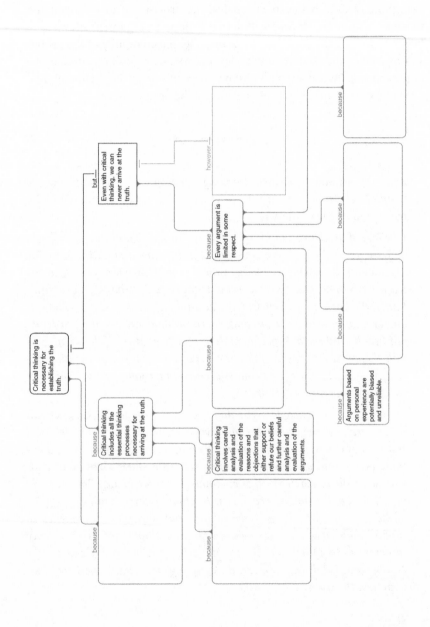

Critical thinking is necessary for establishing the truth.

because — Critical thinking includes all the essential thinking processes necessary for arriving at the truth.

because

because — Critical thinking involves careful analysis and evaluation of the reasons and objections that either support or refute our beliefs and further careful analysis and evaluation of the arguments.

because

but — Even with critical thinking, we can never arrive at the truth.

because — Every argument is limited in some respect.

however

because

because

because — Arguments based on personal experience are potentially biased and unreliable.

Step 3

Based on your identification of the structure of the argument, look for any potential imbalances, omissions or bias in the argument. Make a list of your observations and then answer the three following questions:

1. Does the author sufficiently support their claims? Please explain.
2. Does the author attempt to refute their own arguments (i.e. disconfirm their belief)? How?
3. Does any proposition or any set of propositions suggest to you that the author is biased in any way?

6

Evaluation

> It is the mark of an educated mind to be able to entertain a thought
> without accepting it.
>
> ~ Aristotle (c. 384–322 BC)

As we saw in the last chapter, the ability to analyse an argument (i.e. with
respect to both the structure and the types, or sources, of propositions used
within the argument) allows us to subsequently evaluate the argument.
The Delphi Report describes *evaluation* as a critical thinking (CT) skill that
is used in the assessment of propositions and claims in terms of their
credibility, relevance, logical strength (i.e. with respect to their relationship
with other propositions) and the potential for omissions, bias and imbalance in the argument, thus deciding the overall strength or weakness of an
argument (Facione, 1990b). Specifically, the Delphi Report outlines
a number of sub-skills involved in evaluation, including the following:

- The ability to assess the credibility of statements or other representations,
  which are accounts or descriptions of a person's perception, experience,
  situation, judgment, belief or opinion; and to assess the logical strength
  of the actual or intended inferential relationships among statements,
  descriptions, questions or other forms of representation.
- The ability to assess claims with respect to: recognizing the factors
  relevant to assessing the degree of credibility to ascribe to a source of
  information or opinion; the contextual relevance of questions, information, principles, rules or procedural directions; the acceptability and
  level of confidence to place in the probability or truth of any given
  representation of an experience, situation, judgment, belief or opinion.
- The ability to assess arguments with respect to: judging whether the
  assumed acceptability of the premises of an argument justifies one's

accepting as true (deductively certain), or very probably true (inductively justified), the expressed conclusion of that argument; anticipating, or raising, questions or objections and whether these point to significant weakness in the argument being evaluated; determining whether an argument relies on false or doubtful assumptions or presuppositions and then to determine how crucially these affect its strength; judging between reasonable and fallacious inferences; judging the probative strength of an argument's premises and assumptions with a view toward determining the acceptability of the argument; determine and judge the probative strength of an argument's intended or unintended consequences with a view toward judging the acceptability of the argument; and determining the extent to which possible additional information might strengthen or weaken an argument.

Evaluating the credibility of claims and arguments involves progressing beyond merely identifying the source of propositions in an argument, to actually examining the credibility of those identified sources (e.g. personal experiences, common beliefs/opinions, expert/authority opinion and scientific evidence). Evaluation also implies deep consideration of the relevance of claims within an argument, which is accomplished by assessing the contextual relevance of claims and premises (i.e. the pertinence or applicability of one proposition to another). Evaluating the logical strength of an argument is accomplished by monitoring both the logical relationships among propositions and the claims they infer. Finally, evaluating the potential for omission, bias and imbalance in an argument allows us to progress beyond identifying an argument's underlying motives, to being able to question and adequately address these motives.

In addition, evaluation is a CT skill used to help us establish the truth of a claim. Sometimes, it can be difficult to establish the truth, as establishing the truth is more difficult for some beliefs than for others. Before discussing the abilities that comprise the skill of evaluation, let us consider some claims and attempt to establish their truth. (Hint: In the four beliefs that follow, two cannot be verified as true, but this does not mean we should not think about them and engage in CT when doing so!)

1. Human beings are inherently good.
   Can we establish the truth of this belief? If yes, how difficult will it be to win a debate with someone who believes that *People are inherently bad*?

2. Alcohol consumption during pregnancy disrupts brain development.
Can we establish the truth of this belief? If yes, how might we present
our case to pregnant mothers?

3. Humans will eventually live on Mars.
Can we establish the truth of this belief? If yes, how might we
convince the government to invest in our future?

4. Genetic differences account for differences in intelligence.
Can we establish the truth of this belief? If yes, how do we explain
how genetic differences influence performance on intelligence
tests?

Human beings are inherently good is a claim that requires a moral and
an emotional evaluation, which cannot be verified as either true or false.
What some people see as good, others may interpret as bad. Science
cannot truly resolve this problem, because it is not the kind of problem
that can be resolved by collected data. Nevertheless, philosophers and
psychologists have argued and continue to argue about human nature.
Are we inherently good or inherently bad? Which is more prominent in
our human nature?

It is important that we use CT to analyse and evaluate the arguments
that people present us with when they argue one way or the other. We are
perfectly entitled to voice our own opinion and present our own
argument – we are perfectly entitled to hold one belief or another, but we
should keep in mind that a belief without a supporting argument is open to
being shot down by someone who possesses an opposing belief with
a strong argument base. Although science cannot resolve moral disputes
such as *Human beings are inherently good*, if we make specific assertions
about certain behavioural tendencies, it is possible to look at examples
of what some people might describe as 'good' or 'bad' behaviour. For
example, though we have to avoid labelling behaviour as 'good' or 'bad'
whenever we observe and measure behaviour in the scientific laboratory,
we might be able to evaluate the claim that people are basically selfish,
because, presumably, acting with self-interest is somehow different from
acting for the benefit of others, and we can measure these behaviours and
decide whether or not we act more often with self-interest or more often
with others in mind. We will return to this debate later and consider some
related arguments.

The second belief, *Alcohol consumption during pregnancy disrupts brain
development*, can be empirically tested. In other words, we can evaluate
whether or not this claim is true – we can observe the brain development of

infants in the womb and we can compare the pattern of brain development observed in the children of mothers who drink alcohol during pregnancy with the pattern of brain development observed in the children of mothers who do not drink alcohol during pregnancy. In fact, the belief that *alcohol consumption during pregnancy disrupts brain development* is well-established as a true belief. The only issue in the scientific literature right now is how much alcohol needs to be consumed to cause the brain damage and what are the critical times during pregnancy when alcohol causes the greatest amount of brain damage.

In relation to the third claim, *Humans will eventually live on Mars*, we might believe that humans will eventually live on Mars, but we cannot verify this belief as true. This type of belief represents a possibility, something that may happen in the future, but that has not yet happened. We do not yet know: if Mars can support human life; all the technical issues involved in both transporting and maintaining a human colony on Mars; what might go wrong, either in terms of our physical or mental well-being or whether or not we could stay there long enough to reproduce and build a sustainable community.

The fourth and final belief considered, *Genetic differences account for differences in intelligence*, is still debated in the psychology literature. However, we *can* establish the truth of this belief. For example, research studies that compare the intelligence levels of identical twins (i.e. twins who share an identical gene profile) with non-identical twins (i.e. twins who share approximately 50% of their genes) suggest that some of the variation in intelligence is accounted for by variation in genetic profile. In other words, identical twins are more similar to one another in terms of intelligence than are non-identical twins. On the other hand, some suggest that comparing identical and non-identical twins in this way is problematic and that we cannot easily conclude from these studies that genetic similarities account for similarities in intelligence test performance. For example, identical twins are treated as similar, whereas non-identical twins are treated as different. In other words, the learning environment of identical twins is similar to that of non-identical twins and this might explain why they perform in similar ways when asked to complete intelligence tests. In order to answer *how genetic differences influence performance on intelligence tests*, we must first consider two similar questions: *How do genes influence neurochemical differences in the brain?* and *How do these basic neural differences influence levels of intelligence?* Yet again, these are difficult questions to answer, as there is still a large amount of debate in the scientific literature in relation to both of these questions.

As we have seen in the past few examples, it can be difficult to establish the truth of some claims, thus elaborating the necessity of possessing both analytical and evaluative skills when conducting CT. When we attempt to establish the truth of a claim through the evaluation of its supporting propositions, our main objective is to arrive at some conclusions about the overall strengths and weaknesses of the argument. We can begin evaluating the overall strengths and weaknesses of an argument by asking three questions.

The first question asks: *How strong are the types, or sources, of arguments presented?* As we have seen in the previous chapter, the different types of arguments that may be presented are based on: anecdotal evidence (or stories of personal experience), expert opinion (or an authority opinion), common beliefs, statistics or research findings (e.g. case studies, survey research, correlational research or experimental research). Generally, we evaluate anecdotal evidence and common beliefs as weaker than evidence from empirical research. However, as seen in the last chapter, each source can have its limitations and thus, there remains a need for in depth evaluation.

The second question we must ask is *How relevant and logical are the arguments?* We ask this question because some propositions used within an argument may not be relevant or logically connected to the central claim. If they are irrelevant or illogical, we need to address the issue of irrelevance and ensure that they are excluded from the argument. For example, consider the passage on *How I know Billy likes ice cream* reads:

> *Billy likes ice cream. Every night after dinner he has it for dessert. Whenever he goes grocery shopping with his mom he begs her to buy more. Billy likes to go to the park with his mom, too. One time, when Billy dropped his ice cream on the ground, he started to cry because he did not get to enjoy his treat.*

It is obvious from the excerpt that the irrelevant proposition is that 'Billy likes going to the park with his mom' as it does not reveal a link between *Billy* and *liking ice cream*. As a result, this proposition must be excluded from the argument.

The final question we must ask is whether or not the overall argument is imbalanced in any way. For example, does it exclude important arguments? Is it biased? Are there hidden assumptions that need to be made more explicit? What was the author's purpose for writing this argument?

EVALUATING CREDIBILITY

It is not easy to construct a credible argument. It takes time to find credible evidence to support our arguments. Notably, every link in the chain of reasoning that is used to support our arguments needs to be strong. If we have one weak link, people may quickly begin to doubt our argument. Let us suppose that you are debating the causes of aggression with a friend. Your friend believes that aggression is biologically caused – that people are more or less aggressive by nature. On the other hand, you believe that life experiences and the kinds of environments that people are placed in are far more important predictors of aggressive behaviour. Thus, you want to present some strong objections to your friend's claim that aggression is biologically caused and also to convince your friend that your belief is true. However, you recognize that there are some compelling reasons to believe, as your friend does, that aggression may have a biological basis. As a result, you judge it necessary to weigh up some of the evidence for the biological basis of aggression against arguments that suggest otherwise. For example, your working argument could look something like what is presented on the following page.

Now that you have identified propositions for and against the biological basis of aggression, we must evaluate each with respect to the credibility of its source. In order to consider this issue in depth, we first have to figure out what type of argument we are dealing with. We have dealt with identifying the sources of arguments in the last chapter, with respect to the skill of analysis; but, in terms of the skill of evaluation, we must also focus on the strength or weakness of each source. That is, what type of source would make you more likely to believe the central claim? Please take a moment to consider the strengths and weaknesses of these propositions.

EVALUATING RELEVANCE

Let us suppose that in the heat of the debate on the biological basis of aggression a person says to you:

> Well, you mentioned that men and women have different levels of testosterone – men have more testosterone and this is why men are more aggressive. But, did you know that testosterone has also been implicated in the structural brain differences that underpin gender differences in language ability and spatial ability?

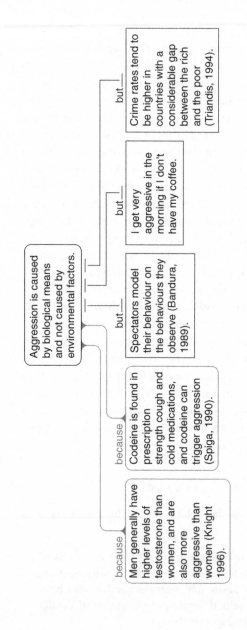

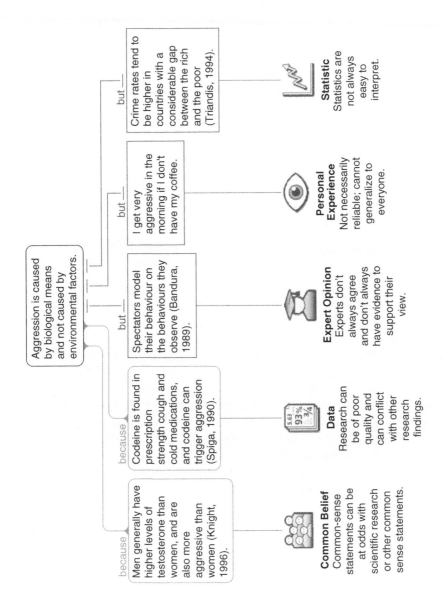

Aggression is caused by biological means and not caused by environmental factors.

because

Men generally have higher levels of testosterone than women, and are also more aggressive than women (Knight, 1996).

Common Belief
Common-sense statements can be at odds with scientific research or other common sense statements.

because

Codeine is found in prescription strength cough and cold medications, and codeine can trigger aggression (Spiga, 1990).

Data
Research can be of poor quality and can conflict with other research findings.

but

Spectators model their behaviour on the behaviours they observe (Bandura, 1989).

Expert Opinion
Experts don't always agree and don't always have evidence to support their view.

but

I get very aggressive in the morning if I don't have my coffee.

Personal Experience
Not necessarily reliable; cannot generalize to everyone.

but

Crime rates tend to be higher in countries with a considerable gap between the rich and the poor (Triandis, 1994).

Statistic
Statistics are not always easy to interpret.

The argument itself might well be vigorously disputed and it might well foster a new debate that sends people off on a different tangent, but is this argument about gender differences in language ability and spatial ability truly relevant here? Is it related to the central claim that aggression is biologically caused?

In order to evaluate an argument, we must also assess the relevance of the propositions included within. Consider the claim: *Watching pornography increases aggressive male behaviour towards females*:

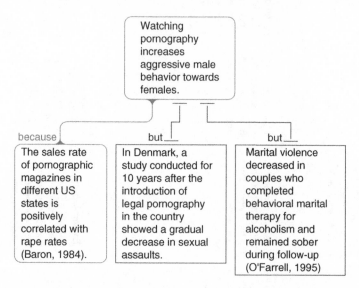

Are all reasons and objections relevant to the central claim? Is there any proposition(s) that does/do not relate to the claim above? Which proposition(s) is/are irrelevant? Please take a moment to consider the relevance of each proposition.

As we may well have evaluated, the third proposition is irrelevant to the central claim. Alcoholism may well be associated with increased levels of marital violence in some instances, but in the absence of any direct link to pornography, this proposition is simply irrelevant. As a result, we must exclude the third proposition and treat this argument as consisting of a claim, one support and one objection.

EVALUATING LOGICAL STRENGTH

The overall structure of an argument needs to be logical if the argument is to be considered strong. In our evaluation of arguments thus far, we have focused a fair bit of attention on individual propositions. However, the overall structure of an argument – the relationships shared among propositions – is very important and individual propositions need to be logically interconnected for the argument structure to be convincing.

Sometimes, we can improve upon the structure of an argument and help demonstrate its logical strength. Consider the argument *Alterations in human biochemistry have an effect on aggression.*

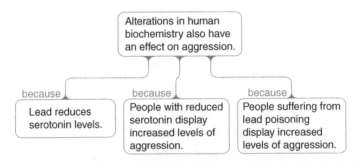

Three propositions are provided to support the central claim. However, two of the propositions, when considered together, actually support the third proposition, rather than directly supporting the central claim. Thus, we could do a better job of revealing the correct logical structure at the base of this argument by placing two of the propositions beneath the third.

Specifically, at the base of this argument, we are trying to explain an intermediate conclusion – we are trying to explain 'how' lead poisoning increases levels of aggression. We can make this explanation explicit if we focus on the logical relationship among the three propositions at the base of this argument. Importantly, we say two things that might make us believe that *People suffering from lead poisoning display increased levels of aggression.* First, we say that *Lead reduces the levels of serotonin in the brain* (serotonin is a neurotransmitter that is related to emotion). Second, we say *People with reduced serotonin display increased levels of aggression.* From these two propositions, we might reasonably deduce that *People suffering from lead poisoning display increased levels of aggression.* This may be an established finding in the scientific literature, but what we are doing here is explaining the relationship between lead poisoning and aggression by reference to the effect of lead on serotonin and the effect of serotonin on emotions.

Now, we might then use this intermediate conclusion as one among, perhaps, many others to argue that *Alterations in human biochemistry have an effect on aggression.*

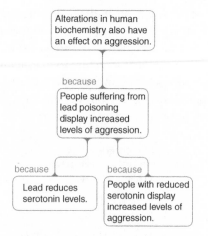

Let us take a look at another argument: *The youth of today are very aggressive*. In the argument map that follows, there are two propositions that support the central claim: (1) *The youth of today watch too much violent TV* and (2) *Watching violent TV makes one aggressive*. These propositions taken together address the two core elements in the conclusion: that is, the subject (i.e. the youth of today) and the predicate (i.e. aggressive). The conclusion states that the youth of today are aggressive, and there is a common element linking the two supporting propositions that make us believe this conclusion to be true – the common element is violent TV. The youth of today watch too much violent TV and watching violent TV makes one aggressive. Thus, we might infer that the youth of today are very aggressive.

EXERCISE 6.1

Study the following argument map and evaluate the relevance and credibility of each proposition. Cross out propositions that either lack credibility or are irrelevant. In addition, suggest alternative arguments wherever possible.

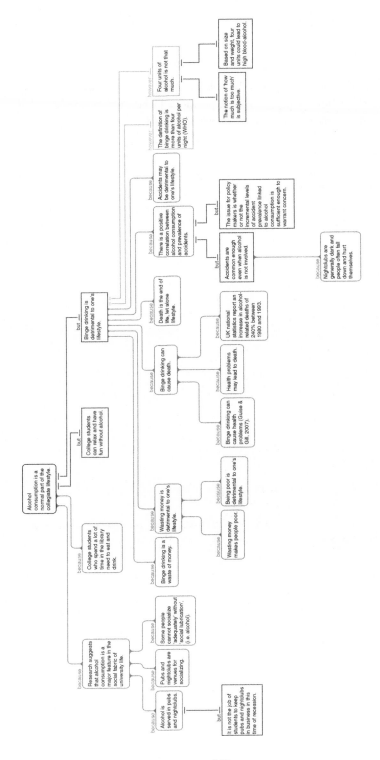

111

EXERCISE 6.2

Ensure the logical strength of the following argument by correctly placing each proposition in its appropriate position. The central claim states that *Genes and hormones dictate sexual orientation*. The argument consists of two supporting lines of reasoning (each containing three propositions). However, in each set of three, two of the three propositions support the third. Please group the six propositions into two sets of three, based on relevance and then decide how best to arrange the arguments in the argument map for purposes of ensuring logical strength. That is, in each group, which two propositions support the third?

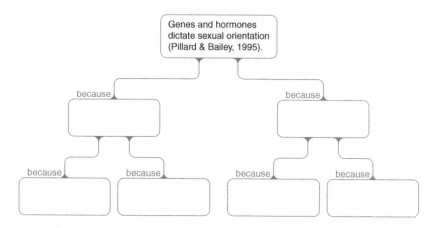

Which Two Support the Third?

1. Monozygotic twins have similar sexual orientation in 52% of cases when at least one twin is homosexual (Whitman, Diamond, & Martin, 1993).
2. People who are genetically similar have similar emotions, thoughts and behaviours.
3. Money et al. (1984) found that homosexuality was several times higher than the average in women who had been exposed to high levels of androgens in utero.
4. Sexual orientation in females is affected by prenatal hormone level.
5. Monozygotic twins are genetically similar.
6. Exposure to high levels of androgens is sometimes linked to an abnormality of the adrenal glands, which usually secretes very low levels of these hormones in women.

EVALUATING BALANCE

Another feature of our overall argument evaluation is the extent to which there is a balance of evidence in an argument structure. When we refer to balance in this context, we are concerned with the number of supporting propositions provided in comparison with the number of objecting propositions. If there is a large relative difference between these counts, then we can consider the argument imbalanced. Such imbalance often implies that the argument's author is in some way biased. An argument may be biased in the sense that a person has a belief or prejudgment that makes them focus only on reasoning that supports their belief. There are two extremes of bias and many shades of difference between these two extremes. The first extreme is where a person wholeheartedly agrees with a claim and offers only supporting arguments (i.e. omitting objections). The second extreme is where a person vehemently opposes a claim and offers only objections (i.e. omitting supports). In both cases, the person may be overlooking some important arguments; *and* in both cases, we need to question their intentions.

Apart from imbalance by omission, arguments can be imbalanced and biased by deliberately pitting weak propositions (e.g. with regard to relevance or credibility) on one side of an argument against strong propositions on the other. Consider the argument: *Television violence increases aggression in the viewer.*

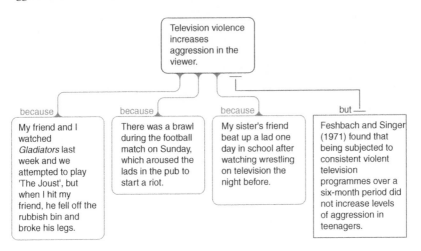

By placing a string of three anecdotes on one side of the debate, supporting the central claim against one good quality experimental study on the other side, we may well wonder if the author is not deliberately pitting the strong against the weak to make us rethink our overall conclusion. Furthermore, the author might be presenting three weak statements against one strong proposition in order to feign a balanced argument, when in reality, the argument is imbalanced. Perhaps television violence has no effect on aggression in the viewer. We would need further, good quality experimental evidence that suggests otherwise if we are to counter-argue the conclusions drawn by the empirical research. Anecdotes are insufficient. We need better reasons if we are to believe the central claim that *Television violence increases aggression in the viewer.*

EXERCISE 6.3

Consider the argument, *We are happy when we are good*, below. Aside from Aristotle's propositions representing an authority position (or

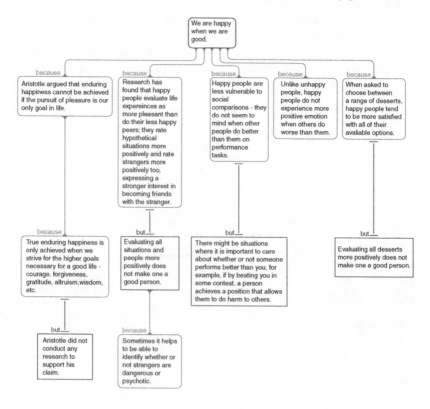

the view of an 'expert' if you wish to describe it thus), the remainder of the argument includes propositions that report research findings. Without questioning the research methods or the quality of the research directly, we can nevertheless ask and answer the following questions relatively easily: How relevant and logical are the arguments? Are they logically connected to the central claim? If they are irrelevant or illogical, please exclude them by crossing them out. Then answer the four following questions:

1. Is the overall argument imbalanced in any way? Please explain.

2. Is the overall argument biased in any way? Please explain.

3. Does the argument exclude important arguments? Please explain.

4. Are there hidden assumptions that need to be made more explicit? Please explain.

SUMMARY AND CONCLUSION

In summary, evaluation is conceptualized as a CT skill that is used in the assessment of propositions and claims in terms of their credibility, relevance, logical strength (i.e. with respect to their relationship with other propositions) and the potential for omissions, bias and imbalance in the argument. Evaluation is a CT skill used to help us establish the truth of a claim. When we attempt to establish the truth of a claim through the evaluation of its supporting argument, our main objective is to arrive at some conclusions about the overall strengths and weakness of the argument. By evaluating the propositions used in an argument, with respect to their credibility, relevance, logical strength and balance of evidence, we can arrive at some conclusions about the overall strengths and weaknesses of arguments.

EXERCISE 6.4

Evaluate the argument on attraction. Take time to assess (1) the credibility, (2) relevance, (3) logical strength and (4) balance of propositions in the argument. If a proposition lacks credibility, relevance or logical strength, exclude it and explain why you did so. Also, explain the balance of the argument.

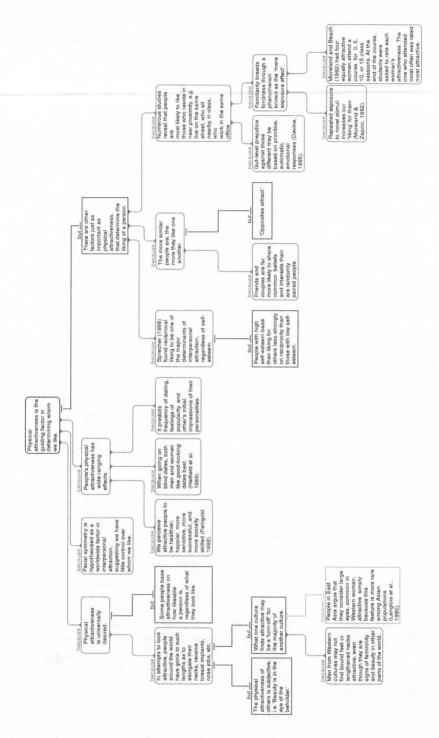

Physical attractiveness is the guiding factor in determining whom we like.

because — Physical attractiveness is universally desired.

but — Some people base attractiveness on how likeable a person is, regardless of what they look like.

because — In attempts to look attractive, people around the world have gone to such lengths as to elongate their necks, receive breast implants, nose jobs, etc.

but — The physical attractiveness of others is subjective, i.e. 'Beauty is in the eye of the beholder.'

but — What one culture finds attractive may be a turn-off for the majority of another culture.

because — Men from Western cultures may not find bound feet or lengthened necks attractive, even though they are signs of femininity and beauty in other parts of the world.

however — People in East Asia argue that they consider large eyes, common in Western women, attractive simply because this feature is more rare among Asian populations (Langlois et al., 1990).

because — Facial symmetry is hypothesized as a worldwide factor in interpersonal attraction, suggesting we have little control over whom we like.

because — People's physical attractiveness has wide-ranging effects.

because — We perceive attractive people to be healthier, happier, more sensitive, more successful, and more socially skilled (Feingold, 1992).

because — When going on blind dates, both men and women like good-looking dates best. (Hatfield et al., 1966).

because — It predicts frequency of dating, feelings of popularity, and other's initial impressions of their personalities.

but — There are other factors just as important as physical attractiveness that determine the liking of a person.

because — Sprecher (1998) found reciprocal liking to be one of the major determinants of interpersonal attraction, regardless of self-esteem.

but — People with high self-esteem base their liking for others less strongly on reciprocity than those with low self-esteem.

because — The more similar people are, the more they like one another.

because — Friends and couples are far more likely to share common beliefs and interests than are randomly paired people.

but — 'Opposites attract.'

because — Numerous studies reveal that people are most likely to like those who reside in near proximity, e.g. live on the same street, who sit nearby in class, who work in the same office.

because — Gut-level prejudice against those different may be based on primitive, automatic, emotional responses (Devine, 1995).

because — Familiarity breeds fondness through a phenomenon known as the 'mere exposure effect'.

because — Repeated exposure to novel stimuli increases our 'liking' for them (Moreland & Zajonc, 1982).

because — Moreland and Beach (1992) had four equally attractive women attend a course for 0, 5, 10, or 15 class sessions. At the end of the course, students were asked to rate each woman's attractiveness. The one who attended most often was rated most attractive.

116

7

Inference

No way of thinking or doing, however ancient, can be trusted without proof.

~ Henry David Thoreau (1817–1862)

Like Bloom's (1956) conceptualization of synthesis (see Chapter 1), the final critical thinking (CT) skill, *inference*, involves the 'gathering' of credible, relevant and logical evidence based on the previous analysis and evaluation of available evidence, for the purposes of 'drawing a reasonable conclusion' (Facione, 1990b, p. 9). Drawing a conclusion always implies some act of synthesis. However, inference is a unique form of synthesis in that it involves the formulation of a set of consequences and conclusions that are derived from a set of arguments or a body of evidence. This may imply accepting a conclusion pointed to by another (e.g. author or speaker) in light of the evidence they present, or 'conjecturing an alternative', equally logical, conclusion or argument based on the available evidence (Facione, 1990b, p. 9). According to the Delphi definition, another important aspect of inference is 'querying the evidence' available, for example, by recognizing the need for additional information or justification and by being able to gather such additional information or justification to draw a conclusion; and to judge the plausibility of utilizing such additional information or justification for purposes of conjecturing an alternative conclusion. Specifically, the Delphi Report outlines a number of sub-skills involved in inference:

- The ability to identify and secure elements needed to draw reasonable conclusions, to form conjectures and hypotheses, to consider relevant information and to deduce the consequences flowing from the information presented.

- The ability to query evidence with respect to: recognizing premises that require support and to formulate a strategy for seeking and gathering information which might supply that support; judging information relevant to decisions regarding the acceptability, plausibility or relative merits of a conclusion, argument or alternative; and determining plausible investigatory strategies for acquiring that information.

- The ability to conjecture alternatives with respect to: formulating multiple alternatives for resolving a problem, postulating a series of suppositions regarding a question, projecting alternative hypotheses, developing a variety of different plans to achieve some goal and projecting the range of possible consequences of decisions or conclusions.

- The ability to draw conclusions with respect to applying appropriate modes of inference in determining what position one should take on a given matter or issue, given the information available; educing logical, inferential relationships and their consequences; and employing reasoning to determine which of several possible conclusions is most strongly warranted or supported by the available evidence, or which should be rejected or regarded as less plausible by the information given.

Notably, in the context of querying evidence and conjecturing alternative conclusions, inference overlaps with evaluation to a certain degree in that both skills are used to assess the acceptability of a claim or an argument. Nevertheless, it remains necessary to query and judge the inclusion of propositions within an argument, before gathering them to draw a conclusion.

Good inference ability depends on good evaluation, and as previously mentioned, though there is a certain degree of overlap between the two, it is also important to note that they differ. Inference differs from evaluation in the sense that the process of inference involves *generating* a conclusion from propositions. Being an autonomous thinker means that you draw your own conclusions. We do not spend our lives simply evaluating other people's thinking; rather, we generate our own conclusions. That said, we must also evaluate our own thinking and subsequent conclusions much the same way as we evaluate the thinking of others.

After inferring a conclusion, we evaluate the argument again and perhaps infer, the second time around, that our original conclusion is false. We might then alter our argument or alter our conclusions, or both. In other words, when applying the skills of evaluation and inference, we progress in a somewhat cyclical manner – from evaluation to inference, back to evaluation and again to inference, again and again. As we do so, our thinking becomes more orderly, more complex, more logical and better . . . so we hope!

INFERENCE IN FORMAL LOGIC

On a daily basis, we draw conclusions from statements, even on a very basic scale. For example, we might be presented with two statements and, from these, draw one conclusion. Syllogistic reasoning, as addressed in Chapter 3, is the classic form of this inference ability that philosophers traditionally studied as part of their basic training, in order to hone their argumentation skills. You might have noted when evaluating the arguments in the previous chapter that some arguments lacked logical strength and coherence in places. It is not unusual to discover that arguments lack essential logic and coherence – we often see this quite clearly after conducting a thorough evaluation of an argument. In conversation and in writing, we often make bold statements and imply logical connections between them. However, the logical connections that we assume to exist are not always there. Syllogisms are a truly great place to start thinking about the skill of inference, because thinking about these three-proposition structures (i.e. two premises and one conclusion) helps us to see clearly many of the common fallacies (or errors) in both our own reasoning and the reasoning of others.

Again, as we discussed in Chapter 3, the foundations of formal logic were laid out by Aristotle in the 4th century BC, through his work with syllogistic reasoning (i.e. the ability to infer the validity of an argument in which a conclusion follows from two premises). The main function of syllogistic reasoning, in the context of formal logic, is to provide methods of testing the validity of arguments. To reiterate, logicians are interested in the logical form of the argument only and dispense with the words which refer to the subject matter by replacing them with variables (e.g. p and q), given that the validity of an argument depends exclusively on its logical form. In the case of the *invalidity* of an argument, there is not necessarily a relationship between the truth and falsity of either the conclusion or its premises. The relation between truth and validity may represent any of the four possible combinations: (1) true-true, (2) true-false, (3) false-true and (4) false-false. Only one of these four possible combinations is impossible – true premises and a false conclusion. Any other combination may occur, even though it may seem counter-intuitive that an argument stemming from false premises can lead to a true conclusion. For example:

All pharaohs were US presidents.

Kennedy was a pharaoh.

Therefore, Kennedy was a US president.

The conclusion is valid, notwithstanding the falsity of both premises. To reiterate, formal logic does not concern itself with the factual truth of statements, but rather the validity of the logical form of the argument. In the context of logical form, a true proposition (i.e. with respect to the truth–validity relationship) can be represented by any proposition, whether it is true or false with respect to its subject matter.

Now, please consider the following premises and the associated conclusions in the following argument map.

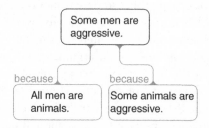

This seems to be a reasonable conclusion, because most people would agree that some men are aggressive. However, consider the following syllogism, which contains the same logical structure as the syllogism above.

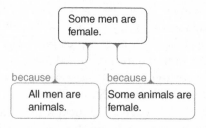

It becomes obvious that this is an invalid argument. What is happening here is that we are using what we know to be true (some men are aggressive) as a *substitute* for logical thinking. In the earlier case, it might be easy to confuse the idea that just because some animals are aggressive, there must be some overlap between men and aggression (i.e. as all men are animals and some animals are aggressive, surely some of the men are aggressive). However, in the second syllogism, the overlap or lack thereof is easier to assimilate (i.e. though men are animals, men are not female).

Again, we might confuse the first syllogism because it seems logical given that all three propositions may very well be true; however, validity and invalidity are not functions of truth, rather logical form. In the next exercise, you are presented with an opportunity to practise considering the validity of syllogisms. In addition to ignoring truth and instead concentrating on form, the following is a list of helpful tips for judging the validity of syllogisms.

A syllogism is judged as valid provided four criteria are met:

1. The middle term must be distributed at least once.
2. No term may be distributed in the conclusion, which was not distributed in one of the premises.
3. No conclusion follows from two negative premises.
4. If one premise is negative, the conclusion must be negative; and if the conclusion is negative, one of the premises must be negative.

EXERCISE 7.1

Read slowly and carefully each of the ten syllogisms. Consider each one in turn. The question you must ask yourself in each case is the same: *Is the conclusion valid?* That is, given the logical relationship between the two premises provided, is the conclusion inferred logically valid?

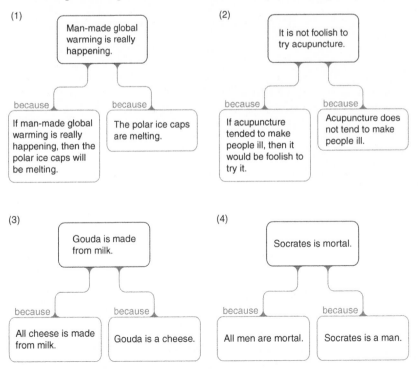

(1)

Man-made global warming is really happening.

because — If man-made global warming is really happening, then the polar ice caps will be melting.

because — The polar ice caps are melting.

(2)

It is not foolish to try acupuncture.

because — If acupuncture tended to make people ill, then it would be foolish to try it.

because — Acupuncture does not tend to make people ill.

(3)

Gouda is made from milk.

because — All cheese is made from milk.

because — Gouda is a cheese.

(4)

Socrates is mortal.

because — All men are mortal.

because — Socrates is a man.

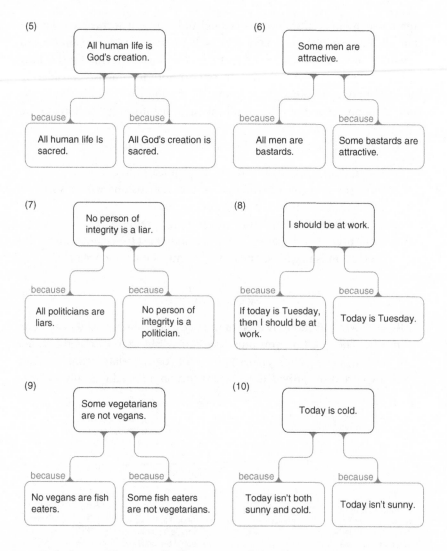

Only three of the ten syllogisms were valid: 3, 4 and 8. Syllogisms 1 and 2 were both invalid because there might be another variable leading to the conclusion. For example, man-made global warming may be happening for reasons other than the *polar ice caps melting*. Likewise, there may be other reasons for why it is *foolish to try acupuncture*. Syllogisms 5 and 7 are both invalid because they both assume an overlap that is simply not there. For example, syllogism 5 is invalid because it is assuming that human life is God's creation because human life is sacred as are God's creation. According to that logic, it would be the same to say:

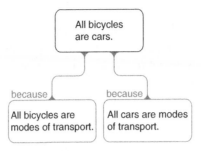

Syllogisms 6 and 9 share the same invalid logic as the earlier example regarding *Some men are aggressive*, albeit add a negation (i.e. *No*). Finally, syllogism 10 is invalid because it does not exclude the possibility of other variables. For example, just because it is not sunny today does not mean it has to be cold – it could be cloudy or rainy.

Notably, many mistakes in judging a syllogism's validity result from our beliefs, attitudes and biases regarding the content of propositions within the syllogism. That is, we let our biases and emotions do the thinking for us. For example, a certain emotion may have been evoked in you, the reader, when considering propositions relating to lawyers, God or even men! Further discussion of the impact of our biases and emotions in decision-making is presented in Chapter 10

Nevertheless, after discussion of formal logic in class, students often ask two questions about the use of syllogisms in CT: (1) *If these are so important, why don't we use them all the time?*; and (2) *Is it feasible to use syllogisms all the time?* The second question actually answers the first. Formal logic is not often used because of feasibility. Though logical form is a valued feature of good CT, so is truth! In reality, regardless of logical form, it is not CT if the premises we work from or the conclusions we infer are false. This explanation is invariably followed by another question from students: *What is the point of learning about syllogisms or formal logic?* The answer is twofold. First, to reiterate from earlier in the chapter, syllogisms are a truly great place to start thinking about the skill of inference, because they help us to see clearly many of the common errors in the logical structure of reasoning – they provide great examples of how arguments should and should not be constructed. Second, as seen in the earlier examples, words such as 'no', 'all', 'some', 'if/then' to name a few, no matter how small or subtle, play a large role in giving the proposition meaning. Though these are commonly used words and are often over-looked relative to more specific ideas and concepts, these subtle words give or withdraw relevance to or from the proposition; and thus, considering syllogisms provides practice in identifying the role of such words and the importance each plays in the explicit or implied meaning of a proposition. After justifying the value of practicing and understanding syllogisms and formal logic, I then teach the more practical aspects of inference (i.e. with respect to critically thinking about real-world situations), namely those related to *informal logic*.

<h3 style="text-align:center">INFERENCE IN INFORMAL LOGIC</h3>

As outlined in the chapter introduction, when using the skill of inference in the context of informal logic, we must gather the information (i.e. propositions) that we have previously analysed and evaluated as credible, relevant and logically sound, and use them to infer a conclusion. Though inference based on informal logic does not adhere to a formulaic method, it is important that we keep the basic principles of syllogistic reasoning in mind. Inference in informal logic is common in scientific thinking as well as most day-to-day applications and is a grounded, practical strategy which stresses the provision of justification for every reason and objection related to a core claim or conclusion (examples of the application of informal logic can be seen in the argument maps presented throughout the previous chapters on analysis and evaluation). For example, scientific understanding is derived from reading many individual research studies. Each study finding should allow us to argue for the existence of some observed relation.

For many scientific questions, there will be several lines of reasoning – many observed relations – that lead to an overall conclusion. In the context of inference in informal logic, an argument with a justifiable conclusion will have lines of reasoning arranged such that:

1. related arguments are grouped together;
2. groups of related arguments are used to derive intermediate conclusions;
3. intermediate conclusions are used to derive higher-level conclusions and so on, until an overall conclusion is derived.

Nevertheless, when we study arguments and examine how intermediate conclusions and high-level conclusions are derived, we often see limited logic and coherence in the overall argument structure.

Consider the argument on attraction:

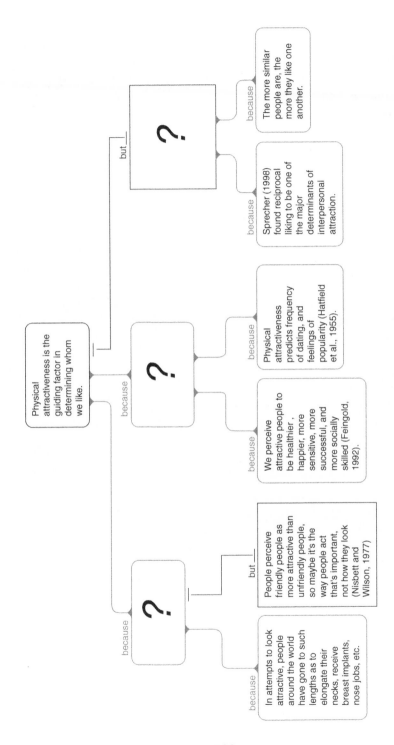

Physical attractiveness is the guiding factor in determining whom we like.

because

?

because

In attempts to look attractive, people around the world have gone to such lengths as to elongate their necks, receive breast implants, nose jobs, etc.

but

People perceive friendly people as more attractive than unfriendly people, so maybe it's the way people act that's important, not how they look (Nisbett and Wilson, 1977)

because

?

because

We perceive attractive people to be healthier, happier, more sensitive, more successful, and more socially skilled (Feingold, 1992).

because

Physical attractiveness predicts frequency of dating, and feelings of popularity (Hatfield et al., 1955).

but

?

because

Sprecher (1998) found reciprocal liking to be one of the major determinants of interpersonal attraction.

because

The more similar people are, the more they like one another.

Without the presence of the three intermediate conclusions, we cannot infer from the three sets of propositions on the third level of the argument map whether the overall conclusion is justified. As a result, the argument lacks coherence and logical strength. Thus, valid, intermediate conclusions must be inferred from the propositions on the third level, which in turn infer the overall conclusion. Please take a moment and consider what these intermediate conclusions might be.

EXERCISE 7.2

Consider the argument concerning the central claim that *Smokers should be given more freedom to smoke and more personal responsibility for the choices they make* on the following page. Please infer the three intermediate conclusions based on each proposition couplet provided on the third level of the argument map. These intermediate conclusions must also infer the central claim (i.e. the overall conclusion).

EXERCISE 7.3

Please infer the intermediate conclusions and central claim in the empty boxes. Begin at the bottom of the argument map and progress upwards. Each intermediate conclusion inferred is important, as it will dictate the conclusion you draw on each ascending level of the argument map.

SUMMARY AND CONCLUSION

In summary, inference refers to the gathering of credible, relevant and logical evidence based on the previous analysis and evaluation of available evidence, for the purposes of drawing a reasonable conclusion. This may imply accepting a conclusion pointed to by an author in light of the evidence they present, or proposing an alternative, equally logical, conclusion based on the available evidence. Though there is some overlap between the CT skills of inference and evaluation (i.e. querying the available evidence), good inference ability depends on good evaluation in order to be able to generate a justifiable conclusion. The ability to infer, or generate a conclusion, can be completed by both formal and informal logic strategies in order to derive intermediate conclusions as well as central claims. After inferring a conclusion, we must re-evaluate our

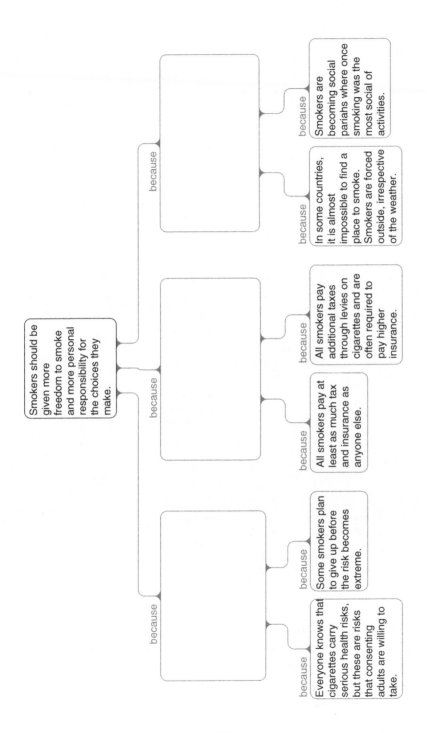

Smokers should be given more freedom to smoke and more personal responsibility for the choices they make.

because

because

Everyone knows that cigarettes carry serious health risks, but these are risks that consenting adults are willing to take.

because

Some smokers plan to give up before the risk becomes extreme.

because

because

All smokers pay at least as much tax and insurance as anyone else.

because

All smokers pay additional taxes through levies on cigarettes and are often required to pay higher insurance.

because

because

In some countries, it is almost impossible to find a place to smoke. Smokers are forced outside, irrespective of the weather.

because

Smokers are becoming social pariahs where once smoking was the most social of activities.

127

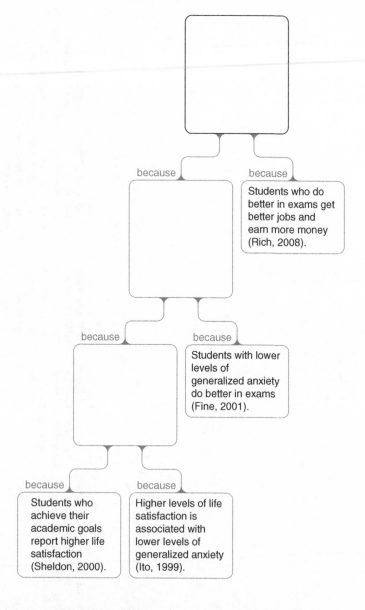

resulting argument. To reiterate, when applying the skill of inference, we progress in a somewhat cyclical manner – from inference back to evaluation and again to inference until we are confident in our overall conclusion. An important by-product of this cycle is that our thinking becomes more complex, more organized and more logical.

8

Reflective Judgment

Knowing a great deal is not the same as being smart; intelligence is not
information alone but also judgment, the manner in which information
is collected and used.

~ Carl Sagan (1934–1996)

Though the conceptualizations of critical thinking (CT) reviewed in the
preceding chapters have shed some light on what it is we mean by CT, at
the same time, it is often acknowledged that CT skills require time to
develop (Dawson, 2008; Halpern, 2014; King & Kitchener, 1994; Kuhn,
1999). However, there is no consensus as to how best to develop CT skills.
For CT to develop to a high level, related metacognitive processes (i.e. in
addition to the self-regulatory functions of metacognition) may be needed
to support CT skill development and to aid in the successful application of
CT to real-world problems.

In Chapter 4, we learned that we will only perform CT skills to the best
of our ability if we are willing to do so. More specifically, we must be willing
to go beyond merely applying CT skills to actually thinking about our own
thinking. But, how do we think about thinking?

In order to think about thinking, we must conduct *reflective judgment*,
in which we reflect upon the information presented to us and what we
already know about that information, so that we may come to a logical
conclusion. Reflective judgment (RJ) is a metacognitive process that can
aid in the support, development and application of CT, particularly in
the context of real-world problems. The ability to think about thinking
(Flavell, 1976; Ku & Ho, 2010b) and the ability to apply CT skills to
a particular problem imply a reflective sensibility and the capacity for RJ
(King & Kitchener, 1994). Like CT, RJ is an important skill for students to
acquire and practise, because it may facilitate their ongoing acquisition and

application of knowledge both inside and outside of school and university (Huffaker & Calvert, 2003; US National Research Council, 2002). According to King and Kitchener (1994), RJ is an individual's understanding of the nature, limits and certainty of *knowing* and how this can affect how they defend their judgments and reasoning in context.

We use RJ every day. When we read the paper or watch the news, we use RJ. Even when we are socializing with our friends, we are forced to reflectively judge situations, especially if we enter into a debate or encounter a problem. Essentially, RJ is our way of thinking about the way in which we think and how we consider making changes to the way we think.

ACKNOWLEDGING UNCERTAINTY

Moreover, RJ involves the ability of an individual to acknowledge that their views might be falsified by additional evidence obtained at a later time (King & Kitchener, 1994). In this context, RJ is our ability to apply reasoning to complex issues we seek to understand and to make judgments even when we recognize that some problems cannot be solved with absolute certainty. A major part of Socrates' teaching was his admission that the only thing he knew was that he knew nothing – a confession of uncertainty. By admitting our own uncertainty, we can come to develop our RJ and become better critical thinkers. Acknowledging this uncertainty is also important because, though we may acknowledge it, others may not; and thus, we can aid them in this acknowledgement. That is, at the core of the Socratic Method (see Chapter 3) is the ability to falsify another individual's claim – revealing to them that what they thought they knew they do not (Guthrie, 1968).

The ability to acknowledge levels of certainty and uncertainty when engaging in CT is important because sometimes the information a person is presented with (along with that person's pre-existing knowledge) provides only a limited source of information from which to draw a conclusion. This is often the case when a person is presented with an ill-structured problem (King, Wood, & Mines, 1990), that is, a problem that cannot be solved with absolute certainty (Wood, 1993). Specific thinking skills are necessary when we realize that some problems cannot be solved with certainty (Dewey, 1933; King & Kitchener, 2004; Wood, 1993); that is, in the context of uncertainty, a combination of CT skills and RJ is necessary in situations where one seeks to arrive at a reasonable conclusion or decide upon a reasonable course of action.

Furthermore, in an ill-structured problem, there can be no one absolutely correct answer. This is because other arguments regarding the same topic can be devised that follow different, though equally strong, lines of argument; or may dispute the claim in an equally logical fashion. A solution to an ill-structured problem is provided by a claim following a justifying argument, in which the strength of the conclusion is based on the strength of the logic and propositions used, as well as the organization of propositions and claims within the structure of the argument. RJ is used when an ill-structured problem is encountered, where the uncertainty associated with the problem indicates that multiple paths of reasoning and action are possible (e.g. 'What is the best way of decreasing global warming?'). Such encounters often lead thinkers to reasonably consider multiple, alternative solutions (e.g. 'Make everyone drive electric cars', or, 'Cut down on cattle farming in order to lower methane emissions'). However, some solutions are deemed better than others based on the organization, complexity and careful consideration of the propositions within the associated argument (e.g. in comparison with the unsupported singular claims above, a more complex and better considered response might propose that 'Although research is still ongoing in this area, mathematical models based on existing research findings suggest that by making small decreases in emissions in all walks of life, whether it be travel, farming, industry or energy production, emissions around the globe will decrease substantially'). Therefore, it is not only the conclusion one reaches, or the inference one draws, correct or otherwise; but also the manner in which one *arrives* at the conclusion, which is important in RJ and likewise, CT. This description of RJ, as involving inferential CT processes, further suggests that there is a strong interdependence between RJ and CT.

EXERCISE 8.1

Consider the two following ill-structured problems. Each ill-structured problem takes the form of a claim in an argument structure. Account for any possible uncertainty by reflectively judging each of these claims and then provide two reasons to support each of them. Then, based on your RJ, provide an alternative to these claims (i.e. in the form of an objection) and provide two reasons to support your alternative.

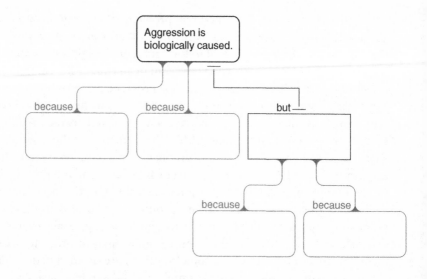

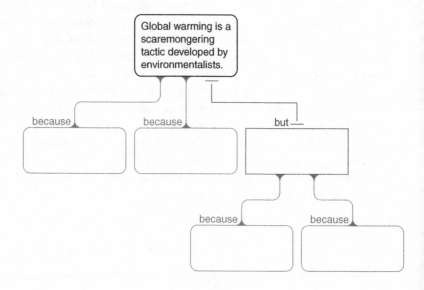

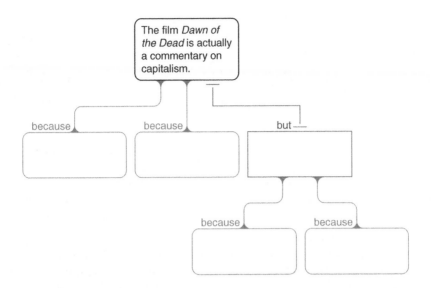

In Exercise 8.1, you may have developed any number of alternative reasons as objections to each claim. As opposed to *aggression is biologically caused*, you may have said that 'aggression is in fact caused by one's environment', which is an equally acceptable argument. With respect to the second example, you may have disagreed with the statement that Dawn of the Dead *is actually a commentary on capitalism* and instead replied that '*Dawn of the Dead* is a one-dimensional horror movie that aims at nothing more than scaring its viewers'. Any one of these alternatives may be acceptable provided they are presented with sufficient support to justify their case. The point to take away from this example is simply that uncertainty very often exists when critically thinking about some issues.

Before moving on, let us take the example of Dawn of the Dead *is actually a commentary on American capitalism* one step further. Let us assume that we have never seen *Dawn of the Dead*, yet we have been asked, as in our previous exercise, to judge whether or not it is a social commentary on capitalism. All we know about the film is what we have heard from others:

1. It is film about zombies.
2. It takes place in a shopping mall in the United States.

3. Some characters in the film help one another.
4. Some characters purposefully sabotage others in order to stay
   alive.

We realize, based on this, that we have little knowledge of the film;
therefore, we cannot elaborate in depth. However, with both RJ and
our previous knowledge concerning relevant information (i.e. capitalism), we make the point that *capitalism ensures private enterprise.*
As a result, we are able to make our first connection between the
topic and our pre-existing knowledge – *shopping malls, like the one in
the film, are filled with private enterprises.* In addition, we know from
other social commentaries on capitalism that some view American
capitalism as 'every man for himself' type of mantra, which is consistent with something else we know about that film: *some people purposefully sabotage others in order to stay alive.* We might now see another
connection between what we know about capitalism and the little
information we have about the film. Thus, at this point, I have two
connections:

1. Capitalism ensures private enterprise.
   Shopping malls, like the one in the film, are filled with private
   enterprises.
   Thus, the location of the film alludes to capitalism.
2. Capitalism has been viewed as possessing an 'Every man for
   himself' type of mantra.
   Some people in the film purposefully sabotage others in order to stay
   alive.
   Thus, some characters fit the mould of what some call the capitalist
   stereotype.

As a result, we are able to infer that *Dawn of the Dead* might
potentially be a social commentary on capitalism. However, we
must also be aware that another person could in fact argue against
our judgment in an equally logical fashion, or may possibly further
justify our position by using different examples or logic. However,
what is important to take from this example is that though we had
little knowledge of the film (apart from what we heard from
others), our previous knowledge of capitalism helped us judge
and draw a conclusion about the film. Now, given your own pre-
existing knowledge, please consider if there was anything that
would have made our judgment stronger?

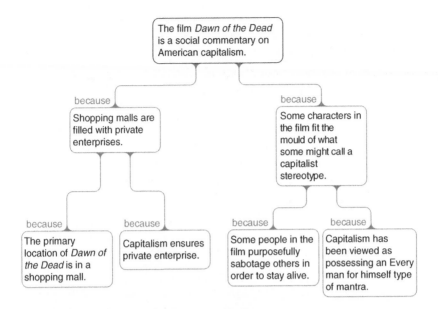

RJ is often considered as a component of CT (Baril et al., 1998; Huffman et al., 1991), because it allows one to acknowledge that epistemic assumptions (i.e. assumptions about one's knowledge) are vital to recognizing and judging a situation in which CT may be required (King & Kitchener, 1994). RJ may also influence how well an individual applies each CT skill (King, Wood, & Mines, 1990). This interdependence between CT and RJ is also consistent with Kitchener and King's (1981) Reflective Judgment Model (RJM, see Table 8.1) in which CT is embedded explicitly.

Research suggests that like CT skills, child and adult development may see a progressive development of RJ ability towards greater levels of complexity and skill. Kitchener and King (1981) created the RJM in order to characterize the development of people's RJ ability. The RJM describes changes in the thinker's recognition of limited knowledge (i.e. uncertainty) and how these changes influence other thinking skills, such as analysis, evaluation and inference. Within the RJM, a series of developmental changes occur in the way people come to understand the process of knowing and reasoning. More importantly, research supports a developmental trajectory of RJ along the lines that

TABLE 8.1 *The Reflective Judgment Model (Adapted from King & Kitchener, 2002)*

Period	Stage	Description
Pre-reflective thought	1	Knowledge is assumed to exist absolutely and concretely; it is not understood as an abstraction. It can be obtained with certainty by direct observation. Beliefs need no justification since there is assumed to be an absolute correspondence between what is believed to be true and what is true. Alternate beliefs are not perceived.
	2	Knowledge is assumed to be absolutely certain or certain but not immediately available. Knowledge can be obtained through direct observation or via authority figures. Beliefs are unexamined and unjustified or justified by their correspondence with the beliefs of an authority figure. Most issues are assumed to have a right answer, so there is little or no conflict in making decisions about disputed issues.
	3	Knowledge is assumed to be absolutely certain or temporarily uncertain. In areas of temporary uncertainty, only personal beliefs can be known until absolute knowledge is obtained. In areas of absolute certainty, knowledge is obtained from authorities. In areas in which certain answers exist, beliefs are justified by reference to authorities' views. In areas in which answers do not exist, beliefs are defended as personal opinion since the link between evidence and beliefs is unclear.
Quasi-reflective thought	4	Knowledge is uncertain and knowledge claims are idiosyncratic to the individual since situational variables dictate that knowing always involves an element of ambiguity. Beliefs are justified by giving reasons and using evidence, but the arguments and choice of evidence are idiosyncratic.
	5	Knowledge is contextual and subjective since it is filtered through a person's perceptions and criteria for judgment. Only interpretations of evidence, events or issues may be known. Beliefs are justified within a particular context by means of the rules of inquiry for that context and by the context-specific interpretations as evidence. Specific beliefs are assumed to be context specific or are balanced against other interpretations, which complicates conclusions.

TABLE 8.1 *(continued)*

Period	Stage	Description
Reflective thought	6	Knowledge is constructed into individual conclusions about ill-structured problems on the basis of information from a variety of sources. Interpretations that are based on evaluations of evidence across contexts and on the evaluated opinions of reputable others can be known. Beliefs are justified by comparing evidence and opinion from different perspectives on an issue or across different contexts and by constructing solutions that are evaluated by criteria such as the weight of the evidence, the utility of the solution and the pragmatic need for action.
	7	Knowledge is the outcome of a process of reasonable inquiry in which solutions to ill-structured problems are constructed. The adequacy of those solutions is evaluated in terms of what is most reasonable or probable according to the current evidence, and it is re-evaluated when relevant new evidence, perspectives or tools of inquiry become available. Beliefs are justified probabilistically on the basis of a variety of interpretive considerations, such as the weight of the evidence, the explanatory value of the interpretations, the risk of erroneous conclusions, consequences of alternative judgments and the interrelationships of these factors. Conclusions are defended as representing the most complete, plausible or compelling understanding of an issue on the basis of the available evidence.

King and Kitchener described. However, RJ development is not a simple function of age or time, but more so a function of the amount of interaction, or active engagement, an individual has in the context of working on ill-structured problems such that the development of higher levels of reasoning and RJ ability can emerge (Brabeck, 1981; Dawson, 2008; Fischer & Bidell, 2006; Terenzini et al., 1995). For example, research by Terenzini and colleagues (1995) found a significant correlation between gains in CT ability and the amount of hours per week students were engaged in study. Similarly, research by King and Kitchener indicated that those who completed a college education show more of an increase in the RJ than those who do not, perhaps as a result of the amount of engagement with ill-structured problems that require RJ. However, it is also possible that RJ development is a function of both interaction and engagement with RJ problems *coupled* with development that occurs as a result of time and maturation, as suggested by Dawson-Tunik et al. (2005) and King and Kitchener (1994), and building on this stance, perhaps an interaction among engagement, time *and* disposition (Dwyer, Hogan, & Stewart, 2015).

Kitchener and King's RJM is a seven-stage model that is broken down into three periods of development. Progress on the RJM (from one stage to another; and from one period to another) is a type of evolution of RJ, in which each progression marks the increasing complexity of the thinking required to justify a belief. The more developed one's RJ, the better one is able to present 'a more complex and effective form of justification, providing more inclusive and better integrated assumptions for evaluating and defending a point of view' (King & Kitchener, 1994, p. 13). Notably, King and Kitchener describe RJ here as a collation of the sub-components of evaluation and inference (i.e. CT skills; again, see Table 8.1) – once again indicating the importance of the interdependency between CT and RJ. However, it is also worth noting individuals do not operate at one stage of development – consistent with Dynamic Skill Theory (Fischer, 1980), they operate at a range of different levels of hierarchical complexity depending on skill area, task, context, degree of support and other variables (e.g. an individual's particular 'level' in one domain does not necessarily predict their skill level in another domain; Bidell & Fischer, 1992; Fischer, 1980; Fischer & Bidell, 2006; Kitchener & Fischer, 1990; Mascolo, 2008).

The relationship between CT and RJ has been confirmed in a number of research studies and the suggestion has been made that CT and RJ develop in an interdependent, cyclical manner (Brabeck, 1981; Dawson, 2008; Dwyer, Hogan, & Stewart, 2015; King & Kitchener, 1994; King, Wood, & Mines, 1990; see Figure 8.1). For example, in research by Brabeck (1981), 119 university students were assessed on both CT and RJ ability. CT was measured using the Watson-Glaser Critical Thinking Appraisal (WGCTA; Watson & Glaser, 1980) and RJ was measured using the Reflective Judgment Interview (Kitchener & King, 1981). Results revealed a positive correlation between both measures ($r = .40, p < .001$). There was also a significant difference between high-scoring and low-scoring critical thinkers on RJ performance.

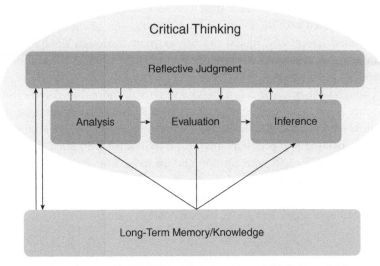

FIGURE 8.1 The Interdependencies among CT Skills and RJ

Based on these findings, Brabeck (1981) suggested that there is an inextricable link between CT and RJ. This link was confirmed by further research conducted by King, Wood, and Mines (1990), which examined the RJ and CT performance of both university undergraduate and graduate students. Results revealed a significant correlation between RJ (as measured by the Reflective Judgment Interview) and CT, measured using both the WGCTA and the Cornell Critical Thinking Test (Ennis, Millman, & Tomko, 1985; $r = .46$, $p < .01$ for both).

Now that we have a better understanding of what RJ is and how it relates to CT, it is necessary to ask what this all means and, more importantly, why is RJ so vital to CT? It is a common assumption in cognitive psychology that the automaticity (i.e. the ability to complete a task without paying attention to it) of cognitive processes is achieved through frequent engagement (Anderson, 1981; Bargh, 1997; Strack & Deutsch, 2004), given that through extensive use, procedural schemas will be constructed for such processes. Thus, with increased practice and engagement with the CT skills of analysis, evaluation and inference, there is (hopefully) a potential for these processes to be conducted, automatically, when encountered with a scenario that requires CT. However, if these processes become automatic, then it implies that little or no attention is paid to the task – which is the antithesis of CT. This is where RJ is at its most important. RJ requires the critical thinker to slow down the process, regardless of whether it is being conducted automatically, and truly consider the nature, limits and certainty associated with the information and knowledge being thought about and applied. Essentially, RJ acts as a slower, more thorough 'double-check' of the analysis, evaluation and inference conducted, whether it is automatic or not.

Though further research is necessary to provide more than correlational evidence alone in support of the link between RJ and CT development, it is reasonable to assume that through the acknowledgement of uncertainty in decision-making and problem-solving, an individual with good RJ will be able to apply CT skills with caution and awareness of alternative conclusions and/or solutions that may be drawn. Consistent with this view, it has been noted that those who show good RJ are more likely to exhibit greater care when *applying* CT skills (King & Kitchener, 2004).

EXERCISE 8.2

Please consider two ill-structured problems (i.e. statements that cannot be verified as absolutely correct) that you have encountered on your own in the past. Develop a conclusion regarding these problems and provide two reasons to support your conclusion. In addition, please offer three alternative conclusions/solutions regarding each problem in the objection boxes, much like the exercise you completed earlier in this chapter. Also, consider each of your solutions in terms of the consequences each solution might evoke.

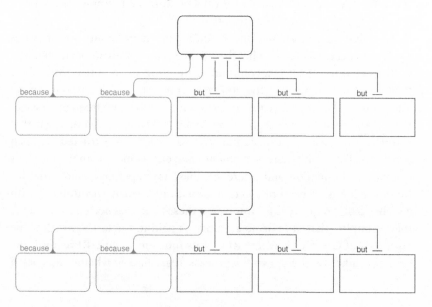

SUMMARY AND CONCLUSION

In summary, a person with a strong willingness to conduct CT has the consistent internal motivation and disposition to engage problems and make decisions by using CT and RJ. RJ involves the logical collection and evaluation of one's own evidence leading to the inference of a conclusion and applied in an effort to solve a problem. This is completed by explaining one's reasoning in a logical and well-organized manner. RJ is a form of thinking in which we acknowledge that uncertainty exists among a variety of problems that we may face in thinking, with respect to academic contexts as well as in everyday situations. As it may be the case that no single absolutely correct answer may exist for certain types of problems (i.e. ill-structured problems), then, it is reasonable to consider multiple, alternative solutions. However, some solutions are deemed better than others based on the careful consideration of facts regarding the problem. Therefore, it is not the conclusion that is important in RJ, but rather the manner in which one arrives at the conclusion through structured thinking.

PART III

CRITICAL THINKING IN REAL-WORLD
SETTINGS

Humanity's natural function is not simply to reason, but rather, reason well.

~ Aristotle (c. 384–322 BC)

9

Applications of Critical Thinking

No problem can withstand the assault of sustained thinking.
~ Voltaire (1694–1778)

As we have learned over the course of the past few chapters, critical thinking (CT) is a metacognitive process that consists of a number of sub-skills (i.e. analysis, evaluation and inference) that, when used appropriately, increases the chances of producing a logical solution to a problem or a valid conclusion to an argument (Dwyer, Hogan, & Stewart, 2011, 2012). The past five chapters have discussed what CT is; presented descriptions and examples of analysis, evaluation and inference; and presented reflective judgment as a blanket term for how we utilize the three core CT skills through a metacognitive sensibility. Now that we have a working definition and conceptualization of what CT is, as well as a description of each of the core skills involved in CT, it is important that we consider how CT is applied in everyday, real-world settings. Thus, in this chapter, we will explore such applications via descriptions and examples of how we might use CT in the context of everyday life.

In order to conduct CT in real-world settings, it is not enough to be able to apply, for example, analysis and evaluation only, or alternatively, analysis and inference only. We must be able to apply analysis, evaluation and inference, *cumulatively*, through our ability to reflectively judge situations, problems and arguments. However, we must identify more specific focuses of application than simply 'situations', 'problems' and/or 'arguments' that require CT.

According to Halpern (2010a, 2014), there are five distinct categories of everyday tasks in which we apply CT: (1) argumentation; (2) verbal reasoning; (3) hypothesis testing; (4) judging likelihood and uncertainty; and (5) problem-solving (see Table 9.1 for a description of each CT

TABLE 9.1 *Real-World Applications of CT (Adapted from Halpern, 2014)*

1. Argumentation	Recognizing the structure of arguments and how to judge their strength or weakness
2. Verbal reasoning	Recognizing what follows what through the use of induction, deduction and falsification
3. Hypothesis testing	Understanding the limits of correlational reasoning and how to know when causal claims cannot be made
4. Judging likelihood and uncertainty	Applying relevant principles of probability and avoiding overconfidence in certain situations
5. Problem-solving	Identifying the problem goal; and generating and selecting solutions among alternatives

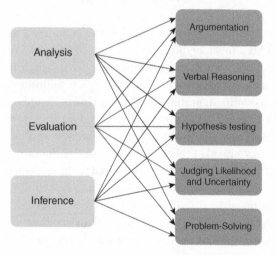

FIGURE 9.1 The Interaction of CT Skills and Applications

application). A large body of research supports the identification of these applications as valid constructs in the modern conceptualization of CT (Butler et al., 2012; Dwyer, 2011; Dwyer, Hogan, & Stewart, 2012, 2014; Halpern, 2006, 2010a, 2014; Ku, 2009). Furthermore, these applications of CT, though labelled differently, reflect the skills identified by the Delphi Report (Facione, 1990b), in that each skill is necessary for successful application(s) of CT (see Figure 9.1 for a diagram exhibiting how these applications interact with the CT skills identified in the Delphi Report). The remainder of this chapter will describe and exemplify each of these applications in greater detail.

ARGUMENTATION

Whether we know it or not, we encounter arguments every day – when we read newspapers, magazines and books; when we socialize with friends and family; when we encounter commercials and advertisements; and even when we watch the news on television. From our investigation of CT thus far, we know that an argument is not just a heated debate between individuals, but rather information we encounter that consists of *at least* two propositions, in which one proposition acts as a claim and the other acts as either a support or an objection. We have also learned that when we need to think critically about an argument, we must analyse and evaluate the argument, so that we may subsequently infer a conclusion.

To reiterate, argumentation is 'a verbal and social activity of reason aimed at increasing (or decreasing) the acceptability of a controversial standpoint ... by putting forward a constellation of propositions intended to justify (or refute) the standpoint' (van Eemeren et al., 1996, p. 5). Given this description of argumentation as a social activity, we must recognize that there are often other people involved in the same arguments as us. We must further recognize that these people may or may not have the same CT skills we have been developing. Some people we enter into arguments with may have better developed argumentation skills or may have less developed argumentation skills than us, but either way we must be cautious. For example, you may feel safe and exude relaxation when driving because you *know* you are a good driver and will not get into an accident. However, if another car comes barrelling down the road from the opposite direction, with a driver who is not as skilled, an accident may still occur, no matter how skilled a driver you are. The point is, when entering into an argument with another individual, like driving, we should be cautious because we do not know what the other person might do.

With respect to exercising caution in argumentation, in addition to analysing and evaluating the sources people use for their arguments, we must also be aware that others may use certain strategies to persuade us to think what they want us to think. Consider television commercials and advertisements, which all use some type of persuasion strategy to get you to buy their product. What types of techniques do they use? According to Halpern (2014), some of the persuasion strategies that are most commonly used include: (1) the bandwagon argument (e.g. *everyone is doing it, so why don't you?*); (2) the use of pity (i.e. an appeal for compassion);

(3) card-stacking (i.e. the use of an unbalanced and biased argument, which purposefully omits important counter-arguments); (4) circular reasoning (e.g. *we need to cut spending as too much money is being spent*); and (5) the slippery slope argument (i.e. an argument that concludes that if an action is taken, other negative consequences will follow; e.g. *if we allow immigration from one country, then immigrants from all other countries will expect the same rights to settle here*). Regardless of the persuasiveness of an argument, again, we must be cautious and willing to analyse and evaluate the argument, so that a balanced and unbiased conclusion can be inferred.

VERBAL REASONING

When you encounter the term *verbal reasoning*, you may automatically think of word problems such as *beagle is to dog as cobra is to* – (e.g. Bennett, Seashore, & Wesman, 1986). You may automatically infer that the answer is *snake*. This is a basic form of verbal reasoning that we use through our ability to classify and categorize things, animals, people and places. A more complex outlook on categorical reasoning would be our ability to apply our reasoning to syllogisms, as in Chapter 7, in which we categorize things, animals, people and places according to the prefixes of each proposition involved (i.e. *All, None* and *Some*). In this respect, verbal reasoning can be conceived of as an application of the CT skill of inference.

According to Halpern (2014), verbal reasoning is essentially our ability to evaluate a series of propositions and identify *what follows what*. In this context, verbal reasoning, in addition to being an application of inference, is also an application of evaluation, in that we must evaluate the logical strength of a series of propositions (see Chapter 6). When we evaluate the logical strength of a piece of reasoning, we must ensure that structure presented is logically sound with respect to, for example, determining that proposition B does in fact follow proposition A.

Consider the following:

A. John enjoyed himself at Imelda's party.
B. Imelda provided John and other guests with a great array of food and drink.

Now consider:

A. John enjoyed himself at Imelda's party.
B. Imelda is afraid of snakes.

The second example is a non sequitur, the Latin for 'does not follow', in that B does not logically follow A. However, this is not to say that B is *irrelevant* in this context (again, see Chapter 6). For example, if the telling of this anecdote were to continue, we might learn that, in addition to being supplied with a wide array of food and drink, someone brought a snake to Imelda's party. As Imelda is afraid of snakes, she started screaming and jumping on furniture in an attempt to escape the presence of the snake. Perhaps, all this excitement was funny to John and, as a result, he had a great time. The point here is that though a piece of information may be relevant to what is being discussed, it is necessary that the propositions involved are presented in a manner where one logically follows the other and avoids non sequiturs.

Verbal reasoning can be considered as two types of reasoning: deductive reasoning and inductive reasoning. *Deductive reasoning* is a type of reasoning where one uses a claim or collection of claims, relevant to the inference of a further conclusion (e.g. examples might be inferred from a general claim or set of claims). On the other hand, *inductive reasoning* refers to a type of reasoning used to infer a conclusion from more specific propositions or examples. An appropriate use of deductive and inductive reasoning in CT is alternating back and forth between the two as a means of 'double-checking' one's reasoning.

The first known use of *deductive reasoning* was in the 5th century BC by the Greek philosopher Parmenides, as a means of justifying claims. It is a reasoning process similar to evaluation in that it is used to decipher the strength or weakness of an argument structure. Deductive reasoning is also similar to inference, given that in application, we must use our past evaluations to decide whether or not the conclusion drawn can be logically inferred. Consider the classic example: *All swans are white.* Using deductive reasoning, we might conclude that *if we go to the park, we will only see white swans.* If we know that it is true that all swans are white, then it must be true that any specific swan we encounter will also be white.

This example is interesting to consider, because traditionally, it was believed by some that all swans were white. We know this to be false because black swans (*cygnus atratus*) do exist. This type of falsification is known as the law of *modus tollens*, which is the Latin for 'the way that denies by denying', referring to a rule of inference that denies the conclusion. According to the logician and philosopher of science, Karl Popper (1934/1959), though a proposition (e.g. *There is a black swan*) cannot be used to prove a claim true (i.e. *All swans are black*), it can be used to prove a claim false (i.e. *All swans are white*). Thus, we must strive to conduct deductive reasoning like deductive falsification and we can do this through rigorous evaluation, which again points to the cyclical nature of evaluation and inference.

Much like the skill of inference, *inductive reasoning* involves the gathering of evidence for the purposes of drawing a conclusion. Generally, we collect a set of premises that are known to us from past observations and obtained evidence, which allows us to draw a previously unknown conclusion. Given that this conclusion may be previously unknown, it is up to us to further validate the truth of this conclusion. That is, we must re-evaluate our inductive reasoning through further testing, given potential problems we may encounter when conducting inductive reasoning, as identified by Popper (1934/1959). For example, through inductive reasoning, we might suppose that if we throw a ball in the air, it will peak and then fall back towards the Earth. However, there is no way to guarantee that if you throw a ball in the air that it will peak and fall back towards Earth; rather, on each occurrence we should *theorize* that the ball will fall back down to Earth, due to the possibility, on one occasion, the ball does not fall back towards Earth. If in the event the ball does not fall back down to Earth, our theory is false; and thus, we must formulate a new theory for outcomes related to throwing balls into the air.

Now, the outcome of throwing a ball into the air and not having it fall back down to Earth is highly unlikely, due to what we know about the laws of physics. Thus, according to Popper, it would be irrational to think the initial theory incorrect. Nevertheless, in situations and on occasions where there is less certainty regarding specific outcomes, it is important that we adequately and appropriately investigate and examine ideas, concepts and theories before accepting them (i.e. instead of relying exclusively on inductive reasoning); and similar to both Socrates and Popper, we can consider adequate and appropriate investigation and examination as being attempts at refuting and/or falsifying such ideas, concepts and theories.

Given the potential problems associated with inductive reasoning, we must re-evaluate what we inferred from our inductive reasoning through the use of deductive reasoning or we can test our conclusions in a scientific manner. For example, from a scientific perspective, we can consider inductive reasoning as developing and testing a hypothesis, in that we gather a rationale from previous research and then formulate a possible outcome, or *hypothesis*, from the rationale (i.e. the initial premises).

HYPOTHESIS TESTING

As we saw in the last example, there is a certain degree of overlap between hypothesis testing and verbal reasoning, specifically, with respect to inductive reasoning. *Hypothesis testing* refers to the examination of a belief that is based on a justified rationale, in order to confirm or disconfirm the belief. Likewise, the goal of hypothesis testing is to make rational predictions about something and subsequently test these predictions (Holland et al., 1986). Based on these descriptions, we can consider hypotheses as justified beliefs or predictions. According to Halpern (2014), a hypothesis is a belief about the nature of the world, in which we believe that there is a relationship between two or more variables. Thus, hypothesis testing is 'one way of finding out about the way the world works' (p. 232). Now that we understand what a hypothesis is, the question becomes, *how* do we test it?

In the late 16th and early 17th centuries, Sir Francis Bacon pioneered what we know as modern scientific methodology for examining and testing hypotheses in order to either confirm or disconfirm them. Much of CT is like hypothesis testing and, likewise, scientific methodology, in that we must analyse and evaluate beliefs and predictions so that we may infer some conclusion relevant to our hypotheses. Thus, in many contexts, we must critically think like a scientist. When scientists conduct experiments, they first identify the relevant factors that will drive their research; and so too should we!

Consider Little Johnny:

> One Sunday in December, Little Johnny decided that he did not want to go to school the following day. He looked out the window and wished as hard as he could that it would snow so much that schools would be closed the following day. The next morning, Little Johnny woke up to discover that it had snowed and that his mother was listening to the radio for school closures. Sure enough, Little Johnny's school was closed that day. Little Johnny was so excited, not just because his school was closed, but because he discovered that he can make it snow just by wishing.

Now, hopefully, you recognize that Little Johnny's finding was a result of correlation (weakly at that) and not cause. Though this may seem obvious to many of us, sometimes the distinction is not so easy to identify. Quite often, in everyday life, results and their interpretations are reported the same as Little Johnny's findings – as causes and not correlations. For example, we might be watching the news one evening and hear a report that the use of fluoridation techniques to provide clean water causes cancer in people who consume it. Before jumping to conclusions, we must consider the manner in which this news was presented to us. We must be sceptical. Perhaps, the researcher at the television news station misinterpreted the findings that were received from the health board. Perhaps the actual findings were that fluoridated water consumption was found to be correlated with cancer. If this is the case, then the news report is grossly incorrect. Thus, we must be sceptical of the findings we observe and those that are presented to us by others. Furthermore, if we care about the implications of these findings, then we should make an effort to examine them ourselves or obtain credible research that either confirms or disconfirms these findings.

How can we help Little Johnny confirm (or disconfirm) his newly found telekinetic capabilities? We can help by thinking like scientists and test Little Johnny's hypothesis that he can make it snow simply by wishing. First, we must identify the variables relevant to our experiment: snowfall (i.e. the dependent variable) and Little Johnny's 'capability' (i.e. the independent variable). Next, we watch the weather forecast for the next predicted snowfall, which is Monday night. We ask Little Johnny that evening to either wish that it snows or ask him not to wish that it snows. We then wait for the next forecast of snow and ask Johnny to do the opposite of what we asked of him Monday evening. In the event that on either night that it snowed and Johnny did not wish for it, then he will see at least it can snow regardless of his 'powers'. In the event that Little Johnny did wish for snow and it did not snow, then we will have some evidence to show that Little Johnny does not have telekinetic abilities.

However, in order to generate stronger belief in the hypothesis that Johnny *does not* have telekinetic powers, it would be prudent to run this experiment over a longer period of time. For example, let us conduct this experiment every night for a year. Furthermore, let us remove the stipulation that snow must be forecasted. This is important because, in the last iteration of this experiment, there was already a good chance that it was going to snow, so Johnny may have been correct in both settings. To truly test this hypothesis, we must have Johnny wish it will snow in July as well as in December, in which case, the time of year will act as a covariate (i.e. an additional variable that may potentially predict or influence the dependent variable – in this context, the outcome of snow or no snow).

Let us not stop there. Why would it be the case that only Little Johnny has this ability? Perhaps Little Susie, who lives 500 miles away from Little

Johnny, has also accurately predicted the weather, as has Little Davy and Little Hayley. Let us test them all. What we are doing here is increasing our sample size. Though it is highly unlikely that anyone can 'make it snow', there are abilities, events and other variables we may wish to evaluate and test on a daily basis. However, testing *one* person's ability is not a good practice as, much like our evaluation of personal or anecdotal evidence in Chapter 6, we cannot generalize the experiences or abilities of one person to an entire population. Thus, we must increase our sample size (i.e. the number of participants in our experiment), as the more people we test, the better able we are to generalize our findings and apply them in real-world settings.

We can continue to make improvements on our experimental design (e.g. increasing our sample size and adding further variables) in an attempt to better explain the 'way the world works' (Halpern, 2014). The important thing is that we derive some empirical under-standing for what it is we wanted to confirm or disconfirm, without being biased one way or another. We must remain sceptical about the information others present us and make an effort to test resulting beliefs, predictions and hypotheses.

JUDGING LIKELIHOOD AND UNCERTAINTY

When we judge the likelihood of an event occurring, we calculate the *probability* (i.e. the study of likelihood and uncertainty; Halpern, 2014) of it happening. The judgment of uncertainty, in this context, refers to our need to be conscious of the fact that the values (i.e. likelihood) derived from a probability assessment (e.g. *There is a 65% chance of rain tomorrow*) are not absolute. That is, like reflective judgment (as discussed in the last chapter), we must recognize our uncertainty of both the situation encountered and the judgments we make. If there is a 65% chance of rain tomorrow, it would be wise to bring an umbrella, even though there is a 35% chance that it will not rain at all.

Specifically, the probability of something happening is the number of ways a specific event can take place over the number of possible outcomes. For example, when flipping a coin, there are two possible outcomes: landing (1) heads or (2) tails. The one, specific event we may wish to observe might be the occurrence of the coin landing tails-up. Thus, there is a 1 in 2, or 50% chance of the coin landing tails-up. Another example can be taken from a deck of playing cards. We know that there are 52 cards in the deck, there are 13 cards per suit and that there are four

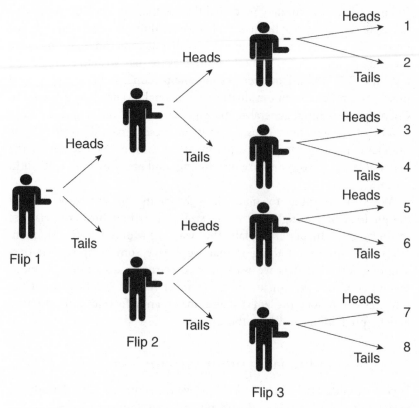

FIGURE 9.2 A Diagram for Calculating the Probability of Flipping Three Tails in a Row

suits. What are the chances, after shuffling the deck, of pulling a spade from the top? We can look at this as 13/52 (i.e. a 13 in 52 chance) or as 1/4 (i.e. a 1 in 4 chance). Either way we look at it, we have a 25% chance of turning up a spade.

Now, what is the chance of flipping a coin twice and having it land tails-up on both flips? We know that there's a 1 in 2 chance on one flip, but how do we calculate this happening twice in succession? What about tails-up on three successive flips? There are two ways we can do this: (1) draw it out or (2) do the math. See Figure 9.2 for how we might draw it out.

Mathematically, we would take the likelihood of tails turning up on one flip (i.e. 1/2) and multiply it by itself (i.e. for the second flip) and once more after (i.e. for the third flip):

$$1/2 \times 1/2 \times 1/2 = 1/8$$

Thus, the likelihood of flipping a coin three times and having it land tails on all three occasions would be 1 in 8, or 12.5%.

Judging likelihoods and uncertainties through probability plays a vital role in most day-to-day situations (e.g. predicting the weather, playing the lottery, playing cards and deciding at which grocery to shop) and more long-term considerations (e.g. taking out life insurance, investing in stocks and shares, medical considerations, retirement options, environmental and societal issues) that require the making of a decision(s). The ability to make decisions through the judgment of likelihood and uncertainty is important because it provides us with both a practical and manageable means of calculating some level of confidence in an event occurring. In this context, the higher the probability of event occurring, the more confident we are that it will happen.

However, the most common problem people have with thinking critically about probability has nothing to do with the application, but rather understanding the true nature of probability and the randomness that governs it. That is, when we assess the probability of an event occurring, we need to understand that we are calculating the likelihood of something happening *in the long run* (Halpern, 2014). That is, we are really evaluating the likelihood of something happening, at a certain rate, over an elongated stretch of time.

Consider again the example of flipping a coin. The one, specific event we may wish to observe might be the occurrence of the coin landing tails up. Thus, there is a 1 in 2, or 50%, chance of the coin landing tails up. So, based on this assessment, some might say if heads comes up on the first flip, then according to the 1 in 2 probability, it seems likely that it will come up tails on the second flip. This would be an incorrect assessment of probability, as coins do not have a memory – every flip is new and is not dictated by what happened previously. Every time a coin is flipped, it will either be heads or tails, a 1 in 2 chance, based on the fact that there are only two outcomes. You could flip a coin three times in row and tails might come up all three times. From the example considered earlier, we know the chance of this happening to be 12.5% – an outcome that hardly reflects a 50/50 likelihood. We must realize that the sequence tails, heads, tails is also only 12.5%, as is tails, heads, heads (again, see Figure 9.2).

However, in the long run (e.g. flipping a coin 100 times), a trend will emerge towards an even split between heads and tails (e.g. 46 times heads and 54 times tails). If we flip a coin a thousand times (i.e. an even longer run), we are likely to see less of a gap (e.g. 490 times heads and 510 tails). The point is, if we are looking to calculate the likelihood of an event occurring in the short-term, potentially, anything can happen (i.e. randomness); and thus, we must recognize our uncertainty of a specific event occurring. On the other hand, if we are calculating something happening in the long run, we have a more useful means of helping us in making decisions.

The caution and uncertainty we must exhibit when evaluating likelihoods is made further important by how probabilities and percentages are presented to us. Sometimes, probabilities are susceptible to misinterpretation, and sometimes, they are just plain wrong. Consider the statement:

92% of all statistics are made up.

Can we take for granted that this statement is true? If it is, then there is a good chance (i.e. 92 in 100) that this statement itself is made up. Often, probabilities and statistics, like the one earlier, are spurious. Thus, it is up to us as critical thinkers to further evaluate whether statements based on probabilities and statistics are likely and credible (see Chapter 6).

With respect to our susceptibility to misinterpreting probabilities and likelihoods, we must be diligent in evaluating not only the numerical values provided (i.e. the percentages) but also the style of language used to deliver these values. There are numerous ways any one probability or likelihood can be presented and subsequently interpreted. For example, consider shampoo commercials on the television. Quite often there is a celebrity in the commercial that is hired to advertise the shampoo. Even more common is that they report that 80% of women surveyed agree that *Shampoo X* is better than leading competitors. This finding suggests to consumers that they have an 80% chance of being more satisfied with Shampoo X than with shampoos produced by leading competitors. Though 80% does seem like a lot, when we look at the small print in the advertisement (i.e. at the very bottom of the screen), it might be that only twenty women were surveyed. It would not be right to generalize the positive review of sixteen women to an entire population. Furthermore, it could be that the women who were surveyed were already consumers of Shampoo X before the survey was conducted. What would be more telling in this situation is how many women switched from Shampoo Y or Z to Shampoo X.

Through critically evaluating the presentation of a likelihood or probability, we can become more familiar with the different manners in which they can be presented and, likewise, become more prudent in the manner we interpret them.

In this context, suppose that:

> A new 'super-flu' has broken out in your town and potentially 750 people could perish. There are two experimental medications that can be given to the infected. (1) One will cure 250 people; and (2) the other has a 1 in 3 chance of saving everyone, though a 2 in 3 chance curing no one. If you were in charge of this important decision, which medication would you prescribe for your town?

Without critically evaluating this hypothetical situation, most people tend to choose the first option. This is curious, given that both of them yield the exact same outcomes. However, the way in which these probabilities are presented (i.e. worded) dictates which will be chosen (i.e. the first option has a positive connotation – *will cure 250 people*; whereas the second option has a negative connotation – *2 in 3 chance of curing no one*). Thus, it is important that we critically evaluate probabilities, just as we critically evaluate arguments, in order to infer the best possible conclusion regarding a given situation.

EXERCISE 9.1

Suppose you decide to participate in a lottery, in which you select 6 numbers out of 45. What are your chances of winning? Do you have a better chance of winning this lottery as opposed to one where you must select 5 numbers out of 50?

PROBLEM-SOLVING

Problem-solving is a real-world application of CT that refers to the ability to identify both the problem at hand and the goal you want to achieve in light of this problem and generate and select solutions to the problem among alternatives. Problem-solving is perhaps the most important application of CT because it can be considered as the foundation of each of the other CT applications. For example, during argumentation, verbal reasoning, hypothesis testing, and judging likelihood and uncertainty, our *goal* is to reach some conclusion. The *problem* involved in each of these cases might be not knowing or not having a position, whereas the solution might be the need to engage alternative arguments and decide which to believe, ensure the logical integrity of a belief we want to promote, overcome factors that may impede our research and ignore false evidence and/or developing methods of determining the chances of something occurring.

In order to better understand the process of problem-solving, we first need to be able to identify a problem. According to Halpern (2014), a problem is the gap between where you are and where you want to be (i.e. a goal). In the context of bridging the gap between where you are and where you want to be, one method of problem-solving would be to find the path that most efficiently gets you to your goal. However, in some cases, there may be numerous routes to your goal and then the problem becomes deciding which path is the best one to take. Thus, a problem is not always a gap that needs to be bridged, but rather a question of which bridge to take!

On a very basic level, a problem refers to any goal that has not yet been attained or accomplished, whereas problem-solving refers to the process of attaining or accomplishing that goal. Given what we know about CT from the preceding chapters, we contextualize problem-solving as a mental process that involves discovering, analysing and evaluating problems, in which the ultimate goal of the problem-solving process is to overcome obstacles and infer a solution that best resolves the issue. The best strategy for solving a problem depends largely on the context of the problem. In some cases, people are better off using what they already know and learning additional information about the issue and then using this knowledge to come up with a solution. In other instances, specific knowledge may not be readily available and, thus, a collation of insight and the ability to 'think outside the box' may be the best and most feasible option.

Similar to arguments, all problems and problem-solving scenarios possess a structure and, for the most part, these scenarios consist of the same basic parts (Newell & Simon, 1972). The most important part of any problem-solving scenario is the goal. The goal is the end-point, where the problem-solver wants to be. The goal has to be defined in such a way that it is very clear to the problem-solver when they have achieved it. Another important part of understanding this scenario is recognizing the reality of the current situation, which is where the problem-solver stands in relation to their goal. In other words, the reality is the amount of steps completed so far and the number of steps that are still necessary to take in order to achieve the desired goal.

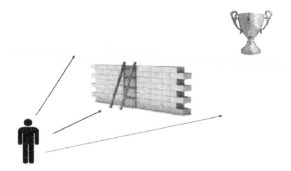

FIGURE 9.3 An Example of a Problem-Solving Scenario

What can potentially stop you from reaching your goal is the actual problem itself (e.g. the gap or the obstacles within the gap). Thus, a problem can be considered as a gap, a barrier or an obstacle, between where you are and where you want to be. You have a problem if you cannot get around an obstacle in order to reach the place you want to be. Alternatively, you may also have a problem when there appears to be many ways around the obstacle, without clarity as to which of the paths will lead to your goal. These paths or ways around an obstacle are referred to as options. In order to understand the problem-situation better, it is important to analyse and tease out the various parts of the problem-solving scenario. If you acknowledge each part in turn, you can face the obstacle that keeps you from your goal head-on. For example, in Figure 9.3, you may decide to reach your goal by going left, or possibly right, or you may decide to get a ladder and go over the barrier. As you can see, sometimes, there are a number of options in which we can solve a problem. However, it is important that we work through each possible solution before acting on one, in order for us to see which one is best.

If we choose to climb the ladder over the barrier, there is a very possible chance that we could fall. Alternatively, if we choose to go to the left of the wall we might get attacked by a rogue alligator! As a result, we should probably choose the option of going to the right of the wall. Though this hypothetical problem-situation presents us with a few silly possibilities, it brings us to another very important factor involved in problem solving, known as the *givens*. A given refers to a piece of information or a rule that places a constraint on the problem. Givens often provide us with the knowledge we need to reach the goal via the best possible route. In this example, there is a goal; a reality, or starting point; an obstacle; and two givens (see Figure 9.4).

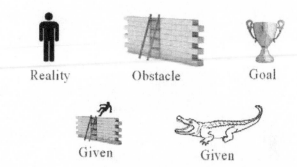

FIGURE 9.4 An Example of the Components of a Problem-Situation

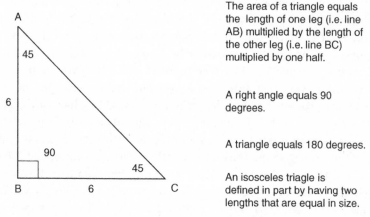

The area of a triangle equals the length of one leg (i.e. line AB) multiplied by the length of the other leg (i.e. line BC) multiplied by one half.

A right angle equals 90 degrees.

A triangle equals 180 degrees.

An isosceles triagle is defined in part by having two lengths that are equal in size.

FIGURE 9.5 An Example of Finding the Area of a Triangle

Not all problems are as easy as the one in the last example. Let us look at another, more difficult problem:

Consider a student in her first geometry class. She is asked to find the area of a right triangle. She is told that the triangle has three sides, in which the length of one leg is 6 and that the angle of the meeting corner is 45 degrees. The student identifies the goal, which is to find the area of the triangle. She also identifies the starting point: the triangle has one length that is 6, one angle that is 45 degrees and another angle that is a right angle. In this context, these three pieces of information act as givens. The problem, or barrier, in this case is that she does not know how to use the information provided to her to find the area of the triangle (see Figure 9.5). The student searches in her text-book and finds a number of additional givens. One given is that the area of a triangle equals the length of one leg (i.e. line AB) multiplied by the length of the other leg (i.e. line BC), with the product divided by two. The student recognizes now that, in order to find the area of the triangle, she has to find the length of the leg (i.e. line AB) not provided to her as an initial given. To find this, the student searches for more information and finds that another given is that a right angle equals 90 degrees. Another given is that all triangles are 180 degrees in total. Based on this, the student creates a sub-goal, which is to find the third angle, which is Angle A. The student subtracts 45 and 90 from 180 and gets 45. Angle A is 45 degrees, the same as angle C. The student searches for more information in her textbook and finds that, given the two congruent angles, which are both 45 degrees, what she has is an isosceles triangle, which is further defined by having two lengths that are equal in size. The student now can now solve her second sub-goal which is to find the length of line AB, which, like the other leg of the triangle, also equals 6. To find the area of the triangle, which is the main goal of the problem, the student follows the formula she found in her research, which tells her to multiply 6 × 6 × ½. The student's solution is 18.

What the student did to solve the geometry problem is a very common problem-solving method known as *means-ends analysis*. This involves finding the difference between the starting point and the goal and setting a sub-goal(s) to reduce that difference. Essentially, *difference reduction* is the practice of selecting a sub-goal(s) that allows us to progress closer to our goal. Simply, means-ends analysis refers to the choosing of an action at each step of the problem-solving strategy (i.e. to reach a sub-goal) in order to move closer to our ultimate goal.

In addition to a potential mean-ends analysis, we can support the problem-solving process by employing a series of steps in an effort to reach our solution (see Table 9.2). This series of steps includes the organization of knowledge and the development of problem-solving strategies.

TABLE 9.2 *Problem-Solving Checklist (Adapted from Hopwood, 1974; Robbins & Judge, 2007)*

1. Define the problem
2. Gather and organize the available information
3. Evaluate possible strategies
4. Generate possible solutions
5. Monitor the progress of the solution strategy
6. Evaluate results of the solution strategy
7. Verify the solution

Essentially this problem-solving procedure, which is similar to many other existing decision-making models (e.g. Hopwood, 1974; Robbins & Judge, 2007), acts as a checklist of steps necessary in the problem-solving process. Notably, while these steps are presented in a sequential order, it is often good practice to go back through steps multiple times until the best (i.e. most logical and feasible) solution is inferred.

Define the Problem

We start the problem-solving process by *defining the problem*. Though it may seem like an easy task, we often mistake the cause or causes of the problem. Likewise, we may sometimes disagree with others over the cause of a problem (Halpern, 2014). If we define the problem incorrectly, the rest of the process will become futile and the solutions we devise will subsequently become irrelevant. Thus, much like an argument, we must analyse the situation we believe is associated with a problem. We can do this by identifying the cause(s) of the problem, the goals we wish to achieve and by asking ourselves *when, where, why, how* and *to whom* is this problem happening.

Gather and Organize the Available Information

Before developing a problem-solving strategy based on our definition of the problem, we must first *gather and organize the information* that we analysed while defining the problem, as well as any other knowledge we may have about the problem. For example, we can organize the goal (and sub-goals), the obstacles, the options and the givens (provided that they are made available), according to the structure of the problem-solving scenario. Next we must evaluate possible problem-solving strategies.

Evaluate Possible Strategies

The problem-solving strategies we use are dictated by both the type of problem encountered and the information we have available. Means-ends analysis, as discussed before, is one such problem-solving strategy. There are also a number of other problem-solving strategies, including working backwards, brainstorming and constructing a problem-solving heuristic.

Sometimes the most efficient way to solve a problem is to simply identify the goal and *work backwards*. This strategy is useful in problems that have various routes to the goal; so, if we know what it is we are trying to achieve, we can reverse engineer the options and givens until a logical progression is obtained. To ensure that this progression actually solves the problem, we must then re-evaluate the problem-solving process from start to finish (i.e. working forward).

Brainstorming is another problem-solving technique and refers to the naming of a numerous (potential) solutions or ideas associated with a potential solution and collating them until the best (i.e. being both logical and feasible) solution is found. We can brainstorm individually or in groups. In the case of brainstorming in groups, it is important that we identify as many possible solutions as we can, while staying open-minded to others' ideas and not passing judgment on any potential solutions until further analyses and evaluations are conducted.

One final technique to consider is constructing a problem-solving heuristic. A heuristic refers to an experience-based plan, which can be utilized for problem-solving. Essentially, heuristics are mental short-cuts – they allow for speedy decisions to be made when an exhaustive search for information or knowledge is impractical (i.e. with respect to the availability, acceptability and applicability of knowledge). The use of heuristics in problem-solving allows us to identify conclusions and solutions without extensive deliberation and/or reflective judgment, given that heuristics are essentially schemas for such solutions (West, Toplak, & Stanovich, 2008). Without the relevant schemas or heuristics, CT and reflective judgment are required. Thus, in order to apply heuristics, one needs not only metacognitive strategies but also declarative memory. For example, our ability to correctly and appropriately (i.e. without bias) apply heuristics in a CT scenario is dependent on one's declarative knowledge of probability, causal reasoning of scientific thinking and logic, and our ability to remember the principles that govern these strategies and concepts (Stanovich, 2008; West, Toplak, & Stanovich, 2008).

Although a heuristic process can result in behaviour that is appropriate for a given purpose (e.g. unreflectively checking whether a stove is hot before placing an object down on it), notably, solutions derived from these heuristics are not always the best to apply, given that they are often made based on 'snap decisions' and not necessarily on any research. West, Toplak, and Stanovich (2008) found that heuristics are often used inappropriately in situations that require CT and that the use of heuristics (and their associated biases) were negatively correlated with CT. Based on their findings, West, Toplak, and Stanovich (2008) indicate that an over-reliance on heuristics, as well as their use in inappropriate settings, results in poor judgments and decisions. Notably, we will examine the use of heuristics in greater detail in Chapter 10, in discussion of judgments, heuristics and cognitive biases.

Generate Possible Solutions

The fourth step in the problem-solving process is the generation of possible solutions. Given the (1) problem-situation, (2) the available information and (3) the problem-solving strategy selected from the previous step (i.e. evaluating possible strategies), we must develop, or generate, a number of possible solutions. For example, we may have participated in a brainstorming session and developed ten possible solutions to a problem. To consider whether these solutions are logical and feasible, we must evaluate them; and we can do this by asking ourselves a number of related questions about both the problem and the solution in question, such as the following:

- What are the consequences (i.e. what will happen when the problem is solved using this solution)?
- Is this solution feasible (i.e. what will we need to do in order to implement this solution)?
- Is this solution cost-effective (i.e. what resources will be needed and will the benefits outweigh the costs of employing this potential solution)?

Monitor the Progress of the Solution Strategy

Like each sub-skill of CT, problem-solving is dependent not just on cognitive or metacognitive skills, but also on our self-regulatory functions of thinking (see Chapter 4). That is, the likelihood of solving a problem is dictated by our ability as well as our *willingness* to engage, regulate and monitor our problem-solving, with respect to the extent to which we are disposed, inclined and motivated to perform such activities (Dwyer, 2011; Dwyer et al., 2016; Pintrich, 2000). Successful problem-solvers have a propensity to monitor their progress in their development of a solution or solutions. Thus, if progress is not being made, we must be willing to re-evaluate our strategy with respect to reconfirming each step in the problem-solving process conducted thus far (e.g. re-evaluating whether the best problem-solving strategy or the most appropriate solution was selected and, if not, subsequently repeating the preceding steps). Notably, one efficient way of monitoring the problem-solving progress is by assessing whether or not the results thus far are commensurate with what we had expected to observe.

Evaluate Results of the Solution Strategy

Similar to monitoring the progress of the solution strategy, after a solution has been inferred, it is important to not only evaluate but also re-evaluate the results of the solution strategy. That is, we must avoid premature celebration and, likewise, avoid jumping to conclusions about the solution. This is an important step because it is necessary to determine whether the solution we chose is indeed the best possible solution to the problem. Similar to the cyclical nature of evaluation and inference, this method of re-checking our work allows us to assess results from our solution on a deeper level. This assessment might be automatic, such as confirming whether your solution to a mathematics problem is correct, or it can be longitudinal, such as in the case of assessing the success of a lengthy intervention.

Verify the Solution

Once the results of a solution have been evaluated and then re-evaluated, we can *verify* its success in light of: whether or not it worked, consequences, feasibility and cost-effectiveness. Simply, we are checking to see whether or not the problem has been solved. Though this overlaps with evaluating results of the solution strategy to a certain extent (i.e. given the re-evaluation of our results), if results remain consistent with our previous evaluations, we can verify the solution as something that works in the context it was used. It is from this point that we can move forward, progressing to our next thinking activity, while at the same time considering what we learned from this problem-solving experience (i.e. new knowledge, understanding and/or skills).

Creative Thinking and Problem-Solving

Throughout this section on problem-solving, the notion of developing both logical and feasible solutions to problems has been promoted. However, as noted earlier, in some cases, relevant knowledge may not be readily available for solving a given problem and, thus, a collation of insight and the ability to *think outside the box* may be an attractive alternative. This ability to 'think outside the box' is often referred to as *creative thinking*. Consider the following anecdote that exemplifies the use of creative thinking in a real-world scenario:

> A high-school principal was notified by the custodian about a persistent problem in the girls' lavatories: some of the female students were leaving 'lipstick kisses' on the mirrors. The custodian had seen to it that notices were left in the lavatories and forwarded to students in class, but to no avail. Every morning the custodian would wipe away the pink and red lip-prints, to only find the mirrors in the evening again covered in kisses. It appeared to the custodian that this had all become a bit of a game.
>
> The principal generally took a creative approach to solving these types of problems and so the next day she asked a few girl representatives from each class to meet with her in the lavatory.
>
> 'Thank you for coming,' said the principal, 'You will see there are several lipstick kisses on the mirrors in this washroom.'
>
> A few of the girls in attendance flashed mischievous grins at one another.
>
> 'As you undoubtedly understand, modern lipstick is designed in such a way as to stay on the lips and as such, it is not easy to clean it from the mirrors. We have therefore had to develop a special cleaning regime and my hope is that when you see the effort involved in the cleaning process, you will help ensure that this does not continue, by spreading the word that we'd all be better off if those responsible for the kisses use tissue paper instead of the mirrors in future.'
>
> It was at this point that the custodian picked up an old mop, stepped into one of the toilet cubicles, dipped the head into the toilet bowl and then used it to clean one of the lipstick-covered mirrors. There were no more lipstick kisses on the mirrors.

Necessity is the mother of invention is a well-known adage that suggests that things are created because they are needed – much like the way we perceive our everyday problems needing solutions. The notion of invention implies the creation of something novel that has not been thought of or created before that can be applied to solve a problem or suit a purpose. Consistent with this perspective, *creative thinking* has been described as producing a solution or conclusion that is (1) unusual or novel and (2) appropriate or valuable (Halpern, 2014; Runco & Jaeger, 2012; Sternberg, 2010). Based on this line of reasoning, we can infer that creative thinking is a useful skill for solving problems – and it often is, much like the principal's creative solution in the earlier anecdote. However, this description only reveals what is ideally produced – a novel and valuable solution – it does not describe what is involved. According to Sternberg (2003), for creative thinking to occur, multiple 'components' must converge: a cognitive style that involves managing the complexities associated with the problem-situation; knowledge of heuristics for generating novel ideas and a work-style characterized by concentrated effort; and ability to be able to set aside problems; as well as high energy and motivation. In a broader context, creativity requires the convergence of six resources: intellectual abilities, knowledge, styles of thinking, personality, motivation and environment (Sternberg, 2006).

Worth noting however, is that creative thinking is not particularly practical (Sternberg, 2002), particularly in the absence of CT. For example, though creative thinking is utilized when relatively novel tasks or situations are encountered (Sternberg, 2005), it is vital that reflective judgment should be engaged when novel tasks or situations are encountered about which we wish to think critically. Though there is certain amount of creativity involved in the synthesis of information necessary to infer a conclusion or solve a problem in a reflective manner, this should be completed via the gathering of credible, relevant and logically sound information, while at the same time acknowledging the limits, certainty and nature of knowledge. That is, we are creating by synthesizing information we have previously analysed and evaluated; and if in doubt, one should not resort to proposing a creative solution before all other avenues involving CT have been considered. This is not to say that creative thinking is a bad thing, but rather, it should be used alongside CT and with caution. Just because a solution is creative does not mean it is feasible.

To exemplify this position to one of my classes, I asked them what they thought might help resolve the recent conflicts in Syria. After deliberating for a few minutes, students returned blank stares– they wanted *me* to advise them what should be done. I advised that one solution would be to 'nuke' Syria. The students' faces changed from that of blank stares to bewilderment and disgust. I quickly added that I did not advocate this position, nor did I support any such violence, but that such a measure would likely put an end to the crisis. I further added that though this solution had great potential to work, it was not feasible, not only from a moral standpoint, but also from political and economic standpoints and thus would be selected against. Again, for solutions to be implemented, they must be both logical and feasible; and so, creative problem-solving must be used with caution.

Sternberg's (2006) description of creative thinking as a convergence of multiple cognitive resources implies that creativity is an important metacognitive process – which it can be. However, as per our previous discussion of what constitutes CT (see Chapter 4), perhaps creative thinking is not appropriate for use when we truly care about our decisions. To reiterate, we all think for different reasons – sometimes we have a clear goal in mind and sometimes we let imagination take over and carry us away in a creative, fantasy world.

Creative thinking generally allows for the free play of imagination, but it is not a prerequisite that it has to be logical – the goal is not necessarily trying to convince people that what we are saying is true and reasonable. If our goal is to decide what to do or what to believe and if we genuinely care about the outcome of our decision-making process, CT is necessary – creative thinking is not. On the other hand, CT is not necessary to think creatively. For example, consider the following scenario and, from it, think about and identify what has transpired within the scenario.

> A man in a pub walks up the bar and asks the bartender for a pint of water. The bartender pulls a gun on the man, points it at him and cocks it. The man looks at the bartender and says sincerely, 'Thank you'.

The point of presenting you with a 'puzzle' such as this, for lack of a better description, is to exemplify what is necessary for *lateral thinking*. You may have developed a number of possible explanations for what has transpired. The most often cited answer that fits the context of the story is that the man in the bar has the hiccups and, upon realizing this, the bartender decides that attempting to scare the man's hiccups away might work better than a pint of water, which it did – hence, the gratitude. Though a vast majority of students to whom I present this puzzle reply that the solution makes sense and seems obvious, (1) it is not the only possible solution and (2) it does not require CT, per se. To some extent, it can be said to require reflection, but by no means requires evaluation.

Lateral thinking, which is a form of creative thinking, has gained notoriety in the past few decades, based on the work of Edward De Bono (1967). Whereas CT is concerned with the reflective inference of reasonable solutions or conclusions, as is creative thinking to some extent, lateral thinking is more concerned with the migration of thinking from what is known across the spectrum of possibilities. That is, lateral thinking involves the provocation and generation of ideas (much like brainstorming), as well as the selection of an idea as a means of breeding and applying new associated ideas (De Bono, 1985). Often, the ideas selected are purposefully outlandish, so that the associated ideas generated from that one outlandish idea can be used to more feasibly solve the problem. For example, consider another scenario:

> A hunter aimed his gun carefully and fired. Seconds later, he realized his mistake. Minutes later, he was dead.

Three (and possibly more) responses (with varying degrees of outlandishness) have been proposed that 'adequately' define the scenario.

1. It was winter. He fired the gun near a snowy cliff, which started an avalanche.
2. The hunter mistook a fellow hunter, wearing camouflage, who had rattled antlers as bait for other deer, for an actual deer. In anger, the second hunter fired back killing the first hunter.
3. He shot an elephant with a low-calibre rifle. Not powerful enough to kill it, the elephant became enraged and trampled him.

The previous two puzzles are often used to demonstrate what is necessary for lateral thinking. As alluded to above, 'puzzles' or problems that have only one solution are not 'lateral'. Also worth noting is that while the development of solutions for these puzzles requires creative thinking, it is the *construction* of such puzzles that require lateral thinking.

According to De Bono, lateral thinking is engaged because attempts at solving problems may prove futile and thus waste time. As a result, 'digging the whole deeper', which is an important facet of CT, may not work; and one must change the direction, or approach, to thinking. However, as discussed in detail in Chapter 8, the use of reflective judgment to gather credible, relevant and logically sound information, while at the same time acknowledging the limits, certainty and nature of knowledge when faced with difficult or novel situations, is more likely to yield a logical and feasible solution, and is thus a better approach to making a decision than that of lateral, creative thinking.

To clarify, De Bono argues for the usefulness of lateral thinking by using the example that life is a game of chess in which we have been provided certain pieces (i.e. the *givens* in problem-situations); however, in real-life situations, the pieces are not given – we just assume they are there; and thus, lateral thinking is necessary to create pieces necessary to play. However, this line of thought does not account for the credibility, relevance or logical strength of these created 'pieces' and, if it were really a case of not having the pieces necessary to play, then recognizing their limits and uncertainty in response to such real-life situations would yield better results than relying on creativity alone. Notably, De Bono's approach to higher-order thinking, such as lateral thinking, has received a great deal of criticism, particularly (and ironically) as a result of focusing primarily on the creation and development of ideas rather than the reliability, validation and efficacy of the lateral thinking approach (Moseley et al., 2005; Sternberg & Lubart, 1999).

> The chief enemy of creativity is good sense.
> ~ Pablo Picasso

So what? is a question you may be asking, particularly after the preceding quote from Picasso. If lateral thinking and, to a large extent, creative thinking are not particularly useful or even practical for CT, then why are they discussed here in a book on CT? These types of thinking are explained here because they have both garnered popularity over the years and are often either confused for or lumped together with CT as an ideal form of (meta)cognition. It would be a disservice to the concept of CT to not explain its difference to other 'popular' forms of thought, such as creative thinking and lateral thinking. Again, this is not to say that creative thinking is a bad thing – it can be used to complement CT. For example, depending on the manner in which we conceive of creative thinking, it can be useful. A famous quote by Steve Jobs goes:

> *Creativity is just connecting things. When you ask creative people how they did something, they feel a little guilty because they didn't really do it, they just saw something. It seemed obvious to them after a while.*

If we treat our conceptualization of creative thinking in this manner, as a means of heightened inference ability (i.e. through the synthesis of credible, relevant and logically sound information), then it can be a helpful process. To reiterate, we can think creatively by synthesizing information we have previously thought about critically (i.e. through analysis and evaluation) – we are not resorting to creativity alone, before all other avenues involving CT have been considered. Thus, given this caveat, we can infuse our CT with creative thinking, but we must do so with caution. Remember, just because a solution is creative does not mean it is logical and feasible.

SUMMARY AND CONCLUSION

In summary, in order to conduct CT in everyday real-world settings, we must be able to apply the skills analysis, evaluation and inference, cumulatively, along with our ability to reflectively judge situations, problems and arguments. The application of these skills as a whole dictates whether our CT will be successful. However, in this context, it is equally important to consider the real-world settings in which we might be expected to apply these skills. Thus, this chapter presented and discussed five distinct categories of everyday tasks in which we apply CT: argumentation; verbal reasoning; hypothesis testing; judging likelihood and uncertainty; and problem-solving. From this discussion, we learned that CT is more than an idealistic conceptualization of how we should think – it is something we use on a day-to-day basis and something we should strive to improve. However, there are a variety of factors that may impede the manner in which we reflect (or do not reflect) in our day-to-day thinking. The focus of the following chapter is to address such situations and the cognitive processes behind them. Such discussion further strengthens the impetus for reflective judgment in real-world settings.

EXERCISE 9.2

Design a problem-solving scenario based on a problem you have recently encountered in your own life. Please identify the goal, reality (or starting point), obstacle, options and givens associated with the problem. How did you go about solving this problem? In light of reading this chapter, brainstorm a list of possible solutions to this problem, not including the one you *actually* used. Based on your brainstorming, develop a series of steps you would choose for your problem-solving procedure. Was the solution you developed here better (i.e. more feasible and logical) than the one you actually used? Why or why not?

Judgment, Heuristics and Biases

Continuous vigilance . . . is impractical.
~ Daniel Kahneman (2011)

Consider for a moment the following problem:

A bat and a ball cost $1.10.
The bat costs one dollar more than the ball.
How much does the ball cost?

For many of you, the answer that automatically sprung to your head was
10¢. However, regardless of how easy this problem is, the solution that most of
you elicited is incorrect. Do the math and you will find that the answer is 5¢.
The ball costs 5¢ and the bat costs $1.05, both of which add to a total of $1.10.
Again, the answer came to many of you almost automatically – without too
much thought. The answering of this problem can be viewed as an intuitive
judgment.

Even those of you who answered the question correctly may have first
instinctively thought the answer was 10¢, but then, just as fast, decided to
ignore this intuition and reflect a little longer on the problem – indicating
a propensity for more reflective judgment.

As we discussed in Chapter 8, reflective judgment is an important aspect of
critical thinking (CT). It is necessary for us to consider our limited knowledge
and (un)certainty regarding specific topics. In this context, we cannot make
snap decisions or judgments; we must avoid relying on intuition alone when
we care about making decisions – we must reflectively judge these situations.

DUAL-PROCESS THEORY

A large body of research in psychology is focused on the differences
between these two types of thought and the manner in which they interact.

Traditionally known as dual-process theory, psychologists often identify what we label intuitive judgment as, for example, *heuristic* (Tversky & Kahneman, 1983), *automatic* (Bargh, 1989; Higgins, 1989), *schematic* (Leventhal, 1984), reflexive (Lieberman, 2003), *implicit* (Weinberger & McClelland, 1991) and System 1 (Stanovich & West, 2000); and what we refer to as reflective thought as, for example, analytical (Epstein et al., 1996; Hamm, 1988; Hammond, 1996; Kahneman, 2011), rational (Epstein et al., 1996; Lieberman, 2003), explicit (Weinberger & McClelland, 1991) and System 2 (Stanovich & West, 2000).[1]

Intuitive judgment has been described in many ways in the past, such as 'the absence of analysis' (Hamm, 1988); 'a capacity for attaining direct knowledge or understanding without the apparent intrusion of rational thought or logical inference' (Dhami & Thomson, 2012; Saddler-Smith & Shefy, 2004); automatic cognitive processing which generally lacks effort, intention, awareness or voluntary control – usually experienced as perceptions or feelings (Kahneman, 2011; Lieberman, 2003); rapid, unconscious data processing that combines the available information by 'averaging it', which has low consistency and is moderately accurate (Hammond, 1996); and similarly, as operating automatically and quickly, with little or no effort and no sense of voluntary control (Kahneman, 2011).

According to Kahneman (2011), examples of System 1 behaviour include:

- answering the question 'What is 2 + 2?'
- completing the phrase 'bread and . . . '
- reading words on large billboards.

On the other hand, reflective judgment, in this context referring to System 2 thinking, has been described as slow, conscious and consistent (Hamm, 1988); and is associated with high cognitive control, slow data processing, high conscious awareness (Cader, Campbell, & Watson, 2005; Hamm, 1988) and the subjective experience of agency, choice and concentration (Kahneman, 2011). Essentially, reflective judgment allocates attention to the effortful mental activities that demand it (e.g. complex computation; Kahneman, 2011). According to Hammond (1996), this type of thinking is generally quite accurate. However, though occasionally

---

[1] Though many refer to System 2 thinking (Stanovich & West, 2000) as analytical judgment/thought, in order to maintain consistency in our own terminology, we will continue to refer to System 2 thinking throughout the remainder of this book as reflective (Lieberman, 2003), given also its consistency with the conceptualization of reflective judgment presented in Chapter 8.

wrong, these errors tend to be quite large, given the amount of complexity behind each judgment (Hamm, 1988; Kahneman, 2011).

According to Kahneman (2011), examples of System 2 thinking behaviour include:

- comparing two washing machines for overall value
- monitoring the appropriateness of one's behaviour in a social situation
- checking the validity of a complex logical argument.

The highly diverse operations of System 2 have one feature in common: they require attention and are disrupted when attention is drawn away. The judgment and decision-making processes associated with reflective thought occur when a question, problem or situation arises for which intuitive judgment processes do not offer an answer or fail to aid in goal achievement (Kahneman, 2011; Lieberman, 2003), for example, in cases where certain outcomes or situational variables deviate from our expectancies. That is, when intuitive judgment processes run into difficulty, reflective judgment is called on in order to support more complex information processing – which may solve the problem for the time being (Kahneman, 2011).

Given that intuitive judgment operates automatically and cannot be voluntarily 'turned off', associated errors and unsupported biases are difficult to prevent, largely because reflective judgment has not been consulted and, thus, is unaware of the error. Even when errors appear obvious, in hindsight, they can only be prevented through the careful, self-regulated monitoring and control afforded by reflective judgment. However, constantly reflectively judging our every thought is not feasible – it is much too slow and much too tedious, especially for making routine decisions (Kahneman, 2011). Thus, the most realistic option is that of using both judgment-making processes, through determining the importance of the decisions and judgments with which we find ourselves faced.

Thus, the types of thinking necessary to make reflective and intuitive judgments are often considered as poles on a continuum (e.g. Cader, Campbell, & Watson, 2005; Hamm, 1988; Hammond, 1981, 1996, 2000). This perspective on human judgment is known as Cognitive Continuum Theory (Hammond, 1981). Cognitive Continuum Theory is an adaptive theory of human judgment that theorizes a continuum of cognitive processes anchored by intuitive judgment and reflective judgment, which represents how judgment situations or tasks relate to cognition (Cader, Campbell, & Watson, 2005; Dunwoody et al., 2000). These two modes of

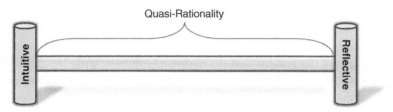

FIGURE 10.1 The Cognitive Continuum Bridged by Quasi-Rationality

thought are considered as existing on a continuum given that thinking is never purely reflective, nor is it completely intuitive (see Figure 10.1); but instead lies somewhere in between these realms of thought. That is, thought is a mixture of both intuitive and reflective judgment (Dunwoody et al., 2000; Hamm, 1988).

The 'mixture' that lies between intuitive and reflective judgment poles has often been referred to as *quasi-rationality* (Cader, Campbell, & Watson, 2005; Dunwoody et al., 2000; Hamm, 1988; Hammond, 1981). More specifically, quasi-rationality refers to the central region on the cognitive continuum and is a form of thought and reasoning that possesses characteristics of both intuitive and reflective judgment (Cader, Campbell, & Watson, 2005; Hammond, 1981, 1996). Quasi-rationality, often referred to as 'common sense' (Dunwoody et al., 2000; Hammond, 1996), is an adaptive form of thought, given that an individual may on some occasions reflect more on their judgments (e.g. through CT) than through automatic, intuitive judgment; or on other occasions, conversely, rely more on the intuitive process. The type of thinking used, or selected, is largely influenced by the type of task or problem-scenario faced – for example, one's experience (or expertise – discussed later in the chapter) in performing a particular task or solving a particular problem will also dictate the kind of thinking selected and its chances for success (Hamm, 1988). Similarly, according to Hamm's (1988) view of Cognitive Continuum Theory, the proportion of intuitive thought used relative to reflective thought is dictated by the individual's expertise or pre-existing knowledge regarding the situation or similar situations and the nature of the task (Hamm, 1988), specifically the complexity, ambiguity and presentation of the task structure and content (Hamm, 1988).

The ability to adapt to problem-situations is both practical and important because we face numerous problems each day, some of which require very little reflection, some which require deeper, more reflective consideration and some which require a 'delicate balance' of both (Langley, 1995).

Being able to decipher these types of problem-situations from one another, through adaptive thinking, is a thinking skill in itself! According to Hammond (1996, p. 175), 'quasi-rationality has many advantages, which may be one of the reasons that the notion of common sense has persisted and been valued by the layperson for so long, despite the fact that virtually no one has convincingly described it'; and though not without limitations, it:

> emerges as a valuable form of cognition because it tries to avoid the irresponsibility of intuition as well as the fragility of analysis [i.e. in this context, reflection]. Quasi-rationality is a superior form of cognition that has been the mainstay of our survival, all the while offering us all the negative consequences of an imperfect form of reasoning.   *(p. 352)*

It is worth noting that though Hammond's conceptualization of analytic judgment/decision-making is for the most part similar with other descriptions of System 2 thinking, including the conceptualization of reflective judgment in this book, there is one large discrepancy that should not be left untreated. According to Hammond (2000), Cader, Campbell, and Watson (2005), and Dunwoody et al. (2000), the better structured a task is, the more *analytically* induced will be the decision-making; whereas with an ill-structured task, decision-making is likely to be intuition-induced. However, the very opposite is posited here. Based on our detailed review of reflective judgment in Chapter 8, we know that in situations where we are faced with an ill-structured problem, the use of reflective judgment is our only choice if we care about our decision, given the uncertainty surrounding the many possible solutions. On the other hand, when dealing with a well-structured problem, for example 5 × 25 (a problem with only one correct solution), a vast majority of you will automatically, intuitively answer: 125. With that said, this critique applies to cognitive processes *only* (i.e. not *tasks*, as outlined by Hammond, 1996). For example, according to Cader and colleagues (2005), if a nurse attempts to support a falling patient, the speed of such an incident makes it near impossible to reflect upon the potential options associated with the problem-situation – an intuitive judgment of automatically 'catching the patient with one's arms' is required.

HEURISTICS, BIASES AND ERRORS

In Cognitive Continuum Theory, neither reflective nor intuitive judgment is assumed a priori to be superior (Dunwoody et al., 2000). However, most contemporary research on judgment and decision-making has focused on the strengths of reflective cognition and the limitations associated with intuitive judgment (Cabantous, Gond, & Johnson-Cramer, 2010; Dhami & Thomson, 2012; Gilovich, Griffin, & Kahneman, 2002). This is because judgments based on reflection can be difficult to dispute and, if used in the context of a well-structured problem, are more often than not correct. However, the limitation of reflective judgment most often cited in research is that it takes too long. Sometimes, 'snap' judgments are what is necessary in a given situation, such as in the example of the nurse catching the falling patient. Obviously, we would prefer to work less when faced with making a decision – this is natural. According to Kahneman (2011), we are lazy thinkers and cognitive misers. This concept is by no means novel. Another Nobel Prize winner, Herbert Simon (1957), noted that rather than engage in extensive, reflective decision-making, people generally settle for a decision or solution that is satisfactory, or simply, 'good enough'. This is why we often choose to go with our gut – our intuition. Thus, often our judgments are simply based on intuitions that simply come to us, which we deem are relatively reasonable to implement. So, if snap judgments are necessary and this type of decision-making requires less effort, why is it consistently cited as 'limited'?

Though System 1 is *generally* good at what it does (Kahneman, 2011) and the intuitive judgments it makes serve us well, a large body of research has been conducted on the manner in which intuitive judgments come to mind and why they are often limited or grossly incorrect – that being as a result of heuristics (Kahneman, 2011; Tversky & Kahneman, 1974). A heuristic is a 'simple' *experience*-based protocol for problem-solving and decision-making, which acts as a mental shortcut – a 'procedure that helps find the adequate, though often imperfect, answers to difficult questions' (Kahneman, 2011, p. 98). Interesting to note is that heuristic stems from the same root as the word *eureka*.

Heuristics sometimes serve us well (e.g. the use of the 'trial-and-error' method, as discussed in Chapter 9). However, they are often misapplied and can lead to faulty reasoning and judgment as a result of systematic biases and errors (Gilovich, Griffin, & Kahneman, 2002; Kahneman, 2011; Kahneman, Slovic, & Tversky, 1982; Slovic, Fischhoff, & Lichtenstein, 1977; Tversky & Kahneman, 1974). According to Kahneman (2011), these errors and biases stem from fundamental problems with intuitive judgment (i.e. System 1 thinking): (1) System 1 often substitutes the question posed with a different question – one in which is more easily answered; and (2) System 1 has a poor understanding of both logic and statistics.

Three Classic Heuristics

Tversky and Kahneman (1974) famously identified three main groups of heuristics: (1) availability; (2) representativeness; and (3) anchoring and adjustment. The availability heuristic is a mental rule of thumb whereby people base a judgment on the ease with which they can bring relevant information, such as an example, to mind.

Consider the classic example:

> Are there more words that begin with the letter 'K', than those with 'K' as the third letter?

Many of you will have answered that there are more words that begin with the letter 'K' given the relative ease with which these words came to mind with words that have 'K' as their third letter (i.e. when searching you memory for words with the letter 'K', *kitten* comes to mind faster than *hake*). In reality, however, there are substantially more words in the English language with 'K' as their third letter than there are with 'K' as their first letter.

Research by Schwarz et al. (1991) is consistent with this perspective. In their study, Schwarz and colleagues asked participants to identify and describe either six or twelve occasions in which they were either *assertive* or *unassertive*. After the recall period, participants were asked to rate their own assertiveness. Given that it easier to recall six events than twelve events (i.e. it should be easier for you to remember six instances of an event compared to twelve), those who were asked to recall six occasions of assertiveness rated themselves as more assertive than those who were asked to describe twelve occasions, as were those who were asked to describe twelve occasions of unassertiveness relative to those asked to describe six occasions of unassertive behaviour.

The second heuristic identified by Tversky and Kahneman (1974) is the representativeness heuristic, which is a mental shortcut we take when making judgments about the probability of an event or occurrence. When individuals rely on this heuristic, they are generally wrong as a result of substituting what they perceive as representative of the real world for the actual likelihood of something (Kahneman, 2011; Tversky & Kahneman, 1982). For example:

> Which outcome is more likely when playing at a fair roulette table?
> BRRBRB
> or
> BBBRRR

Hopefully, after our discussion of judging likelihood and uncertainty in real-world scenarios, with respect to coin-flipping, in Chapter 9, you will realize that both occurrences are equally likely. Nevertheless, without such knowledge, many individuals indicate that the first is more likely because it represents what they consider as being *random*. Again, intuition has a very poor understanding of statistics and indeed the nature of true randomness (Kahneman, 2011).

Another example, developed by Tversky and Kahneman (1974), is as follows:

> Steve is very shy and withdrawn, invariably helpful. A tidy soul, he has a need for order and structure and a passion for detail.
> Is Steve a farmer or a librarian?

Most people indicate that Steve is a librarian, because the description is commensurate with what they would conceive of as a librarian. However, Steve is statistically more likely a farmer, given that there are more farmers than there are librarians. Perhaps you said that Steve is a farmer. This may have resulted from the fact that you were, to a certain degree, prepped for a folly in thinking (given that these examples are provided to exploit errors in judgment). However, it may also have arisen from another example of the representativeness heuristic. On one occasion in class, when teaching through this very example, one student raised his hand and made the point that he picked Steve (correctly) as a farmer over a librarian, not because of anything to do with the description, but for the simple reason that he knew of no female farmers and no male librarians. I asked the rest of the class if anyone else had made their judgment based on this logic, and astoundingly, around thirty students (about 10% of the class) raised their hands – they had substituted one representativeness heuristic for another. When teaching the 'Steve problem', I have since adopted the name *Jamie* for the title character.

The third and final category of heuristics identified by Tversky and Kahneman (1974) is the anchoring and adjustment heuristic. The use of this occurs when an individual utilizes the initial piece of information presented to them (often a number value) as a starting point and subsequently makes a judgment or decision by adjusting away from this anchor. For example, consider the following two questions in turn:

> Was Winston Churchill more or less than 40 when he died?
> How old was Churchill when he died?

I am sure a vast majority of you realize that Churchill was well over 40 when he died, but nevertheless, the indication that perhaps he was around 40 when he died (as in the first question) has primed you to consider that he was not as old as you initially thought. Perhaps 55–65 years old is reasonable to suggest. However, this would be wrong. According to Kahneman (2011, p. 122), intuition comprehends information by attempting to make it true (i.e. it takes additional cognitive effort to assimilate information and simultaneously assess its truth) and, thus, 'the selective activation of compatible thoughts produces a family of systematic errors that make us gullible and prone to believe too strongly whatever we believe'. Now, consider the following questions:

Was Winston Churchill more or less than 120 when he died?
How old was Churchill when he died?

Though 120 years old may seem like a preposterous age to many of you (and thus, you will of course have said younger), it may have allowed you to adjust your answer to an age somewhere between 85 and 95, which, in its own right, would be a big age. Interestingly, this would be accurate. Churchill died at 90 and it seems that the more preposterous anchor was in fact the more reasonable one. Herein lies the contradictory nature of heuristics – people very often fall prey to following an anchoring heuristic because, in many situations, anchoring is the reasonable thing to do. Sometimes, when we are presented with difficult questions, we have a tendency to clutch at straws and the anchor is a plausible straw (Kahneman, 2011).

Another classic example of the anchoring and adjustment heuristic is that of shopping for a used car at a dealership. Imagine you find a car that you are interested in purchasing and you ask the salesman for the price. The salesman might tell you that the car costs $8,900. Though you realize that used car salesmen are stereotyped as being notorious for overcharging on cars, it remains that the counter-offer you propose is based on the *initial* suggestion and may still be very much over the actual value of the car. Kahneman (2011) recommends that when in situations where negotiation is likely, be sure to be the first person to offer a price!

Kahneman's Modern Outlook on Heuristics

As alluded to earlier in describing the representativeness heuristic, people have a tendency to substitute what they perceive as representative of the real world for the actual likelihood of something happening. People also have a tendency to substitute a similar, though easier question for the question they were actually asked. According to Kahneman and Frederick (2002), heuristics all share a common element – they process information through *attribute substitution*. This perspective is consistent with past research theory on heuristics and intuitive judgment, as a heuristic is described in this context as being used 'when the individual assesses a specified target attribute of a judgment object by substituting a related heuristic attribute that comes more readily to mind' (Kahneman, 2003, p. 466).

For example, according to Kahneman (2011), you might be asked 'How much would you contribute to save an endangered species?' You may answer this question as if you were asked 'How much emotion do I feel when I think of dying dolphins?' In the first question – the one that was actually asked – the target attribute may not be easily accessible or may *require* reflective thought (i.e. it may be that a number of variables must be considered, such as: *Is contribution referring to time, money or effort?* and also *What is considered an endangered species?*), whereas the second question – the one you substituted – is related to the target question and is highly accessible (e.g. I like dolphins and the thought of them dying saddens me).

Since the work of Tversky and Kahneman (1974), numerous other heuristics and biases have been proposed and researched (e.g. naive diversification; escalation of commitment; and recognition, similarity, fluency and effort heuristics, to name a few). One notable, recent heuristic is the affect heuristic (Kahneman & Frederick, 2002), which draws upon an emotional response, such as in the dolphin example (i.e. the thought of dolphins dying saddens me). The identification of the affect heuristic by Kahneman and Frederick stems from their reading and interpretation of research by Strack, Martin, and Schwarz (1988), in which college students were asked the following questions:

How happy are you with your life in general?
How many dates did you have last month?

The size of the correlation between the two questions was small when asked in this order. However, the correlation between the two was significantly large when the order was switched (i.e. when the dating question was asked first). Why? This research indicates that individuals who were asked the dating question first were primed by being asked a question about their romantic life, which elicited an emotional reaction. This reaction heavily influenced the manner in which the following question was answered. That is, when asked a broad, difficult question such as 'How happy are you these days?', individuals who were just asked about how frequently they date have information related to their romantic life readily available and easily accessible and are likely to draw more heavily upon this information than they are to search for other facets of their life for consideration. That is, given the effects of both the availability heuristic and attribute substitution, the dating question automatically evokes an emotion-based evaluation of one's satisfaction with their love-life; and the emotion carries over to the next question, ultimately leading to the answering of the *how happy are you with your life* with a response that reflects their happiness with their love-life (Kahneman, 2003).

Consistent with this perspective is research by Slovic et al. (2002), who highlight how individuals' basic affective reactions can be used as a heuristic for wide-ranging evaluations, regardless of the complexity of the question. For example, it is a common observation of educators that when students are asked difficult questions and they do not know the answer (i.e. when they lack the required knowledge), they more often than not respond with a related, affect-based belief or attitude. This example is also consistent with research by Kahneman and Ritov (1994) and Kahneman, Ritov, and Schkade (1999), which proposed that the emotional basis of attitudes (i.e. *automatic affective valuation*) has a major role in dictating the judgments and decisions that individuals make.

In Being & Nothingness (1943), the French philosopher, Jean Paul Sartre suggests that every time an individual acts, they are making a choice in that they have chosen to commit that act as opposed to not acting, or acting in an alternative manner. In this sense, each and every day is filled with potential decisions. For example, in 2005, it was estimated that the average US supermarket carried 40,000 specific products available for purchase (Trout, 2005). If you want to buy a loaf of bread, you might need to decide whether you wanted a small or large loaf, white or brown, with or without seeds, with or without crust, pan or barrel, etc. – approximately five decisions over a simple loaf of bread. The choices for a cup of coffee are even more staggering: in 2003, a leading coffee chain boasted a possibility of over 19,000 beverage combinations. Though most of the time we choose based on habituation or other automatic processes (Bargh, 2002), that is, we remain reinforced by choices made in the past, other times, novel and/or considered choices are necessary. In addition to emotion, fatigue also impacts the manner in which judgments and decisions are made in novel situations – particularly, *decision fatigue.*

Decision fatigue (Baumeister, 2003) refers to the decreased accuracy and/or quality of processing in decision-making or self-regulation as a result of the amount of previous engagement with problem-situations that required decisions or judgements; that is, people often make poor decisions after having made many decisions or worse decisions than if they had to have made less previous decisions. Consistent with the latter description, decision fatigue often occurs later in the day (Danziger, Levav, & Avnaim-Pesso, 2011). Similarly, given that attention and processing associated with executive function is limited and, as such, resembles a form of strength or energy that can be depleted, past research also indicates that this resource is also diminished as tasks requiring self-regulation are increased (i.e. ego depletion; Baumeister, 2002; Muraven, Tice, & Baumeister, 1998; Vohs & Heatherton, 2000; Vohs et al., 2014). According to Vohs et al. (2014), ego depletion and decision fatigue of an individual's reserve of cognitive resources have been linked to multiple negative behavioural and decision-making outcomes, including inappropriate sexual responses (Gailliot & Baumeister, 2007), prejudicial responding (Richeson & Shelton, 2003), intellectual underachievement (Schmeichel, Vohs, & Baumeister, 2003), ineffective self-presentation (Vohs, Baumeister, & Ciarocco, 2005), impulsive overspending (Vohs & Faber, 2007) and overeating by dieters (Vohs & Heatherton, 2000).

Furthermore, according to Hammond (1996), while the positive view of intuitive judgment cites and celebrates its successes, at the same time, its failures are either ignored or forgotten. This observation is quite ironic, given its likeness to the availability cascade, which is a self-reinforcing chain of events that leads to the development of a large-scale collective belief – an associate of the affect heuristic – for example, starting from a media report of a minor event or report, leading to public panic and government action, such as the Love Canal affair of 1979 and the Alar scare of 1989 (Kahneman, 2011; Kuran & Sunstein, 1999). The availability cascade exemplifies people's inability to cope with risks, especially small ones – people either ignore them or allot them too much weight (Kahneman, 2011). According to Slovic and Peters (2006), people have a tendency to 'imagine the numerator' only (e.g. the number of deaths caused by eating apples with pesticides – what you see in the media) and 'neglecting the denominator' (the number of people who eat apples with pesticides).

NATURALISTIC DECISION-MAKING

Given that heuristics are often misapplied and can lead to imperfect answers, as well as faulty reasoning and judgment, resulting from systematic biases and errors (Dhami & Thomson, 2012; Gilovich, Griffin, & Kahneman, 2002; Kahneman, 2011; Kahneman, Slovic, & Tversky, 1982; Slovic, Fischhoff, & Lichtenstein, 1977; Tversky & Kahneman, 1974), most contemporary research on judgment and decision-making has focused on the strengths of reflective cognition and the limitations associated with heuristic-based, intuitive judgment. However, not all intuitive judgments are produced as a result of heuristics, as the accurate intuitions of experts are better explained by the effects of prolonged practice (Kahneman, 2011). That is, some intuitions reflect experience-based strategies, such as those required in practice.

In the realm of *naturalistic decision-making* (i.e. how people make practical decisions in real-world settings; Klein, 2008), experience/expertise-based intuitions can be explained according to the recognition-primed decision (RPD) model. The RPD is based on qualitative data derived from interviews conducted with fireground commanders regarding occupation-related emergency events/problem-situations (Klein, 1989, 2008). The fireground commanders reported that they 'were not "making choices", "considering alternatives" or "assessing probabilities". They saw themselves as acting and reacting on the basis of prior experiences; they were generating, monitoring and modifying plans to meet the needs of the situations' (Klein, 1989, p. 139).

Specifically, the RPD describes how people apply their experience/expertise in the form of a repertoire of patterns (Klein, Calderwood, & Clinton-Cirocco, 1986). These patterns organize the primary variables (e.g. potential causal factors) operating in the situation that is to be judged. More specifically, these patterns allow individuals to quickly identify relevant environmental cues, anticipated outcomes, possible goals for a given situation and, subsequently, select an appropriate reaction(s). Simply, when faced with a situation that requires a decision within or relevant to one's expertise domain, that individual can quickly apply the patterns they have learned to their current situation (Klein, 2008). Thus, individuals *can* successfully make rapid, intuitive-based decisions, without reflectively comparing options.

In addition to this concept of 'pattern-matching' and similar to a trial-and-error heuristic[2] (see Chapter 9), individuals who are expert can

---

[2] Notably, though the trial-and-error strategy is a heuristic and is similar to this concept of mental simulation, the latter is slightly different than the trial-and-error method discussed in Chapter 9, given that it is based on expertise/experience and thus can be conceptualized more as a general schema, rather than what is discussed as a heuristic.

rapidly, mentally simulate how a certain decision will work if applied (de Groot, 1965; Kaempf et al., 1996). Notably, this concept is similar to Simon's conceptualization of *satisficing* (i.e. searching for and identifying the first feasible solution/decision), but also suffers a negative connotation given that it is the first *feasible* solution and not necessarily the *best* solution – one that is 'satisfactory', or simply one that is 'good enough' (Dhami & Thomson, 2012).

To digress briefly, the notion of satisficing can be argued to stem from traditional perspectives on scientific determinism. According to scientific determinism, uncertainty is a concept confined to the subjective nature of human thought, as the concept does not exist in the human world. If an individual were to have infinite cognitive resources, infinite time and all the necessary information, then certainty would be assured. This concept is commonly referred to as *Laplace's Demon*. According to Laplace (1902):

> Given an intelligence which at a certain moment would know all the forces by which nature is set in motion and all positions of all the items of which nature is composed, if moreover this intellect were vast enough to submit these data to analysis, it would embrace in a single formula the movements of the largest bodies in the universe and those of the tiniest atom; to it nothing would be uncertain and the future just like the past would be present to its eyes.

For example, Laplace argued that an intellect, such as the demon's, would know the exact location of where each and every descending snowflake would land as a result of absolute knowledge.

However, there is no such demon and humans are subject to limited cognitive resources, limited time and limited information. This concept, known as *bounded rationality*, was also developed by Nobel Prize winner Herbert Simon. According to bounded rationality, individuals can never be completely rational (i.e. consistent with the aforementioned perspective on quasi-rationality) and are limited by the boundaries of time in that they are not privy, in advance, to the results of their decisions. Thus, individuals choose the optimal judgment or decision identified within the confines of these limitations (i.e. satisficing); however, that is not to say that the judgment or decision is the most optimal, but rather, 'good enough' for an entity that is not Laplace's demon.

With more specificity to intuition and central to this discussion of RPD, Simon (1992, p. 155) argues:

Intuition is nothing more and nothing less than recognition ... the situation has provided a cue; this cue has given the expert access to information in stored memory; and the information provides the answer.

Hammond (1996, p. 167) criticizes this perspective because if intuitive judgment is reduced to *nothing more and nothing less than recognition*, then 'Simon robs this concept of almost everything that has attracted all students of intuition'. Hammond continues by exemplifying, if

'Richard Feynman just wrote down the solutions out of his head without ever writing down the equations, was he merely recognising information stored in his memory? If so, where did he get this information? Not from anyone else.'

What Hammond fails to address in his criticism is twofold: (1) that Feynman likely used more reflective judgment than intuition in his administration of formulae (thus, nullifying this example as irrelevant) and (2) the role of what we conceptualized, in Chapter 2, as comprehension in stored memory. Recall that comprehension is a cognitive function that integrates novel information with existing information, along with, perhaps, other novel pieces of information. Two (or more) separate items or chunks of information may be integrated, depending on how the thinker deems them relevant to one another, through schema construction; and create what Hammond refers to as these 'novel and attractive solutions'. Thus, contrary to Hammond's perspective, it is reasonable to conclude that intuition is nothing more than recognition – recognition of schemas that allow for automatic judgment.

On the other hand, notably, Klein focuses on the *recognition* function of naturalistic decision-making and the RPD and avoids describing it as an intuitive process; rather, he describes RPD, consistent with Cognitive Continuum Theory, as an integration of intuition and reflection (2008). In the context of CT, this reflection refers to one's ability to analyse and evaluate particular situations. Specifically, the pattern-matching is the intuitive component of RPD, whereas the mental simulation requires the reflective component of RPD. Klein (2008, p. 458) notes the importance of this integration in that, with reference to applying this model to the example of fireground commanders, 'A purely intuitive strategy relying only on pattern matching would be too risky because sometimes the pattern matching generates flawed options. A completely deliberative and analytical strategy would be too slow; the fires would be out of control by the time the commanders finished deliberating.'

It is further worth noting that though experience is the critical component of expertise, within the field of judgment and decision-making research, experience is very often observed to be unrelated to the accuracy of expert judgements and sometimes negatively correlated with accuracy (Goldberg, 1990; Hammond, 1996; Kahneman, 2011; Stewart et al., 1992), perhaps as a result of overconfidence (Kahneman, 2011) or perhaps as a result of large amounts of experience in doing the wrong thing (Hammond, 1996). However, if empirical evidence indicates that experience is not a crucial factor in predicting accuracy, then the question remains as to why RPD and other decision-making models that focus on the importance of experience are rational to promote. Simply, the answer boils down to the structure of the situation or, more specifically, the structure of the task.

To reiterate, the type of thought, or the proportion of intuitive thought used relative to reflective thought, depends on the nature of the task (Hamm, 1988; Hammond, 1996). This is important to consider given that tasks vary with respect to the complexity, ambiguity and presentation of the task structure and content (Hamm, 1988). That is, there also exists a continuum between reflection-inducing tasks and intuition-inducing tasks (Hammond, 1996). For example, in an ill-structured problem, experience may not necessarily aid the decision-making process, given the associated uncertainty. However, in a well-structured problem, where there is only one correct solution, relevant experience in the domain associated with the problem will aid the decision-making processes, perhaps automatically, because the individual can respond based on factual knowledge. Based on that logic, and consistent with discussion in this chapter and in Chapter 8, in the event that an ill-structured problem is encountered, more reflective judgment might be the only option in the search for a reasonable solution.

SUMMARY AND CONCLUSION

In summary, the ability to adapt to problem-situations is both practical and important because we face numerous problems each day, some of which require very little reflection; some which require deeper, more reflective consideration; and some which require a 'delicate balance' of both (Langley, 1995). Though most contemporary research on judgment and decision-making has focused on the strengths of reflective judgment, which is associated with cognitive control, conscious awareness, consistency and accuracy (Cader, Campbell, & Watson, 2005; Hamm, 1988; Kahneman, 2011), and the limitations associated with heuristic-based, intuitive judgment, it remains that reflective judgment can be a slow process, which can be easily disrupted from loss of attention. Thus, reflective judgment is not always practical.

Though the type of judgments made largely depend on external factors, for example, the task structure or situational variables, they also depend on internal factors, for example, the motivation of an individual to suppress 'gut' instinct, emotion and intuition (Lieberman, 2003; Weber & Johnson, 2009), as well as an individual's expertise and experience relevant to the problem or situation (Weber & Johnson, 2009). Depending on the presence of task-relevant expertise and experience, as well as the task structure, intuitive judgment has been argued as a viable option, given emerging acknowledgement of its benefits (e.g. Dane & Pratt, 2007; Hammond, 1996; Hamm, 1988; Hodgkinson et al., 2008, 2009; Salas, Rosen, & DiazGranados, 2010), especially in the field of organizational psychology. Although the importance of intuitive, expertise-based judgment is recognized as an important tool in organizational settings, given its observed success as a practical cognitive application, it is also important to acknowledge that the use of intuitive judgment alone is not sufficient (Dhami & Thomson, 2012) and should be employed, when possible, in conjunction with reflective judgment (Hamm, 1988; Hammond, 1996; Klein, 2008; Simon, 1987).

The mixture of intuitive and reflective judgment, known as quasi-rationality, is an adaptive form of thought, the strengths of which, as a construct, are its robustness and flexibility; and its weaknesses are imprecision and inconsistency. Whereas the former allows for individuals to cope with ever-changing situations, the latter may induce inaccuracy and the potential for both irrationality and interpersonal conflict (Hammond, 1996). With that said, although a judgment process based on heuristics can result in appropriate behaviours in certain situations (e.g. unreflectively looking both ways before crossing a street), in the context of CT, such processes more often than not result in poor judgments and decisions about what to believe and what to do. Much of the research conducted on heuristics and biases have implications for the manner in which CT is applied – reflective thought in CT may require the application of causal reasoning, probabilistic reasoning, hypothetical thought, theory justification, assessment of the covariation of events, scientific reasoning, disjunctive reasoning, the tendency to think statistically and the tendency to think of alternative explanations (Facione, 1990b; Halpern, 2014; Kahneman, 2011; West, Toplak, & Stanovich, 2008). Thus, in order to think critically, one must embrace the notion of reflective judgment and the sole use of heuristics (and associated biases) should be avoided (West, Toplak, & Stanovich, 2008). However, caution of intuition and promotion of reflective judgment are not enough for the CT to develop – as you will see, the development and improvement of CT skills have been the focus of a large body of research. The purpose of the following chapter is to discuss research that has examined both strategies designed to improve CT and methods of how we can best discern whether or not CT ability has improved.

11

Critical Thinking Instruction and Assessment

The direction in which education starts a man will determine his future life.

~ Plato (c. 427–347 BC)

According to Willingham (2007, p. 8), 'virtually everyone would agree that a primary, yet insufficiently met, goal of schooling is to enable students to think critically', and that this insufficient meeting of critical thinking (CT) goals may stem from, Willingham argues, the inability to teach CT due to its domain-specific nature. Though the goal of enabling students to think critically is quite often insufficiently met (Kuhn, 1991; Lloyd & Bahr, 2010), the latter half of Willingham's assertion has been largely disputed by the CT research literature. That is, CT is a domain-general skill (i.e. it does not require knowledge of any specific academic field) and a large body of research reveals that not only can CT be taught, but it can also be improved by such instruction (e.g. Butchart et al., 2009; Dwyer, Hogan, & Stewart, 2012; Gadzella, Ginther, & Bryant, 1996; Hitchcock, 2004; Reed & Kromrey, 2001; Rimiene, 2002; Solon, 2007).

Teachers and students can use a variety of different strategies to facilitate CT ability, but given that CT takes time to develop (Halpern, 2014; King, Wood, & Mines, 1990), the most prominent among these strategies are those aimed at providing extended training in CT. In this context, the overall pattern of findings in the literature helps to situate the importance of CT in educational settings and aid our understanding of both the nature of CT assessment and why strategic CT instruction is a critical factor in enhancing CT ability. Thus, in this chapter, a selective review of previous research examining both the effects of various CT training interventions and CT assessment strategies is presented.

CRITICAL THINKING ASSESSMENT

CT courses have been taught at universities in varying academic domains including history, law, nursing, philosophy, psychology and sociology (to name just a few), all with the goal of improving CT performance. Such CT courses have also been informed by varying conceptualizations of CT (e.g. Ennis, 1987; Facione, 1990b; Halpern, 2014; Paul, 1993). According to Couch (2012, p. 8), 'too many people today use the term critical thinking in ways that are vague and at cross-purposes with how others use the term'. As a result, the varying conceptualizations of CT can make it difficult for researchers and teachers to understand or agree on its key components. These difficulties may impede the ability of researchers and teachers to construct an integrated theoretical account of not only how best to *train* CT skills, but also how best to *measure* CT skills. According to Knight (2007), a clear, unambiguous conceptualization of CT is necessary for fair and valid assessment of students' CT ability. This is important to consider as the matching of the conceptualizations used to teach and assess performance is vital in determining the success of the intervention (Romiszowski, 1981). As a result, researchers and educators must consider the wide array of CT measures available, in order to identify the best and the most appropriate, based on the CT conceptualization used for training. Popular measures of CT performance include the California Critical Thinking Skills Test (CCTST; Facione, 1990a), the Cornell Critical Thinking Test (CCTT; Ennis, Millman, & Tomko, 1985), the Watson-Glaser Critical Thinking Assessment (WGCTA; Watson & Glaser, 1980) and the Ennis-Weir Critical Thinking Essay Test (EWCTET; Ennis & Weir, 1985).

It has been noted by some commentators that these different measures of CT ability may not be directly comparable (Abrami et al., 2008). For example, the CCTST consists of thirty-four multiple-choice questions (MCQs) and measures CT according to the same core skills as identified by the Delphi Report (Facione, 1990b): analysis, evaluation and inference, as well as inductive and deductive reasoning. The CCTT consists of fifty-two MCQs that measure skills of CT associated with induction; deduction; observation and credibility; definition and assumption identification; and meaning and fallacies. The WGCTA consists of eighty MCQs that measure the ability to draw inferences, recognize assumptions, evaluate arguments, use logical interpretation and apply deductive reasoning (Watson & Glaser, 1980). The EWCTET is an essay-based assessment of the test-taker's ability to analyse, evaluate and respond to arguments and debates in real-world

TABLE 11.1   *Topics Assessed by EWCTET (Adapted from Ennis & Weir, 1985).*

Getting the point
Seeing the reasons and assumptions
Stating one's point
Offering good reasons
Seeing other possibilities (including other possible explanations)
Responding appropriately to and/or avoiding:
   Equivocation
   Irrelevance
   Circularity
   Reversal of an *if-then* (or other conditional) relationship
   The Straw Person Fallacy
   Overgeneralization
   Excessive scepticism
   Credibility problems
   The use of emotive language to persuade

situations (Ennis & Weir, 1985). The authors of the EWCTET provide what they call a 'rough, somewhat overlapping list of areas of CT competence', which is measured by their test (Ennis & Weir, 1985, p. 1). This list can be seen in Table 11.1.

In addition, the reported reliability and validity of different CT measures also vary, which has led Abrami and colleagues (2008, p. 1104) to ask: 'How will we know if one intervention is more beneficial than another if we are uncertain about the validity and reliability of the outcome measures?' Abrami and colleagues add that, even when researchers explicitly declare that they are assessing CT, there still remains the major challenge of ensuring that measured outcomes are related, in some meaningful way, to the conceptualization and operational definition of CT that informed the teaching practice. To reiterate, the matching of the conceptualizations used to teach and assess performance is vital in determining the success of the intervention (Romiszowski, 1981). However, too often the relationship between the concepts of CT that are taught and those that are assessed is unclear; and a large majority of studies in this area include no theory to help elucidate these relationships.

The format of many existing CT assessments (i.e. based on MCQs) makes CT measurement further problematic. The MCQ format is less than ideal because it allows test-takers to simply guess when they do not know the correct answer, instead of demonstrating their ability to critically analyse and evaluate problems and infer solutions to those problems (Ku, 2009). Furthermore, as argued by Halpern (2003b), the MCQ format of the CCTST makes the assessment a test of verbal and quantitative knowledge rather than CT (i.e. because one selects from a list of possible answers rather than determining one's own criteria for developing an answer; Ku, 2009). The measurement of CT through MCQs is also problematic given the potential incompatibility between the conceptualization of CT that shapes test construction and its assessment using MCQs. That is, MCQ tests assess cognitive capacities associated with identifying single right-or-wrong answers and, as a result, this approach to testing is unable to provide a direct measure of test-takers' use of metacognitive processes such as CT, reflective judgment and disposition (Halpern, 2014; Ku, 2009).

Furthermore, a large body of research suggests exercising caution when interpreting scores from the CCTT and the WGCTA (Berger, 1985; Helmstadter, 1985; Hughes, 1992; Malcolm, 1992; Modjeski & Michael, 1983), which are two such MCQ-based CT assessments, which 'are not without their own weaknesses' (Tsui, 1999, p. 191). Moreover, the CCTST, another one of the most commonly used MCQ-based CT assessments, suffers further drawbacks. Though the CCTST measures CT and CT sub-skills according to the Delphi Report definition and framework, it is not necessarily ideal for evaluating gain in intervention studies. For example, according to Jacobs (1995), the various CCTST forms (i.e. Forms A, B and 2000) are characterized by different levels of difficulty and should therefore not be used for purposes of measuring individual differences or gains from pre- to post-testing. In addition, each version of the CCTST (i.e. Forms A, B and 2000) contains a different number of questions per sub-scale. Thus, Jacobs (1995) recommends that one form should be used as both a baseline measure and a covariate when examining intervention group differences. This, however, is less than an ideal situation as this does not allow for the adequate measurement of CT gain (i.e. from pre-test to post-test).

In response to problems associated with MCQ-based CT assessments in general, it has been recommended that a better measure of CT might ask open-ended questions, which would allow test-takers to demonstrate whether or not they spontaneously use a specific CT skill (Dwyer, 2011; Ku, 2009). One commonly used CT assessment that employs an open-ended format is the EWCTET (Ennis & Weir, 1985). However, this test has been criticized for its domain-specific nature (Taube, 1997), the subjectivity of its scoring protocol and its bias in favour of those proficient in writing (Adams et al., 1996). At the current time, both MCQ and open-ended tests for assessing CT have their respective limitations.

One recent CT assessment, the Halpern Critical Thinking Assessment (HCTA; Halpern, 2010a), attempts to overcome this issue by combining the two response formats into one test (Ku, 2009), thus facilitating more reliable and valid CT measurement. The HCTA asks open-ended questions based on believable, everyday situations and examples categorized under the CT applications of argumentation; verbal reasoning; hypothesis testing; judging likelihood and uncertainty; and problem-solving (see Chapter 9), followed by specific questions that probe for the reasoning behind the answer. The multi-part nature of the questions makes it possible to assess the ability to use specific CT skills when the prompt is provided (Ku, 2009). This format and the sub-scales assessed provide a valid means of assessing CT. Test reliability is robust, with reported internal consistency ranging between $\alpha = .73$ and $\alpha = .88$ (Butler, 2012; Butler et al., 2012; Dwyer, Hogan, & Stewart, 2012; Halpern, 2010a).

Furthermore, future research on CT interventions could also move beyond measuring CT performance according to standardized tests that rely upon quantitative assessment, to include qualitative analyses of how students come to answer CT questions/problems. For example, research by Ku and Ho (2010b) examined students' CT ability using the HCTA, but did so by asking each student to 'talk aloud' when critically thinking about each question on the assessment. Results revealed that those who were proficient at CT engaged in more metacognitive activities and processes, including self-regulatory planning and evaluation skills. This type of qualitative examination can potentially shed greater light upon the nature of the skills used by students during CT and, more specifically, may also shed light on the relationship between metacognitive processes such as self-regulatory planning, the increase (or decrease) in disposition and motivation towards CT and the coupling (or decoupling) of self-regulatory functions of thinking and CT ability over time.

Moreover, it should be an aim of future research to develop a method of assessing various dispositional, attitudinal, epistemological and motivational factors towards learning and thinking in a manner other than self-report. Perhaps a method of researcher observation can be developed to measure such dispositional traits. Ku (2009) suggests that the HCTA can be used to do this, in that its open-ended nature of questioning requires students to exhibit dispositional traits in order to answer sufficiently.

However, Ku's recommendation is largely speculative, given that it is not accompanied by a clear method in which to either quantify or operationally observe disposition.

CRITICAL THINKING INSTRUCTION

Though the relationship between CT training and assessment is often unclear in CT interventions, researchers have attempted to group CT intervention studies in an effort to examine whether or not CT can be improved via explicit instruction and how it is best improved (Dwyer, 2011; Lloyd & Bahr, 2010). As noted in Chapter 2, research suggests that efforts to promote schema construction through some form of training can aid in the reduction of *intrinsic* cognitive load (Pollock, Chandler, & Sweller, 2002; van Merriënboer, Kirschner, & Kester, 2003), because those who possess relevant schemata, or some level of expertise in a knowledge or skill domain, are better equipped to assimilate information with high element interactivity than are those who do not possess the relevant knowledge or skills (Pollock, Chandler, & Sweller, 2002; Sweller, 2010). Specifically, training in CT may provide students with the opportunity to develop the CT schemas necessary to decrease the intrinsic cognitive load associated with the application of CT in situations of high element interactivity and also facilitate enhanced CT performance. This is reasonable to suggest given the large body of research which indicates that CT instruction can enhance CT ability.

For example, a recent meta-analysis by Alvarez-Ortiz (2007) examined fifty-two studies that investigated a wide range of teaching strategies designed to improve CT. The meta-analysis was specifically conducted in order to answer the question as to whether or not participation in philosophy courses improved CT ability. The criteria for inclusion in the meta-analysis were that studies must have had an intervention designed to enhance CT; a sample consisting of under-graduate students; CT as a dependent variable, measured by an objective MCQ test; conducted quantitative analysis (i.e. including data for an overall effect size, means, standard deviations and sample sizes); and a pre/post-test design. Notably, of the fifty-two studies, only twenty-nine used an intervention that explicitly taught at least some CT and only twelve of those used dedicated CT instruction (Alvarez-Ortiz, 2007). The remaining studies used interventions that taught other subjects, including philosophy, nursing, classics and history, psychology, politics and sociology and mathematics, but did not teach CT. Results of the meta-analysis revealed that participation in courses that taught at least some CT (effect size of .30 SD, CI [.16, .43]) yielded better CT performance than courses that did not explicitly teach CT in some form (effect size of .12 SD, CI [.08, .17]).

In another recent meta-analysis of CT interventions, conducted by Abrami et al. (2008), 3,720 studies that focused on CT were identified, and of those, 117 were deemed suitable for inclusion. Criteria for inclusion were:

(1) accessibility – the study must be publicly available or archived;
(2) relevancy – the study addresses the issue of CT development, improvement, and/or active use;
(3) presence of intervention – the study presents some kind of instructional intervention;
(4) comparison – the study compares outcomes that resulted from different types or levels of treatment (e.g. control group and experimental group or pre-test and post-test);
(5) quantitative data sufficiency – measures of relevant dependent variables are reported in a way that enables effect size extraction or estimation;
(6) duration – the treatment in total lasted at least 3 hours; and
(7) age – participants were no younger than 6 years old.

(Abrami et al., 2008, p. 1108)

The 117 studies yielded 161 independent effect sizes, from which Abrami and colleagues (2008) reported a significant effect ($g+$ =.34) of all CT courses included in the meta-analysis on CT performance. However, of these 161 effects, only 91 were measured using standardized CT assessments (which yielded an average effect size of $g+$ =.24), only 101 were from true ($g+$ =.34) or quasi-experiments ($g+$ =.36) and only 16 were derived from the effects of instructional training ($g+$ = 1.00).

Abrami and colleagues used Ennis's (1989) typology of four CT courses (i.e. general, infusion, immersion and mixed) to differentiate CT training methods. In the *general* approach to CT training, actual CT skills and dispositions 'are learning objectives, without specific subject matter content' (Abrami et al., 2008, p. 1105). The *infusion* of CT into a course requires specific subject matter content upon which CT skills are practised. In the infusion approach, the objective of teaching CT within the course content is made explicit. In the *immersion* approach, like the infusion approach, specific course content upon which CT skills are practised is required. However, CT objectives in the immersed approach are *not* made explicit. Finally, in the *mixed* approach, CT is taught independently of the specific subject matter content of the course.

Comparing the four CT course types, results of the meta-analysis revealed that courses using the mixed approach had the largest effect on CT performance ($g+$ =.94), followed by the infusion approach ($g+$ =.54), the general approach ($g+$ =.38) and the immersion approach ($g+$ =.09), respectively. It is important to note that the immersion approach (which had the smallest effect) is the only approach that does not make CT objectives explicit to students. This finding indicates that making CT objectives and requirements clear to students may be an important part of any course design aimed at increasing CT ability (Abrami et al., 2008). Furthermore, Abrami and colleagues concluded that the enhancement of CT ability is greatly dependent upon how CT is taught and, more specifically, that the *mixed* and *infusion* approaches to teaching CT worked best as students were explicitly taught how to use and apply CT skills to other course content. This finding is consistent with more recent research, which indicates that explicit CT instruction is an effective method of enhancing CT skills (Bensley et al., 2010; Dwyer, Hogan, & Stewart, 2012; Marin & Halpern, 2011).

Though these meta-analyses have provided many interesting results, the issue of the inclusion of non-controlled studies should be considered. For example, though both meta-analyses discussed earlier included the criterion that studies incorporated into the meta-analysis must have compared outcomes that resulted from different types or levels of treatment (e.g. control group/experimental group design *or* pre- to post-testing), this criterion did not ensure that all studies contained a control group (i.e. many studies used a pre- to post-testing design only). As a result, the effect sizes reported in both meta-analyses are derived from a mixed sample of controlled and non-controlled studies and should therefore be interpreted with caution. Notably, the inclusion of a control group or a similar experimental group with which to compare a CT intervention is necessary in order to confidently conclude that gains in CT observed are a result of the CT intervention and not simply the result of practice effects or maturation effects. For example, previous research has shown that CT skills can increase over time, without the aid of a CT intervention, as a result of maturation or experience (Pascarella & Terenzini, 1991).

Following an in-depth review of the available literature on CT interventions, five research studies have been selected for further detailed discussion (i.e. Gadzella, Ginther, & Bryant, 1996; Hitchcock, 2004; Reed & Kromrey, 2001; Rimiene, 2002; Solon, 2007), because they all (1) examined CT performance as a dependent variable; (2) provided participants with explicit instruction in CT; (3) assessed an adult sample (e.g. undergraduate students); (4) conducted quantitative analysis of the results (i.e. including data for an overall effect size, means, standard deviations and sample sizes); and importantly, (5) to some degree described the conceptualization of CT used as the basis to instruct and train CT skills within the intervention. The last criterion for inclusion in this selective review is particularly important to consider because, due to the many varying conceptualizations of CT available, there is no definitive method of how best to teach and measure CT. Having said that, only a handful of studies that examined the effects of CT instruction/ training on CT performance have described in any detail the conceptualization of CT used as the basis to instruct and train CT skills. Quite often, the detail that is provided in this context is very limited. In addition, it is important to note that though all five studies reviewed later also compared CT performance outcomes that resulted from different types or levels of treatment (e.g. pre- and-post-test design), this does not mean that they all included a control group, which is a common problem in CT intervention research. Although the importance of including a control group was discussed earlier and will continue to be an important criterion of experimental rigour in CT intervention research, the main purpose of this selective review is to demonstrate the variety of different conceptualizations of CT used in past CT training research and to critically examine the issues of alignment between conceptualization, training and assessment of CT.

Gadzella, Ginther, and Bryant (1996) investigated the effects of a fourteen-week long CT course on the CT performances of 113 first-year university students. Students in the intervention were assessed prior to commencement of the CT course via the administration of the WGCTA, Form A (Watson & Glaser, 1980). During the course, students 'were taught CT skills and given problems (and brought some of their own) which were analysed by the whole class, small groups and individual students' (Gadzella, Ginther, & Bryant, 1996, p. 5). According to the Gadzella and colleagues, the main focus of CT instruction was the analysis and solving of problems. Though the authors do not describe their conceptualization of CT in great detail, they do provide two definitions of CT – by Chaffee (1988) and Dressel and Mayhew (1954) – which they claim were the basis for the conceptualization of CT taught to students. Chaffee (1988, p. 29) defined CT as 'active, purposeful and organised efforts to make sense of our world by carefully examining our thinking and the thinking of others, in order to clarify and improve our understanding'. Dressel and Mayhew (1954) defined CT as 'exclusively linked with abilities that are needed for solving problems, selecting pertinent information for problem-solving, recognising assumptions, formulating hypotheses, drawing valid conclusions and judging the validity of inferences' (Gadzella, Ginther, & Bryant, 1996, p. 3).

As addressed by Gadzella, Ginther, and Bryant (1996), as well as Watson and Glaser (1980, 1994), the WGCTA was developed in light of both research conducted by Glaser (1941) and Dressel and Mayhew's definition of CT. These influences are evident as there is a great deal of congruence between Dressel and Mayhew's definition and what the WGCTA measures (e.g. they both highlight the skills of recognizing assumptions, evaluation and inference). After completion of the course, students completed the WGCTA, Form B. Results revealed a significant gain in CT ability from the pre-test assessment (M = 47.69, SD = 10.03) to post-test assessment (M = 51, SD = 7.88) with an effect size of d =.37. Notably, gains in CT were not compared with those of a control group.

Research by Hitchcock (2004) examined the effects of a computer-assisted CT course on CT performance (i.e. computer-assisted instruction was provided to students as a series of tutorials). A total of 402 undergraduate students participated in the study, of which 278 completed both pre- and post-testing. Students in the intervention were assessed prior to the commencement of the CT course using either Form A or Form B of the CCTST.

After completion of the pre-test, students engaged in 15.8 hours of computer-assisted CT training over the duration of thirteen weeks. The components of CT trained in this study were based on LeBlanc's (1998) book, *Thinking Clearly*. There were two class-based MCQ assignments on the nature of argumentation, which were completed by the students in groups. Students also completed exercises derived from LeBlanc's (1998) *Thinking Clearly*, as well as MCQs and exercises from the computer-software LEMUR, which was used as a means of presenting computer-assisted CT instruction. There was also a course website available to students, in which answers to the textbook exercises were posted, as were additional MCQ exercises and past exams with answers. However, the extent to which students used the software or website was not monitored. As this was a compulsory course, students were also assessed via midterm and final examinations, in which the former covered up to and

TABLE 11.2 *Critical Thinking Skills Taught to Students in Hitchcock (2004)*

Identifying arguments
Standardizing arguments
Necessary and sufficient conditions
Language (definitions and fallacies of language)
Accepting premises
Accepting relevance
Arguments from analogy
Arguments from experience
Causal arguments

including *accepting premises*, and the latter covered all topics, as listed in Table 11.2. Although the skills identified in Hitchcock's conceptualization and those measured by the CCTST are not entirely congruent, some of the components of CT identified by Hitchcock (e.g. identifying arguments, accepting premises, accepting relevance and arguments from experience) are measured by the CCTST as sub-components of the skills of analysis and evaluation (see Chapters 4–6). After completion of the course, students completed the CCTST post-test (i.e. either Form A or B – the opposite of what was completed at pre-testing). Analysis of change over time revealed that the students showed a significant gain in CT performance of 6.44% points on the CCTST – an effect size of .49 SD. However, it is important to note that much like Gadzella, Ginther, and Bryant (1996), a control group was not included for comparison purposes in Hitchcock's study.

Solon (2007) examined the effects of infusing CT into an introductory psychology course (i.e. teaching an introductory psychology course by means of having students critically think about the topics encountered). Fifty-one students participated. Twenty-six students were allocated to a control group condition (i.e. students attended an introductory psychology course without the infusion of CT). Twenty-five students were allocated to the experimental group, in which, over the duration of the course, students were required to think critically about a variety of psychology topics. Solon's list of CT skills applied to each topic is presented in Table 11.3. Students in the experimental group also completed ten reading and writing homework assignments, derived from chapters 4–7 of Diane Halpern's (2003a) *Thought & Knowledge: An Introduction to Critical Thinking*; and part II of Meltzoff's (1998) *Critical Thinking about Research: Psychology and Related Fields*. More specifically, these homework

TABLE 11.3 *Solon's Conceptualization of Critical Thinking*

Critical thinking as a set of basic and generic reasoning skills, including
the ability to identify and/or distinguish between:
1. Inferences and non-inferences
2. Assumptions (covert as well as overt) and conclusions
3. Consistent and inconsistent statement sets
4. Deductive and inductive reasoning
5. Valid and invalid arguments
6. Credible versus seriously questionable claims and courses
7. Meaningful versus vague, ambiguous and/or meaningless language
8. Relevant versus irrelevant evidence
9. Scientific versus pseudo-scientific procedures

assignments involved deductive reasoning, argument analysis, thinking as hypothesis testing and understanding probabilities, likelihood and uncertainty (Halpern, 2014). Ten hours of in-class activity were devoted to a review of Halpern, Meltzoff and related exercises.

Both the experimental and control groups were administered the CCTT (Form Z) as pre- and post-tests. Solon acknowledged that the issue of compatibility between what is taught as part of CT training and what is measured is important to consider, for purposes of clarifying whether or not it is the training of certain skills that is responsible for their improvement. Solon also noted that the conceptualization of CT skills taught to students in his study and the manner in which CT skills were assessed was compatible, as the CT abilities laid out in this conceptualization of CT were 'observable, measurable and readily lend themselves to objective standardised testing, as in the Cornell' CT test (Solon, 2007, p. 96). The level of compatibility between what was taught and what was measured can be seen through comparison of Table 11.3 (i.e. what was taught in the study) and what the CCTT measures (i.e. induction; deduction; observation and credibility; definition and assumption identification; and meaning and fallacies).

Notably, the results of Solon's research revealed that those who participated in the CT-infused psychology course performed significantly better on CT ability than the control group on post-testing with an effect size of .66 *SD*, CI [.08, 1.24]. Results also revealed that students in the experimental group showed a significant gain in CT ability with an effect size of .87 *SD*, CI [.28, 1.47]. As the control group did not demonstrate a significant gain in CT ability ($p = .49$), the results suggest that the gain observed in CT ability in the experimental group was not a result of a practice effect (i.e. the same form of the CCTT was used at both pre- and post-testing). It is worth noting that the research conducted by Solon (2007) was one of the richest and most informative CT intervention studies reviewed, not only because it was a controlled study, but also because a more detailed account, relative to the other studies, was provided for how the CT conceptualization used in the intervention aligned with both the training and assessment.

Reed and Kromrey (2001) also reported improvements in CT ability, as a result of infusing CT into a US history course. Students met for three hours per week for fifteen weeks. Following pre-testing on the EWCTET (Ennis & Weir, 1985) and the California Critical Thinking Dispositions Inventory (CCTDI; Facione & Facione, 1992), twenty-nine students in the experimental group were (a) explicitly taught Richard Paul's (1993) model of CT (i.e. *Elements of Reasoning*, which focuses on elements of good, quality thinking, reasoning and disposition; see Table 11.4) and (b) trained to use Paul's elements of reasoning to analyse primary source documents and historical problems.

Students completed homework assignments that required the use of Paul's model and were provided with a packet of handouts that graphically displayed and further explained the model. Finally, students participated in classroom discussions, which focused on the elements and standards set forth within Paul's (1993) model. Twenty-three participants in the control group completed the same assignments as part of their history course, but did not receive any CT instruction. Upon completion of the course, both groups again completed the EWCTET and the CCTDI.

Results revealed no differences between the CT and control groups on the EWCTET or the CCTDI at pre-testing, suggesting that both groups were adequately matched prior to the intervention. Results from post-testing revealed that those who received the CT training scored signifi-cantly higher than the control group on the Ennis-Weir test with an effect size of $f = .83$; and that there was no difference between the groups on CCTDI scores. The null-finding on the CCTDI suggests that the improve-ment in CT ability made by the CT training group was not a result of change in students' disposition toward thinking.

Rimiene (2002) investigated the effects of a three-month long CT course on the CT performances of 77 university students, in comparison with a control group of 150 students who did not attend the CT course. Students were randomly allocated to their respective groups. All students were assessed prior to commencement of the CT course on both the CCTST and the CCTDI. There were no differences between groups on pre-test performance, suggesting that both groups were appropriately matched.

TABLE 11.4 *Paul's Elements of Reasoning (Adapted from Paul, 1993)*

Elements of Reasoning	Description
Purpose of thinking	Take time to state purpose clearly. Distinguish purpose from other related purposes. Choose significant and realistic purposes.
Question at issue	Take time to clearly state the question at issue and express it in several ways to clarify its meaning and scope. Break the question into sub-questions. Identify if the question has one correct answer or requires reasoning from more than one point of view.
Information	Gather sufficient information and restrict claims to those supported by the data readily available. Search for information that both refutes and supports the information. Information used should be clear, accurate and relevant to the question at issue.
Interpretation and inference	Infer only what the evidence implies. Check inferences for their consistency with each other. Identify assumptions that lead to the conclusions made.
Concepts	Identify key concepts and provide clear explanations and consider alternative concepts or alternative definitions to concepts.
Assumptions	Clearly identify assumptions and determine whether they are justifiable and consider how assumptions shape the bias/balance of the reasoning, or point of view.
Implications and consequences	Trace and consider all the implications and consequences that follow from the reasoning.
Points of view	Identify the point of view; seek others and identify their strengths as well as weaknesses. Strive to be fair-minded in evaluating all points of view.

The CT course 'was based on the precepts of humanistic psychology and meaningful learning, and the aims were to introduce students to CT theory, to develop CT skills and to strengthen motivation for CT' (Rimiene, 2002, p. 18). Both Facione, Facione, and Giancarlo (1997) and the Delphi Report (Facione, 1990b) were cited in Rimiene's conceptualization of skills necessary for CT – both of which name analysis, evaluation and inference as core CT skills. During the course, 'students learned the principles and stages of CT, the main criteria of successful thinking and solved different problems' through various forms of active learning including 'brainstorming, problem-solving, reflexive writing, active listening, purposeful research, co-operative learning, conversations, discussions, debates, projects and demonstration' (Rimiene, 2002, pp. 18–19). After completion of the course, all students were again assessed on both the CCTST and the CCTDI.

Results revealed that though there was no difference between groups at pre-testing, students in the CT group scored significantly higher than those in the control group on overall CT (d = 1.57), analysis (d = .85), evaluation (d = 1.13), inference (d = 1.30), inductive reasoning (d = 1.10), deductive reasoning (d = 1.30) and overall disposition towards thinking (d = .62) at post-testing. Results also revealed that students in the CT group scored significantly higher on overall CT (d = 1.09), analysis (d = .37), evaluation (d = .82), inference (d = 1.10), inductive reasoning (d = .64), deductive reasoning (d = 1.17) and overall disposition towards thinking (d = .49) at post-testing when compared with pre-testing. There were no differences between pre- and post-test scores for the control group.

The findings from this study are interesting to consider given that both CT ability and disposition of those who participated in the CT course increased from pre- to post-testing. Though CT ability may have developed over time as a result of instruction, it is also possible that improved dispositions towards thinking may have been the catalyst for growth in CT ability. The latter possibility is consistent with both Marzano's (1998, 2001) view on the powerful role of positive self-system changes on educational outcomes (see Chapter 1) as well as previous research and theory that suggests that not only are self-regulatory functions of CT (e.g. dispositions) and CT abilities correlated, but that these metacognitive processes are dependent on one another in order to conduct CT (Ennis, 1996, 1998; Halpern, 2006, 2014; Ku, 2009; Ku & Ho, 2010a; Perkins & Ritchhart, 2004; Valenzuela, Nieto, & Saiz, 2011). In light of past research (e.g. Reed & Kromrey, 2001), it seems likely that beneficial effects of training on CT ability can be observed in absence of any changes in self-regulated thinking dispositions. Nevertheless, the impact that such dispositional factors may have on CT ability should not be overlooked, given that both theory and research suggest that the two are intimately related (Dwyer et al., 2014; Dwyer, Hogan, & Stewart, 2011, 2012, 2015; Ennis, 1998; Facione et al., 2002; Halpern, 2006, 2014; Ku & Ho, 2010a; Marzano, 1998).

SUMMARY AND CONCLUSION

On balance, it is clear that a variety of different conceptualizations of CT have been used as the basis to instruct and train CT skills. However, the degree of alignment between conceptualizations of CT, training methods and measures of CT used can vary considerably from one study to the next; and it is unclear precisely what impact these variations have on the quality of interventions and their overall impact on students. What is clear is that research indicates that the crucial factor in improving CT is the explicit teaching of CT itself (Alvarez-Ortiz, 2007; Bensley et al., 2010; Marin & Halpern, 2011).

Abrami and colleagues' (2008) meta-analysis also suggests that making CT learning objectives explicit to students is vital to improving CT ability. However, as Abrami and colleagues' meta-analysis was conducted in light of very broad distinctions between different types of CT training courses, less is known about how more specific pedagogical and educational strategies, including different presentation strategies and study methods (e.g. argument mapping, outlining and other text-based presentation/study methods); as well as learning/study environments (e.g. in-class, online, collaboratively, isolated, etc.), impact overall training benefits.

While researchers (e.g. Solon, 2007) have begun to broach the critical issue of the alignment of CT theory, training and measurement in intervention studies, less research has focused on the manipulation of specific instructional design strategies for training CT (Dwyer, 2011; Lloyd & Bahr, 2010). Across studies, it may be possible to broadly evaluate whether or not some instructional tools are better than others. This issue is important to consider because, in addition to the way in which CT is taught and assessed, research suggests that the manner in which CT is presented and learned (i.e. through instructional tools and learning strategies), also impacts the enhancement of CT ability. Thus, in the following chapter, we will discuss a number of pedagogical and learning strategies and tools that have been observed in the research literature to have a beneficial effect on CT.

12

Pedagogical and Learning Strategies

The function of education, therefore, is to teach one to think intensively and to think critically ... The complete education gives one not only power of concentration but worthy objectives upon which to concentrate.

~ Martin Luther King Jr. (1929–1968)

In the last chapter, we learned that numerous conceptualizations of critical thinking (CT) have been used to inform the instruction and assessment of CT. We also learned that this can be problematic, as we cannot always be sure that the manner in which CT is taught matches the way in which it is assessed; and subsequently, whether CT is being accurately assessed. Thus, in order to ensure the success of a CT intervention, it is necessary to provide clear guidelines regarding how CT is taught and assessed, as well as the goals of the CT intervention. We also learned that not only can CT be taught, but it is done so best when the CT element of instruction is made explicit to students. However, within the CT research literature, there is not a very strong focus on explicit experimental manipulation of instructional tools and strategies within CT intervention study trials (Dwyer, 2011; Lloyd & Bahr, 2010). More specific pedagogical and learning tools are important to consider in providing CT instruction because past research suggests that such tools and strategies may facilitate significant growth in CT abilities. For example, research suggests that *active learning* (e.g. Burbach, Matkin, & Fritz, 2004), online learning or *e-learning* (e.g. Butchart et al., 2009; Dwyer, Hogan, & Stewart, 2012; Newman et al., 1996), *collaborative learning* (e.g. Engelmann et al., 2010; Engelmann & Hesse, 2010; Kuhn et al., 2008; Wegerif & Dawes, 2004) and *argument mapping* (Butchart et al., 2009; Dwyer, Hogan, & Stewart, 2011, 2012; van Gelder, 2000) may have beneficial effects on overall CT and its associated skills and applications.

Thus, in the current chapter, we will discuss the use and efficacy of active learning, e-learning, collaborative learning and argument mapping as educational tools in CT instruction.

ACTIVE LEARNING

In the Introduction to this book, the point was made that too much class and study time is devoted to didactic instruction and the reading of textbooks, while not enough time is devoted to actively analysing and evaluating knowledge as it is acquired and constructed (Hogan, 2006). Specifically, educators spend about 80%of class time didactically lecturing to students (Fischer & Grant, 1983; Smith, 1983), whereas students only pay attention to approximately 50% of this didacticism (Pollio, 1984). Furthermore, research suggests that didactically teaching students for durations longer than fifteen minutes at a time can substantially decrease attention to the source of instruction thereafter (Wankat, 2002). Thus, in order to keep students attentive, they must be actively engaged, in some manner, with their learning (e.g. through class exercises).

According to Mayer (2004), students must be cognitively active during learning and educators must provide students with guided practice. This type of active learning provides students with a form of *scaffolding* (Wood, Bruner, & Ross, 1976), whereby students are guided didactically by their educator (and each other) and also actively *learn by doing*. The concept of scaffolding is quite similar and largely consistent with Vygotsky's (1978) theory of the *zone of proximal development* (ZPD), which is the gap between what a student can learn with and without help. Scaffolding is used to bridge the gap that is the ZPD and begins with passive learning (i.e. through didactic instruction), in which a student starts out as a novice in a specific subject area and is guided by someone who is more expert than the student (e.g. a teacher helps to develop a student's CT skills). Notably, guiding students through the provision of feedback is another important aspect of the active learning process, as active learning is more effective if students receive feedback on their performance (e.g. Butchart et al., 2009). For example, according to Marzano's (1998) meta-analysis, feedback on both the type of strategy used to improve learning and the efficacy of its utilization produced a significant gain in student achievement (with an effect size of 1.31). Furthermore, feedback can provide additional opportunities to evaluate and reflect upon one's own thinking (Dwyer, 2011).

Once the student becomes more comfortable with the types of problem/question(s) faced, the teacher gradually becomes less involved with the student's learning. It is then the student begins 'learning by doing' (i.e. active learning), given enough instruction is initially provided. Essentially, learning through scaffolding is much like an apprenticeship (Rogoff, 1998).

Research suggests that people learn more through active learning (e.g. Hake, 1998; Laws, Sokoloff, & Thornton, 1999; Perry et al., 1996; Redish, Saul, & Steinberg, 1997) and, more specifically, that the intensive, active practice of CT skills increases CT ability more so than didactic teaching of CT (Burbach, Matkin, & Fritz, 2004; Tsui, 2002). Active learning strategies are diverse and can be used alongside many other educational strategies, including e-learning, collaborative learning and argument mapping.

E-LEARNING

e-Learning is a method of instruction delivered through the use of multimedia technologies on a computer (e.g. software programmes or the Internet) designed to foster the transfer of information for purposes of achieving specific learning goals (Clark, 2005; Huffaker & Calvert, 2003). A report by the US National Research Council, which surveyed 1,206 public schools, suggests that the use of e-learning resources in conjunction with students' application of metacognitive processes (e.g. CT) can potentially improve learning (Huffaker & Calvert, 2003).

Past research has shown that online e-learning instruction can have a beneficial effect on learning in a variety of training contexts (e.g. Agarwal & Day, 1998; Brown, 2001; Chen, 2009; Hugenholtz et al., 2008; Johnson et al., 2004). e-Learning can prove efficacious provided that certain guidelines are adhered to (Clark, 2005; Mayer, 2003). For example, Mayer (2003) proposed that in order to design a multimedia e-learning course appropriately, the designer of the course must adhere to three basic 'cognitive assumptions' about learning. These assumptions are that (1) people process information both visually and phonologically (Mayer, 1997; Paivio, 1986); (2) people possess a limit for the amount of information that can be processed by either the visuospatial or the phonological coding system (Baddeley, 2000; Cowan, 2000; Miller, 1956); and (3) people learn more through active learning (e.g. Hake, 1998; Laws, Sokoloff, & Thornton, 1999; Redish, Saul, & Steinberg, 1997).

With respect to the design of e-learning courses, Clark (2005) proposes that e-learning is an efficacious method of both encouraging active learning (i.e. by providing students with the opportunity to complete multimedia exercises) and minimizing cognitive load. The use of e-learning interfaces can be used to reduce cognitive load in a variety of different ways, for example, by explaining complex visual content with audio narration and by using integrated visuospatial presentation strategies to reduce levels of element interactivity. Furthermore, students who participate in an e-learning course are able to engage in learning at a time and place that suits them (Clark, 2005) and can thus avoid clashes with other compulsory courses (e.g. in asynchronous e-learning, which is not instructor-led – instead, instruction is pre-recorded and made available online). In this context, the option to rewind and replay recordings and instructions also facilitates different learners who work at differences paces to optimize the rate of delivery to suit their own needs.

COLLABORATIVE LEARNING

In addition to the potential benefits of utilizing active learning and e-learning in CT instruction, research also suggests that providing students with opportunities to learn collaboratively or in computer-supported (e.g. e-learning-based) collaborative learning (CSCL) environments may enhance CT (e.g. Engelmann et al., 2010; Engelmann & Hesse, 2010; Kuhn et al., 2008; Wegerif & Dawes, 2004; Yang, 2002). It has been argued by Paul (1987, 1993) that dialogue, a fundamental component of collaborative learning, is necessary for CT. Furthermore, given that CT is often employed in scenarios that require debate and argumentation and that argumentation is a social activity (van Eemeren et al., 1996), it seems reasonable to recommend that CT ability may be optimized in collaborative learning settings.

The use of active dialogues in CT education is advantageous because it provides students with an opportunity to explain and question their own beliefs and arguments in light of the thinking and opinions of others involved in the dialogue. Notably, the opportunity to *elaborate* upon beliefs and arguments within a dialogue is in itself beneficial to CT, given that elaboration facilitates the construction of (new) knowledge (Dansereau, 1988; Newbern et al., 1994; Wittrock, 1986). In this way, the thinkers involved in the dialogue are actively engaged in collaborative learning.

The use of collaborative learning (and likewise, CSCL) is further recommended for use in CT instruction as previous research indicates that the use of CSCL strategies can facilitate: (1) higher grades on academic course assessments; (2) reasoned discussion among students; and (3) aid in focusing students to transfer these dialogic skills to curriculum-based learning (Engelmann et al., 2010; Engelmann & Hesse, 2010; Hwang, Shi, & Chu, 2011; Johnson, Johnson, & Stanne, 2000; Ma, 2009; Wegerif & Dawes, 2004). According to Johnson, Johnson, and Stanne (2000), there are over 900 research studies that have indicated positive effects of collaborative learning over and above other learning strategies, including individual and competitive learning. Furthermore, in Johnson, Johnson, and Stanne's (2000) meta-analysis of 164 high-quality studies, a number of cooperative learning strategies were shown to enhance scholastic performance; in particular, *learning together*, which was shown to enhance academic achievement significantly more than both competitive learning ($d = .85$) and individual learning ($d = 1.04$). Slavin (1995) describes a number of reasons why collaborative learning enhances academic performance, including both motivational and cognitive factors. According to Slavin, when students share a common goal and work together, they positively reinforce each other during their collaborative work, which motivates them to achieve higher standards of performance. Similarly, students are motivated to help one another in collaborative learning environments because it is in their own interest to do so. That is, as students involved in group projects are graded based on what the group achieves, as opposed to their own individual efforts, it is in the interest of each student to motivate and help their peers to work hard and perform well.

ARGUMENT MAPPING

Argument mapping, as introduced in Chapter 3, is a method of visually representing arguments using a 'box and arrow' diagrammatic format, with the aim of simplifying the reading of an argument structure and facilitating the assimilation of core statements and relations (i.e. the argument is made unambiguous and explicit, with no need for attention switching from paragraph to paragraph or from page to page in a linear text, in search for reasons and objections to the central claim around which the argument map is constructed). It is an active, educational learning tool that can be employed in both e-learning settings (e.g. through the use of argument mapping software, such as Rationale; van Gelder, 2007) and collaborative learning settings (e.g. the collaborative development of an argument map through a debate or dialogue). To reiterate, the argument map (again, see Figure 3.2 and Chapters 4–8 for examples) uses a 'box and arrow' design in which the boxes represent propositions (i.e. the central claim, reasons, objections and rebuttals) and the 'arrows' among propositions indicate the inferential relationships linking the propositions together (van Gelder, 2002). Thus, the provision of an arrow between two propositions indicates that one is evidence for or against another.

Similarly, colour can be used in an argument map to distinguish evidence for a claim from evidence against a claim. For example, in the software package Rationale™ (van Gelder, 2007), green represents a support and red represents an objection to the claim above. More generally, an argument map is designed in such a way that if one proposition is evidence for another, the two will be appropriately juxtaposed (van Gelder, 2001) and the link explained via a relational cue, such as *because, but* and *however.*

Modern argument mapping software, such as Rationale™ (van Gelder, 2007), allows for the creation of one's own argument map, by means of typing text into blank boxes and dragging these newly created propositions to their appropriate locations on the map. Single propositions, or entire branches of the argument, can be removed or dragged to another location, and edited in the process, in order to facilitate the reconstruction and easy manipulation of an argument map. This aspect of argument mapping is also useful when analysing and evaluating arguments. For example, if an individual observes an error in reasoning within an argument map, they can edit or delete propositions, add propositions, and edit or remove an entire chain of reasoning. Similarly, they can relocate propositions or chains of propositions to a new location on the map, and thus deepen their analysis and evaluation of propositions and argument structures in the process. In this sense, the manner in which propositions and chains of reasoning can be manipulated within an argument map may encourage deeper analysis and evaluation of the argument, as well as further refinements of its inferential structure.

A Brief History of Argument Maps

In Chapter 3, we discussed the important contributions to both informal logic and CT made by Stephen Toulmin – one of which was an example of the first modern argument mapping technique. However, Toulmin was not the first person to use argument maps or diagrams. Argument maps have existed for well over a century (Buckingham-Shum, 2003). In fact, the historical roots of modern argument mapping can be traced as far back as Socrates. Perhaps, the most famous pedagogical interaction in history takes place in Plato's *Meno.* Socrates, concerned about the nature of learning and knowledge, questions a young slave boy about the most basic principles of geometry. The exchange hinges upon Socrates literally drawing a set of figures in the dirt at their feet. He *displays* the concepts they are considering. The slave boy is rendered knowledgeable as he explicates the ideas implicit in the Socratic graphic designs. So begins a long and important relationship between philosophical inquiry and graphicacy – the use and understanding of figures, graphs, concept maps and other representational devices.

Consider also Petrus Ramus, the influential 16th-century philosopher, pedagogue and logician whose work shaped the teaching of logic for over one hundred years. As Walter J. Ong (1958) has shown, Ramus' work and influence was directly related to the development of the printing industry and his insights about the visual presentation of materials on the printed page. Ramus explicitly addressed the importance of the spatial arrangement of tables and text, seeing it as an integral part of the logical and pedagogical economy of his work. That is, he saw the arrangement of signs on the page as more than a matter of taste, and began the modern printing practice of combining tables, figures and text. This attention to the non-arbitrary logic of graphical representations resulted in his influence affecting not only what people thought, but also how people displayed their thinking (Ong, 1958).

A less obscure example is John Venn, the inventor of the Venn diagram, whose concerns for graphical representations of logical relations have had a wide-ranging impact to this day. He understood his diagrams as more than a mere heuristic (Venn, 1881). In his view, the search for new representational devices is part and parcel of the search for new ideas. Along these same lines, Charles S. Peirce, inspired by Venn, developed alternative modes for representing logical relations; a system that looked more like concept mapping than propositional calculus. Peirce's existential graphs, unlike Venn's diagrams, were built as a comprehensive system of logical expression (Shin, 2002). Peirce, like Venn and Ramus, reflected explicitly on the benefits of some graphical systems over others and on the non-trivial relation between graphicacy and philosophical inquiry, claiming that we need to build representational devices – moving beyond linear text – in order to adequately present some of the most important ideas in philosophy and logic.

The style of argument mapping endorsed by Toulmin, van Gelder and others dates back to 1826, when the practice was conducted by the logician Richard Whately, in his book *Elements of Logic* (Reed, Walton, & Macagno, 2007). Whately (1826) presented a hierarchical chain of

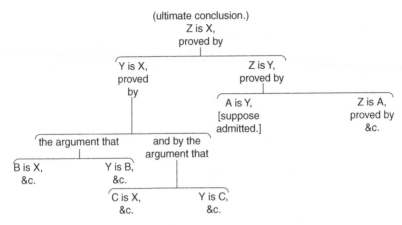

FIGURE 12.1 An Example of Whately's Model of Mapping

arguments (see Figure 12.1), which sought to reduce the structure of an argument to the necessary, relevant propositions such that logic and reasoning could be applied by the reader (Reed, Walton, & Macagno, 2007).

As Toulmin's ideas spread among those in the field of informal logic and argumentation during the late 1950s, the value of argument maps was soon recognized, resulting in the regular appearance of argument mapping in textbooks (e.g. Scriven, 1976; Fisher, 1988). Though the argument maps Toulmin developed were relatively simple, more recent attempts have been made to create maps of very complex arguments. For example, Robert Horn (1999) devised a set of seven maps (consisting of in excess of 750 propositions) that present arguments in relation to the question, *Can computers think?* Horn's argument mapping strategy (or *information mapping*) organized and presented arguments in a graphical array to facilitate easier assimilation of the structure of arguments, for such purposes as improving teaching and learning (Horn, 2003; Monk, 2001). Horn's work demonstrates that increasingly complex, ill-structured arguments (which may be difficult for a majority of the population to comprehend) can be translated into a manageable representation. Notably, Horn and Weber (2007) have also applied this mapping strategy to a range of social problems, in an effort to facilitate the reasoning and consensus of groups working to solve complex social problems.

Although argument maps have been in existence for almost 200 years (Buckingham-Shum, 2003; Reed, Walton, & Macagno, 2007; van Gelder,

2007), only recently has argument mapping technology become user-friendly. In the past, argument mapping was a slow and tedious task of drawing out measured boxes, filling them in with the appropriate text and accurately connecting them with arrows using only pen and paper. As a result, they have not been widely used as learning tools, despite the possibility that they may provide considerable advantages over standard prose as a medium for presenting reasoning. With the advent of various argument mapping software programmes, such as Rationale™ (van Gelder, 2007), the time required to construct an argument map has been substantially reduced, as the construction of an argument using this software needs only the choice of an appropriate box and associated relational cue, the typing of text into the box and the selection of an appropriate location for the box in the argument structure (i.e. in relation to other propositions).

Why Use Argument Maps?

To reiterate, an argument map is a diagrammatic version of any prose-based argument made in speech or text form. Diagramming can offer advantages over traditional text-based presentation of information because the indexing and structuring of information can potentially support essential computational processes (i.e. comprehending propositional relationships; Berkowitz, 1986; Larkin & Simon, 1987; Oliver, 2009; Pollock, Chandler, & Sweller, 2002; Robinson & Kiewra, 1995; Tindall-Ford, Chandler, & Sweller, 1997). In addition, as diagrams can group all the necessary information together based on relatedness, it makes the search for specific, relevant information more efficient, which in turn supports perceptual inferences (i.e. 'seeing' the conclusion; Larkin & Simon, 1987, p. 98). Thus, assimilating information and inferences from an argument map is believed to be substantially easier than assimilating information and inferences within potentially unaccommodating linear text. In addition, asking students to produce diagrams, such as argument maps, can provide teachers with valuable insights into a student's 'mental model of the argument in question' (Butchart et al., 2009). Furthermore, such information can be used to support teachers in offering feedback to students or scaffolding student learning from simple to complex levels of argument comprehension, analysis and evaluation. Logically, as expertise in argument mapping grows, so does the ability to present a well-structured argument, which allows for improvement in writing ability as well.

Though other forms of mapping strategies exist, such as *concept mapping* and *mind mapping* (Buzan & Buzan, 1997), they differ from argument mapping based on the manner in which they are organized and the way in which each 'proposition' is presented. For example, concept mapping is a mapping method in which a set of terms, numbers, sentence fragments or full sentences (which represent propositions) are joined by a set of lines and arrows, based on some relation (Reed, Walton, & Macagno, 2007). Similarly, mind mapping is a method of concept mapping in which words or phrases are integrated with coloured (or non-coloured) pictures (i.e. used to represent a concept), in which the coupled pictures and text are connected via lines or arrows to demonstrate some type of relationship.

The problem with many concept mapping techniques is that they do not present an argument per se. Instead, they present a graphical structure that may act as a representation of a separate text, which might be used to diagram: the links among concepts, decision-making schemes, a set of plans or instructions, or, at best, act as an argument overview – which does not represent the argument in full. Thus, because the text of the argument and the diagram may often be separate entities, concept mapping may become more cognitively demanding by adding the necessity of switching attention from text to diagram and vice versa (e.g. Chandler & Sweller, 1991; Pollock, Chandler, & Sweller, 2002; Tindall-Ford, Chandler, & Sweller, 1997; see Chapter 2).

In addition, if the reader of a concept map is not familiar with the information from the text that the map is derived, then the map itself becomes meaningless. For example, in Figure 12.2, the mind map presents a relational link between 'Dry wall' and 'Interest rate' in the context of 'Supply and demand' (Budd, 2004), yet presents neither explanation nor a relational cue (e.g. *because, next, causes, but, alternatively*) as to the nature of the link. There are neither sentences nor any inferential structures to facilitate comprehension. Thus in this context, concept mapping strategies may not necessarily be useful pedagogical aids that are open to analysis by everyone.

Past research examining the efficacy of concept mapping and mind mapping techniques is mixed, which may be as a result of the issues described in the preceding paragraphs. For example, while research by Wheeler and Collins (2003) suggests that concept mapping may have beneficial effects on CT, research by Boyadjian-Samawi (2006) indicates otherwise. With respect to mind mapping, research by Farrand, Hussain, and Hennessy (2002) indicate that mind mapping has a beneficial effect on memory performance. However, research by D'Antoni et al. (2010) found

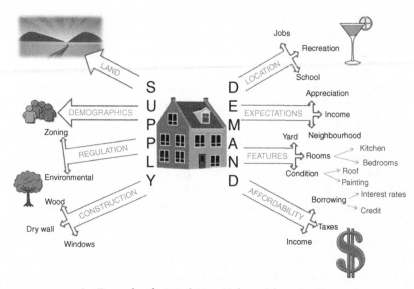

FIGURE 12.2 An Example of a Mind Map (Adapted from Budd, 2004)

that students who studied through the mind mapping technique performed no better than students who studied from standard note-taking
on tests of immediate recall. Notably, D'Antoni and colleagues further
found no significant effect of mind mapping on CT from pre- to post-
intervention or in comparison with students who participated in
a standard note-taking intervention.

Furthermore, though these mapping strategies are used primarily to
represent concepts, decision-making schemes and the organization of
plans (which they may do adequately), they are not specifically designed
to present arguments. That is, there is no strict usage of relational cues
within these concept mapping strategies because of their many applications, such as creating instructions, procedures and heuristics, or simply
linking concepts, rather than exclusively linking propositions within an
argument. However, in argument mapping, relational cues such as *because,*
but and *however* are necessary and must be used consistently, as they are
what 'glue' the structure of the argument together. Pedagogically, the
existence of these cues within an argument map is important as adequate
use of relational cues may help students and teachers to avoid cohesion
deficits (Dee-Lucas & Larkin, 1995; Duchastel, 1990). Thus, while argument
mapping is similar to other mapping strategies in some respects, due to the
nature of argument mapping (i.e. strictly dealing with argument

structures), it specifically focuses on the logical and evidential relationships among propositions.

As discussed in the last chapter, Alvarez-Ortiz's (2007) meta-analysis found that academic courses which provided at least some CT instruction facilitated CT ability better than academic courses that did not provide CT instruction. Notably, it was also found in Alvarez-Ortiz's (2007) meta-analysis that students who participated in CT courses that used at least some argument mapping infused within the course achieved gains in CT ability with an effect size of .68 SD, CI [.51, .86]. In courses where there was 'lots of argument mapping practice' (LAMP), there was also a significant gain in students' CT performance, with an effect size of .78 SD, CI [.67, .89]. The effect sizes for LAMP studies compared favourably with other CT intervention strategies reviewed in the last chapter, including teaching CT through philosophy (.26 SD) and computer-supported CT training (.49 SD). The effect size for LAMP studies was derived by Alvarez-Ortiz (2007) from a number of separate studies (e.g. Donohue et al., 2002; Butchart et al., 2009; Twardy, 2004; van Gelder 2000, 2001), which all indicate that the infusion of argument mapping into CT training has beneficial effects on CT ability. Other recent studies on argument mapping similarly suggest that its infusion into CT instruction has beneficial effects on CT ability (Dwyer, Hogan, & Stewart, 2011, 2012; van Gelder, Bissett, & Cumming, 2004).

Such beneficial effects could potentially be due to argument mapping's organizational features, which may help decrease the demands associated with *extraneous* cognitive load (again, see Chapter 2), while simultaneously enhancing various key cognitive processes (e.g. awareness of argument structure for analysis and coordinated evaluation of propositions marked as supports and rebuttals). There are a number of potential reasons for why argument mapping (and its associated features) has been shown to facilitate enhanced CT ability in past research. First, unlike standard text, argument maps represent arguments through dual modalities (visual-spatial/diagrammatic and verbal/propositional), thus facilitating the latent information-processing capacity of individual learners. Second, argument maps utilize Gestalt grouping principles that facilitate the organization of information in working memory and long-term memory, which in turn facilitates ongoing comprehension, analysis, evaluation and inference activities necessary to further promote the development of CT and reflective judgment skills in the classroom. Third, argument maps present information in a hierarchical manner, which also facilitates the organization of information in working memory and long-term memory for purposes of enhancing comprehension and promoting CT skills of analysis, evaluation, inference and reflective judgment.

In relation to the first reason, dual-coding theory and research (Paivio, 1971, 1986), Mayer's (1997) conceptualization and empirical analysis of multimedia learning and Sweller and colleagues' research on cognitive load (Sweller, 2010), suggests that learning can be enhanced and cognitive load decreased by the presentation of information in a visual-verbal dual-modality format (e.g. diagram and text), provided that both visual and verbal forms of representation are adequately integrated (i.e. to avoid attention-switching demands). That is, in order to keep cognitive load at a minimum, effort must be made to present information to students in a way that maximizes the potential of dual-modality forms of representation, such that students can successfully integrate the information in working memory and apply it through CT. Given that argument maps (AMs) support dual-coding of information in working memory via integration of text into a diagrammatic representation, cognitive resources previously devoted to translating prose-based arguments into a coherent, organized and integrated representation are 'freed up' and can be used to facilitate deeper encoding of arguments in AMs, which in turn facilitates subsequent, higher-order thinking processes (Halpern, 2014; Maybery, Bain, & Halford, 1986).

The second related reason for why argument mapping is hypothesized to enhance CT is because AM also makes use of Gestalt grouping principles. Research suggests that when to-be-learned items are grouped according to Gestalt cues, such as proximity and similarity, they are better stored in visual working memory (Jiang, Olson, & Chun, 2000; Woodman, Vecera, & Luck, 2003). For example, Jiang, Olson, and Chun (2000) examined how visual stimuli are organized in working memory by asking participants to identify target stimuli in a series of change-detection tasks, based on both spatial configuration (i.e. location) and colour. Results revealed that when the spatial organization, or relational grouping cues denoting organization (i.e. similar colour, close proximity), is absent, memory performance is worse, and that when multiple spatial organization cues (such as colour and location) are used, recall is better. These findings suggest that visual-based information in working memory is not represented independently, but in relation to other pieces of presented information and that the relational properties of visual and spatial information may be critical for successful CT.

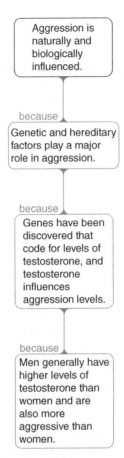

FIGURE 12.3 An Example of a Branch from an Argument Map

The third reason for why argument mapping is hypothesized to enhance CT is because it presents information in a hierarchical manner. The active construction of an argument map involves the extraction and summarization of key arguments and sub-arguments from a text. This active reconstruction and hierarchical ordering of arguments has been shown to benefit learning (Dwyer, Hogan, & Stewart, 2011; Taylor, 1982; Taylor & Beach, 1984). In addition, when arguing from a central claim, one may present any number of argument levels which need to be adequately represented for the argument to be properly conveyed (see Figure 12.3). For example, an argument that provides a (1) support for a (2) support for a (3) support for a (4) claim has four levels in its hierarchical structure. More complex or 'deeper' arguments (e.g. with three or more argument levels beneath a central claim) are difficult to represent in text due to its linear nature; and yet it is essential that these complex argument structures are understood by a student if their goal is to analyse or evaluate the argument and to, subsequently, infer their own conclusions.

The linear nature of text sometimes makes it troublesome to assimilate information because the reader must often switch attention from one paragraph, or even one page, to another and back and forth, in order to create some structural representation of the argument. This is consistent with research that suggests that individuals often have difficulty in extracting key propositions and evidence from text (c.f. Brem, 2000; Phillips, Norris, & Macnab, 2010). On the other hand, the hierarchical nature of AM allows the reader to choose and follow a specific branch of the argument in which each individual proposition is integrated with other relevant propositions in terms of their inferential relationship.

SUMMARY AND CONCLUSION

The current chapter discussed and recommended a number of pedagogical and learning tools (i.e. active learning, e-learning, collaborative learning and argument mapping) for use in CT instruction, in order to facilitate the development of CT abilities. These recommendations were made as existing research suggests that they all, when employed appropriately, enhance CT and CT sub-skill ability. They are also interesting to consider as a group of educational strategies and tools that can be collated and used simultaneously. That is, *argument mapping* can be used in *e-learning* settings, where students work *collaboratively* to *actively* construct, analyse and evaluate their own and each other's arguments; and then, work to infer a conclusion(s). This recommendation is not simply an idealistic hope for future CT instruction and education in general. Extant research has examined two or more of these educational tools (i.e. active learning, e-learning, collaborative learning and argument mapping) in a single instructional environment. For example, in past research, CT interventions that infused active learning, e-learning and argument mapping (e.g. Butchart et al., 2009; Dwyer, Hogan, & Stewart, 2012; van Gelder, 2000, 2001; van Gelder, Bissett, & Cumming, 2004) yielded beneficial effects on CT performance. Furthermore, recent research has also found beneficial effects of active, collaborative, argument mapping–based e-learning on CT performance (Dragon et al., 2011; Scheuer et al., 2012). Overall, it is recommended that future research should be conducted to further confirm the positive effects of active learning–based argument mapping as instructional support in collaborative, e-learning settings, given the existing research that indicates potentially beneficial CT enhancement effects of argument mapping, active learning, collaborative learning and e-learning strategies.

13

Summary and Conclusions

The important thing is not to stop questioning. Curiosity has its own reason for existing.
~ Albert Einstein (1879–1955)

As we discussed in the Introduction to this book, there is an exponential increase in the annual output of knowledge and, thus, it is not only the ability to draw upon knowledge that is necessary to achieve success in educational settings, but also the capacity to think critically. The teaching of critical thinking (CT) skills in higher education has been identified as an area that needs to be explored and developed (Association of American Colleges & Universities, 2005; Australian Council for Educational Research, 2002; Higher Education Quality Council, 1996). CT is a metacognitive process used to reflectively judge a situation, problem or argument, consisting of a number of sub-skills (i.e. analysis, evaluation and inference) and dispositions that, when used appropriately, increases the chances of producing a logical solution to a problem or a valid conclusion to an argument. Such skills are vital in educational settings because they allow students to go beyond simply memorizing information, to actually gaining a more complex understanding of the information being presented to them (Halpern, 2014). CT skills are not only important in the academic domain, but also in social and interpersonal contexts where adequate decision-making and problem-solving are necessary on a daily basis (Ku, 2009). Over the last several decades, educators, employers and organizations around the world have openly expressed concern about student preparedness for this 21st-century world (e.g. Association of American Colleges and Universities, 2010; Bureau of Labor Statistics, 2011; Butler et al., 2012; Halpern, 2010b; Hunt, 1995).

Though, the development of CT skills is often endorsed because these skills allow students to transcend lower-order, memorization-based learning strategies to gain a more complex understanding of the information or problems they encounter (Halpern, 2014; Pollock, Chandler, & Sweller, 2002); despite this, there has been little agreement on how to define CT, resulting in the existence of many diverse conceptualizations of CT. Consequently, the varying conceptualizations of CT can make it difficult for researchers and teachers to understand or agree on its key components and impede their ability to construct an integrated theoretical account of how best to train and measure CT.

Accordingly, the purpose of this book was to present a modern, detailed description of CT – one that can be employed in educational settings and used by *both* educators and students in order to adapt to the new knowledge economy of the 21st century – in order to overcome past, potential confusion as to what it is to think critically. In our discussion of CT throughout this book, we explored historical and conceptual perspectives on CT, the foundational processes necessary for CT, practical guidelines for CT assessment and instruction, as well as pedagogical and learning strategies that are likely to enhance CT performance. A number of active learning exercises were also presented throughout the book, in order to provide our student readers an opportunity to practise their CT skills and to provide the teacher population of our readers with examples and discussion of the types of CT exercises they should be administering in the classroom.

In Chapter 1, we discussed various frameworks of thinking processes that are necessary for CT (i.e. memory, comprehension, analysis, evaluation, inference and reflective judgment). Broadly speaking, two major components of thinking were distinguished, variously described as lower-order thinking skills (i.e. memory and comprehension) and higher-order thinking skills (i.e. CT and reflective judgment). Based on the discussion of thinking frameworks and the identification of the thinking processes necessary for CT, Chapter 2 examined these thinking processes in more detail, by reference to empirical research from the field of cognitive psychology (e.g. Baddeley, 1986, 2000; Chase & Simon, 1973; Chi, Glaser, & Rees, 1982; Kotovsky, Hayes, & Simon, 1985), which was important given that the ability to think critically about specific information is directly affected by one's ability to recall and understand the information one is required to think about (Dwyer, Hogan & Stewart, 2014; Halpern, 2014; Maybery, Bain, & Halford, 1986).

Specifically, short-term, working memory is a multi-component system for processing, encoding and retrieving information within brief periods of time, and through manipulation of that information within short-term storage, it can be transferred into long-term memory (i.e. a region of memory that enables relatively permanent storage of information), where it is presumably represented as a form of knowledge. According to Sweller (1994), the acquisition of knowledge is dependent upon schema construction, because it is only once a schema (i.e. knowledge) has been constructed that information can be comprehended.

Research suggests that memory and comprehension are interconnected processes (Sweller 1994, 1999, 2005) that are necessary for the application of CT skills (e.g. Halpern, 2014; Maybery, Bain, & Halford, 1986). Furthermore, research indicates that in order to improve learning and avoid cognitive load, efforts should be made to assimilate information multiple times – first, to understand the information and again to remember the information (Pollock, Chandler, & Sweller, 2002).

In Chapter 3, historical and conceptual perspectives on CT and brief discussions of the nature and use of falsification, formal logic and informal logic were presented. CT has a long and rich history, dating back 2,400 plus years to the time of Socrates. The work conducted by Aristotle on what we know as classical, formal logic alongside more recent endeavours in informal logic and argumentation have also largely contributed to what we know as CT. That is, by being able to assess the logical structure of an argument and the subject matter of that reasoning, we are able to begin to think critically about that subject. Furthermore, recognition of the important links among CT, logic and argumentation, as well as subsequent work in these fields have provided us with a means of visually representing our thinking in a graphical manner.

In Chapter 4, we discussed the many definitions of CT and pinpointed exactly what it is we mean by CT through a discussion of metacognition, self-regulatory functions of thinking, the Delphi model of CT (Facione, 1990b) and the various CT skills. The Delphi Report has shed some light on what CT is, given the consensus agreement of forty-six experts who indicated that CT is 'purposeful, self-regulatory judgment' (Facione, 1990b, p. 3), consisting of analysis, evaluation and inference. We used the Delphi model as a basis for the conceptualization of CT presented in this book.

We use analysis, evaluation and inference when we care about what to do and believe. When we want to decide what to do or what to believe, we can choose to think in a careful, logical, reasonable way. We weigh up our own reasons and objections when deciding what to do, and our decisions about what to do very often hinge upon what we believe. We can question our beliefs and the arguments that support our beliefs. This sceptical mode of thinking is a core part of what we call CT. Furthermore, arguments are hierarchical structures. Whether we are trying to decide what to do or what to believe, an argument of sorts ensues, in which we have a core idea/belief, a set of propositions (i.e. reasons and/or objections) that either support or refute the core idea/belief, and, if we like, additional sets of propositions that support these reasons and objections and in turn add to the complexity of our argument.

Chapters 5–8 focused on the description and practical use of the CT skills of analysis, evaluation, inference and reflective judgment, respectively. Analysis is a CT skill that is used to detect, examine and identify the propositions within an argument, their sources (e.g. research, common beliefs and personal experience), the role they play (e.g. the main conclusion, reasons provided to support the conclusion and objections to the conclusion) and the inferential relationships among propositions. When it comes to analysing the basis for a persons' belief, we can extract the structure of their argument for analysis (from dialogue and prose) by looking for arguments that support or refute the belief, and by looking for arguments that support this first level (or tier) of arguments, and so on. What we see as a result is a hierarchical structure, in which we can analyse each independent proposition by identifying what types of arguments others are using when trying to persuade us to share their point of view. Being able to analyse the structure of an argument and the types, or sources, of propositions used within an argument allows us to begin *evaluating* the argument.

Evaluation is a CT skill that is used in the assessment of propositions and claims in terms of their credibility, relevance, logical strength (i.e. with respect to their relationship with other propositions) and the potential for omissions, bias and imbalance in the argument. Evaluation is used to help us establish the truth of a claim. When we attempt to establish the truth of a claim through the evaluation of its supporting argument, our main objective is to arrive at some conclusions about the overall strengths and weaknesses of the argument. By evaluating the propositions used in an argument, with respect to their credibility, relevance, logical strength and balance of evidence, we can arrive at some conclusions about the overall strengths and weaknesses of arguments.

The final core CT skill, inference, refers to the gathering of credible, relevant and logical evidence based on the previous analysis and evaluation of available evidence, for the purposes of drawing a reasonable conclusion. This may imply accepting a conclusion pointed to by an author in light of the evidence they present, or proposing an alternative, equally logical, conclusion based on the available evidence. Though there is some overlap between the CT skills of inference and evaluation (i.e. querying the available evidence), good inference ability depends on good evaluation in order to be able to generate a justifiable conclusion. The ability to infer, or generate, a conclusion can be completed by both formal and informal logic strategies in order to derive intermediate conclusions as well as central claims. After inferring a conclusion, we must re-evaluate our resulting argument. To reiterate, when applying the skill of inference, we progress in a somewhat cyclical manner – from inference back to evaluation and again to inference until we are confident in our overall conclusion. An important by-product of this cycle is that our thinking becomes more complex, more organized and more logical.

Reflective judgment is a skill that 'umbrellas' analysis, evaluation and inference, in that reflective judgment is necessary to adequately conduct these three core CT skills. Reflective judgment involves the logical collection and evaluation of one's own evidence, leading to the inference of a conclusion and applied in an effort to solve a problem. This is completed by explaining one's reasoning in a logical and well-organized manner. Reflective judgment is a form of thinking in which we acknowledge that uncertainty exists among a variety of problems that we may face in thinking, with respect to academic contexts as well as in everyday situations. As it may be the case that no single, absolutely correct answer may exist for certain types of problems (i.e. ill-structured problems), it is reasonable to consider multiple, alternative solutions. However, some solutions are deemed better than others based on the careful consideration of facts regarding the problem. Therefore, it is not the conclusion that is important in reflective judgment, but rather the manner in which one arrives at the conclusion through structured thinking.

Chapter 9 investigated the many applications of CT in real-world settings (i.e. argumentation, verbal reasoning, hypothesis testing, judging likelihood and uncertainty, and problem-solving). From this discussion, we learned that CT is more than an idealistic conceptualization of how we should think – it is something we use on a day-to-day basis and something we should strive to improve. Notably, in order to apply CT in these types of real-world settings, we must be able to apply the skills analysis, evaluation and inference, cumulatively, along with our ability to reflectively judge situations, problems and arguments. The application of these skills as

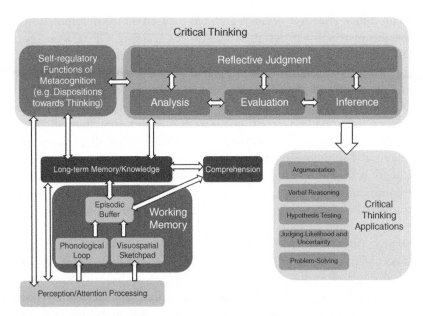

FIGURE 13.1 An Integrative Framework of Critical Thinking

a whole dictates whether our CT will be successful. See Figure 13.1 for the integrative framework of CT developed from Chapters 2–9.

Chapter 10 presented the opposite of reflective judgment – intuitive judgment – and discusses and evaluates not only the differences between these two forms of judgment but also the cognitive biases and heuristics that can negatively impact our thinking when we rely too heavily on intuitive thought. The types of thinking necessary to make reflective and intuitive judgments are often considered as poles on a continuum – thinking is never purely reflective, nor is it completely intuitive but instead lies somewhere in between these realms of thought. The chapter indicates that though reflective, CT is the ideal method for thinking about things we care about, it is not practical all of the time. Our judgments are always going to be a mix of intuitive and reflective forms of judgment, and it is important that we recognize this, so that we may in turn recognize our own uncertainty.

Chapters 11 and 12 discussed the nature of CT assessment and instruction; and CT development through pedagogical and learning strategies. A large body of research indicates that CT can be taught and is best done so through making CT learning objectives explicit to students (e.g. Abrami et al., 2008; Alvarez-Ortiz, 2007; Dwyer, Hogan, & Stewart, 2012;

Solon, 2007). However, less research has focused on the manipulation of specific instructional design strategies for training CT (Dwyer, 2011; Lloyd & Bahr, 2010). Thus, a number of pedagogical and learning tools (i.e. active learning, e-learning, collaborative learning and argument mapping) were discussed and recommended for use in CT instruction, in order to facilitate the development of CT abilities. These recommendations were made as existing research suggests that they all, when employed appropriately, enhance CT and CT sub-skill performance. They are also interesting to consider as a group of educational strategies and tools that can be collated and used simultaneously. Overall, it is recommended that future research should be conducted to further confirm the positive effects of active learning-based argument mapping as instructional support in collaborative, e-learning settings, given the existing research that indicates potentially beneficial CT enhancement effects of argument mapping, active learning, collaborative learning and e-learning strategies.

In conclusion, despite the consensus agreement of the forty-six-member Delphi committee regarding a CT definition and the skills that comprise CT, confusion exists over what it is to think critically. As a result of this confusion, there is a large body of extant research on CT that uses various conceptualizations, instructional strategies and methods of assessing CT. Accordingly, the purpose of this book was to rectify this confusion and present a modern, detailed description of CT – as a metacognitive process used to reflectively judge a situation, problem or argument, consisting of a number of dispositions and sub-skills (i.e. analysis, evaluation and inference) that, when used appropriately, increases the chances of producing a logical solution to a problem or a valid conclusion to an argument – which can be used by both educators and students in order to adapt to the new knowledge economy of the 21st century.

REFERENCES

Abrami, P. C., Bernard, R. M., Borokhovski, E., Wade, A., Surkes, M. A., Tamim, R., & Zhang, D. (2008). Instructional interventions affecting critical thinking skills and dispositions: A stage 1 meta-analysis. *Review of Educational Research, 78,* 4, 1102–1134.

Adams, M. H., Whitlow, J. F., Stover, L. M., & Johnson, K. W. (1996). Critical thinking as an educational outcome: An evaluation of current tools of measurement. *Nurse Educator, 21,* 23–32.

Agarwal, R. & Day, A. E. (1998). The impact of the Internet on economic education. *Journal of Economic Education, 29,* 99–110.

Allen, R., Feezel, J., & Kauffeld, F. (1967). *A taxonomy of concepts and critical abilities related to the evaluation of verbal arguments (Occasional Paper No. 9).* Madison, WI: Wisconsin Research and Development, Center for Cognitive Learning.

Alvarez-Ortiz, C. (2007). *Does Philosophy Improve Critical Thinking Skills?* Unpublished Master's Thesis, University of Melbourne, Australia.

Anderson, J. R. (Ed.). (1981). *Cognitive skills and their acquisition.* Hillsdale, NJ: Erlbaum.

Anderson, J. R. 1990. *The adaptive character of thought.* Hillsdale, NJ: Erlbaum.

Anderson, L. W. & Krathwohl, D. R. (2001). *A taxonomy for learning, teaching, and assessing: A revision of Bloom's taxonomy of educational objectives.* New York: Addison-Wesley.

Anderson, R. D. (1983). A consolidation and appraisal of science meta-analyses. *Journal of Research in Science Teaching, 20,* 497–509.

Andolina, M. W., Jenkins, K., Zukin, C., & Keeter, S. (2003). Habits from home, lessons from school: Influences on youth civic engagement. *Political Science and Politics, 36,* 2, 275–280.

Anicha, C. L., Ode, S., Moeller, S. K., & Robinson, M. D. (2011). Toward a cognitive view of trait mindfulness: Distinct cognitive skills predict its observing and nonreactivity facets. *Journal of Personality, 80,* 2, 255–285.

Association of American Colleges & Universities. (2005). *Liberal education outcomes: A preliminary report on student achievement in college.* Washington, DC: AAC&U.

Association of American Colleges & Universities. (2010). Raising the bar: Employers' views on college learning in the wake of the economic downturn. Retrieved from the AAC&U website: www.aacu.org/leap.

Athanassiou, N., McNett, J. M., & Harvey, C. (2003). Critical thinking in the management classroom: Bloom's taxonomy as a learning tool. *Journal of Management Education*, *27*, 5, 533–555.

Atkinson, R. C. & Shiffrin, R. M. (1968). Human memory: A proposed system and its control processes. In K. W. Spence & J. T. Spence (Eds.), *The psychology of learning and motivation*, 2, 89–195. New York: Academic Press.

Australian Council for Educational Research. (2002). *Graduate skills assessment: Stage one validity study*. Australia: Dept. of Education, Science and Training.

Ayres, P. & Sweller, J. (2005). The split-attention principle in multimedia learning. In R. E. Mayer (Ed.), *The Cambridge handbook of multimedia learning*, 135–146. New York: Cambridge University Press.

Baddeley, A. D. (1986). *Working memory*. Oxford: Oxford University Press.

Baddeley, A. D. (2000). The episodic buffer: A new component of working memory? *Trends in Cognitive Sciences*, *4*, 417–423.

Baddeley, A. D. (2002). Is working memory still working? *European Psychologist*, *7*, 85–97.

Baddeley, A. (2012). Working memory: Theories, models and controversies. *Annual Review of Psychology*, *63*, 1–29.

Baddeley, A. D., Eldridge, M., & Lewis, V. (1981). The role of subvocalisation in reading. *The Quarterly Journal of Experimental Psychology Section A*, *33*, 4, 439–454.

Baddeley, A. D. & Hitch, G. (1974). Working memory. In G. H. Bower (Ed.), *The psychology of learning and motivation: Advances in research and theory*, 8, 47–90. New York: Academic Press.

Baddeley, A. D. & Wilson, B. A. (2002). Prose recall and amnesia: Implications for the structure of working memory. *Neuropsychologia*, *43*, 4, 583–587.

Bargh, J. A. (1989). Conditional automaticity: Varieties of automatic influence in social perception and cognition. *Unintended Thought*, *3*, 51–69.

Bargh, J. A. (1997). The automaticity of everyday life. In R. S. Wyer (Ed.), *The automaticity of everyday life: Advances in social cognition*, 10, 1–61. UK: Psychology Press.

Bargh, J. A. (2002). Losing consciousness: Automatic influences on consumer judgment, behavior, and motivation. *Journal of Consumer Research*, *29*, 2, 280–285.

Baril, P. B., Cunningham, B. M., Fordham, D. R., Gardner, R. L., & Wolcott, S. K. (1998). Critical thinking in the public accounting profession: Aptitudes and attitudes. *Journal of Accounting Education*, *16*, 4, 381–406.

Bartlett, F. (1932). *Remembering: A study in experimental and social psychology*. New York: Cambridge University Press.

Barton, K. & McCully, A. (2007). Teaching controversial issues . . . Where controversial issues really matter. *Teaching History*, *127*, 13.

Basson, A. H. & O'Connor, D. J. (1968). *Introduction to symbolic logic*. London: University Tutorial Press.

Baumeister, R. F. (2002). Ego depletion and self-control failure: An energy model of the self's executive function. *Self and Identity, 1,* 2, 129–136.

Baumeister, R. (2003). The psychology of irrationality: Why people make foolish, self-defeating choices. *The Psychology of Economic Decisions, 1,* 3–16.

Bennett, G. K., Seashore, H. G., & Wesman, A. G. (1986). *Differential aptitude test.* Windsor, UK: Psychological Corporation & NFER-Nelson.

Bensley, D. A. (1998). *Critical thinking in psychology: A unified skills approach.* Pacific Grove, CA: Brooks & Cole.

Bensley, D. A., Crowe, D. S., Bernhardt, P., Buckner, C., & Allman, A. L. (2010). Teaching and assessing critical thinking skills for argument analysis in psychology. *Teaching of Psychology, 37,* 91–96.

Berger, A. (1985). Review of Watson-Glaser critical thinking appraisal. In J. V. Mitchell (Ed.), *Ninth mental measurements yearbook,* 1692–1693. Lincoln, NE: University of Nebraska, Lincoln, Buros Institute of Mental Measurements.

Berkowitz, S. J. (1986). Effects of instruction in text organization on sixth-grade students' memory for expository reading. *Reading Research Quarterly, 21,* 2, 161–178.

Bidell, T. R. & Fischer, K. W. (1992). Cognitive development in educational contexts. In A. Demetriou, A. Efklides, & M. Shayer (Eds.), *Neo-Piagetian theories of cognitive development: Implications and applications for education,* 9–29. UK: Routledge.

Bishop, S. R., Lau, M., Shapiro, S., Carlson, L., Anderson, N. D., Carmody, J., & Devins, G. (2004). Mindfulness: A proposed operational definition. *Clinical Psychology Science and Practice, 11,* 3, 230–241.

Bloom, B. S. (1956). *Taxonomy of educational objectives: The classification of educational goals. Handbook 1: Cognitive domain.* New York: McKay.

Boekaerts, M. & Simons, P. R. J. (1993). *Learning and instruction: Psychology of the pupil and the learning process.* Assen: Dekker & van de Vegt.

Boomer, G. (1992). Negotiating the curriculum. In G. Boomer, N. Lester, C. Onore, & J. Cook (Eds.), *Negotiating the curriculum: Educating for the 21st century,* 4–13. London: Falmer.

Boyadjian-Samawi, Z. (2006). The effect of concept mapping on critical thinking skills and dispositions of junior and senior baccalaureate nursing students. Doctoral dissertation: Widener University School of Nursing. *Dissertation Abstracts International, 67,* 47.

Brabeck, M. M. (1981). The relationship between critical thinking skills and development of reflective judgment among adolescent and adult women. Paper presented at the *89th Annual Convention of the American Psychological Association,* Los Angeles, August 24–26.

Brem, S. K. (2000). *Helping students ask effective questions about scientific claims: Navigating the 'sound bite' environment.* US Department of Education, Research Report 143.

Brewin, C. R. & Smart, L. (2005). Working memory capacity and suppression of intrusive thoughts. *Journal of Behavior Therapy and Experimental Psychiatry, 36,* 1, 61–68.

Broadbent, D. E. (1958). *Perception and communication.* New York: Oxford University Press.

Brown, A. (1987). Metacognition, executive control, self-regulation, and other more mysterious mechanisms. In F. Reiner & R. Kluwe (Eds.), *Metacognition, motivation, and understanding,* 65–116. Hillsdale, NJ: Erlbaum.

Brown, K. G. (2001). Using computers to deliver training: Why employees learn and why? *Personnel Psychology, 54,* 271–296.

Brown, K. W., Ryan, R. M., & Creswell, J. D. (2007). Mindfulness: Theoretical foundations and evidence for its salutary effects. *Psychological Inquiry, 18,* 4, 211–237.

Buckingham-Shum, S. J. (2003). The roots of computer supported argument visualization. In P. A. Kirschner, S. Buckingham-Shum, & C. Carr (Eds.), *Visualizing argumentation: Software tools for collaborative and educational sense-making,* 3–24. London: Springer-Verlag.

Budd, J. (2004). Mind maps as classroom exercises. *Journal of Economic Education, 35,* 1, 35–49.

Burbach, M., Matkin, G., & Fritz, S. (2004). Teaching critical thinking in an introductory leadership course utilizing active learning strategies: A confirmatory study. *College Student Journal, 38,* 3, 482–493.

Bureau of Labor Statistics. (2010–2011). Occupational outlook handbook, 2010–2011 edition. Retrieved from www.bls.gov/oco/ocos021.htm.

Burton, C. L., Strauss, E., Hultsch, D. F., & Hunter, M. A. (2006). Cognitive functioning and everyday problem solving in older adults. *The Clinical Neuropsychologist, 20,* 3, 432–452.

Butchart, S., Bigelow, J., Oppy, G., Korb, K., & Gold, I. (2009). Improving critical thinking using web-based argument mapping exercises with automated feedback. *Australasian Journal of Educational Technology, 25,* 2, 268–291.

Butler, H. A. (2012). Halpern critical thinking assessment predicts real-world outcomes of critical thinking. *Applied Cognitive Psychology, 26,* 721–729.

Butler, H., Dwyer, C., Hogan, M., Franco, A., & Almeida, L. (2012). Extending the validity of Halpern critical thinking assessments: Cross-national applications. *Thinking Skills & Creativity, 7,* 112–121.

Buzan, T. & Buzan, B. (1997). *The mind map book.* London: BBC Books.

Cabantous, L., Gond, J. P., & Johnson-Cramer, M. (2010). Decision theory as practice: Crafting rationality in organizations. *Organization Studies, 31,* 11, 1531–1566.

Cacioppo, J. T., Petty, R. E., & Kao, C. F. (1984). The efficient assessment of need for cognition. *Journal of Personality Assessment, 48,* 306–307.

Cader, R., Campbell, S., & Watson, D. (2005). Cognitive continuum theory in nursing decision-making. *Journal of Advanced Nursing, 49,* 4, 397–405.

Chaffee, J. (1988). *Thinking critically* (2nd ed.). Boston: Houghton Mifflin.

Chandler, P. & Sweller, J. (1991). Evidence for cognitive load theory. *Cognition and Instruction, 8,* 4, 351–362.

Chase, W. G. & Simon, H. A. (1973). Perception in chess. *Cognitive Psychology, 4,* 5–81.

Chen, C. M. (2009). Personalized e-learning system with self-regulated learning assisted mechanisms for promoting learning performance. *Expert Systems with Applications, 36*, 5, 8816–8829.

Chi, M. T. H., Glaser, R., & Rees, E. (1982). Expertise in problem solving. In R. S. Sternberg (Ed.), *Advances in the psychology of human intelligence*, 7–77. Hillsdale, NJ: Erlbaum.

Chiesa, A., Calati, R., & Serretti, A. (2011). Does mindfulness training improve cognitive abilities? A systematic review of neuropsychological findings. *Clinical Psychology Review, 31*, 3, 449–464.

Clark, R. C. (2005). Multimedia learning in e-courses. In R. E. Mayer (Ed.), *The Cambridge handbook of multimedia learning*, 589–615. New York: Cambridge University Press.

Colucciello, M. L. (1997). Critical thinking skills and dispositions of baccalaureate nursing students – A conceptual model for evaluation. *Journal of Professional Nursing, 13*, 236–245.

Cooperative Institutional Research Program. (1995). 1994 Nine Year Follow-Up Survey (of 1985 Freshmen). Higher Education Research Institute at UCLA.

Couch, M. (2012). Approaching critical thinking. In M. Couch (Ed.), *Center for catholic studies, critical thinking: Summer seminars*, 10, 8–9. South Orange, NJ: Seton Hall University.

Cowan, N. (2000). The magical number 4 in short-term memory: A reconsideration of mental storage capacity. *Behavioral & Brain Sciences, 24*, 87–185.

Cowan, N. (2008). What are the differences between long-term, short-term, and working memory? *Progress in Brain Research, 169*, 323–338.

Craik, F. I. M. (1983). On the transfer of information from temporary to permanent memory. *Philosophical Transactions of the Royal Society of London, 302*, 341–359.

Craik, F. I. M. & Tulving, E. (1975). Depth of processing and the retention of words in episodic memory. *Journal of Experimental Psychology: General, 104*, 3, 268–294.

Craik, F. I. M. & Watkins, M. J. (1973). The role of rehearsal in short-term memory. *Journal of Verbal Learning and Verbal Behaviour, 12*, 6, 599–607.

D'Antoni, A. V., Zipp, G. P., Olson, V. G., & Cahill, T. F. (2010). Does the mind map learning strategy facilitate information retrieval and critical thinking in medical students? *BMC Medical Education, 10*, 61.

Daly, W. M. (2001). The development of an alternative method in the assessment of critical thinking as an outcome of nursing education. *Journal of Advanced Nursing, 36*, 1, 120–130.

Dane, E. & Pratt, M. G. (2007). Exploring intuition and its role in managerial decision making. *Academy of Management Review, 32*, 1, 33–54.

Dansereau, D. F. (1988). Cooperative learning strategies. In C. E. Weinstein, E. T. Goetz, & P. A. Alexander (Eds.), *Learning and study strategies: Issues in assessment, instruction and evaluation*, 103–120. Orlando, FL: Academic Press.

Danziger, S., Levav, J., & Avnaim-Pesso, L. (2011). Extraneous factors in judicial decisions. *Proceedings of the National Academy of Sciences, 108*, 17, 6889–6892.

Darling-Hammond, L. (2008). How can we teach for meaningful learning? In L. Darling-Hammond (Ed.), *Powerful Learning*, 1–10. San Francisco: Jossey-Bass.

Davies, M. W. (2008). 'Not quite right': Helping students to make better arguments. *Teaching in Higher Education*, 13, 3, 327–340.

Dawson, T. L. (2008). *Metacognition and learning in adulthood*. Northampton, MA: Developmental Testing Service, LLC.

Dawson-Tunik, T. L., Commons, M. L., Wilson, M., & Fischer, K. W. (2005). The shape of development. *International Journal of Cognitive Development*, 2, 63–196.

De Bono, E. (1967). *The use of lateral thinking*. London: Jonathan Cape.

De Bono, E. (1985). *Six thinking hats*. Boston: Little Brown.

Dee-Lucas, D. & Larkin, J. H. (1995). Learning from electronic texts: Effects of interactive overviews for information access. *Cognition and Instruction*, 13, 3, 431–468.

De Groot, A. D. (1965). *Thought and mind in chess*. The Hague, The Netherlands: Mounton.

Del Missier, F., Mäntylä, T., & Bruine de Bruin, W. (2010). Executive functions in decision making: An individual differences approach. *Thinking & Reasoning*, 16, 2, 69–97.

Demetriou, A. (2000). Organisation and development of self-understanding and self-regulation: Toward a general theory. In M. Boekaerts, P. R. Pintrich, & M. Zeidner (Eds.), *Handbook of Self-Regulation*, 209–251. London: Academic Press.

Dewey, J. (1910). *How to think*. Boston: Heath & Co.

Dewey, J. (1933). *How we think: A restatement of the relation of reflective thinking to the educative process*. Lexington, MA: Heath & Co.

Dhami, M. K. & Thomson, M. E. (2012). On the relevance of cognitive continuum theory and quasirationality for understanding management judgment and decision making. *European Management Journal*, 30, 4, 316–326.

Donohue, A., van Gelder, T., & Cumming, G. (2002). *Reason! project studies, 1999–2002*. Melbourne: The University of Melbourne.

Dragon, T., McLaren, B. M., Mavrikis, M., & Geraniou, E. (2011). Scaffolding collaborative learning opportunities: Integrating microworld use and argumentation. Paper presented at the *International Workshop on Adaptive Support for Team Collaboration*, held in conjunction with the *International Conference on User Modeling, Adaptation and Personalization*, Girona, Spain, July 11–15.

Dressel, P. L. & Mayhew, L. B. (1954). *General education: Exploration in education*. Washington, DC: American Council on Education.

Duchastel, P. C. (1990). Examining cognitive processing in hypermedia usage. *Hypermedia*, 2, 221–233.

Duff, K., Schoenberg, M. R., Scott, J. G., & Adams, R. L. (2005). The relationship between executive functioning and verbal and visual learning and memory. *Archives of Clinical Neuropsychology*, 20, 1, 111–122.

Dunwoody, P. T., Haarbauer, E., Mahan, R. P., Marino, C., & Tang, C. C. (2000). Cognitive adaptation and its consequences. *Journal of Behavioral Decision Making*, 13, 1, 35–54.

Dwyer, C. P. (2011). The evaluation of argument mapping as a learning tool. Doctoral Thesis, National University of Ireland, Galway.

Dwyer, C. P., Harney, O., Hogan, M. J., & O'Reilly, J. (2014). Using interactive management to define and cultivate critical thinking competencies. *Educational Technology Research & Development, 62,* 687–709.

Dwyer, C. P., Harney, O., Hogan, M. J., & Kavanagh, C. (2016). Facilitating a Student-Educator Conceptual Model of Dispositions towards Critical Thinking through Interactive Management. *Educational Technology & Research,* doi: 10.1007/s11423-016-9460-7.

Dwyer, C. P., Hogan, M. J., & Stewart, I. (2011). The promotion of critical thinking skills through argument mapping. In C. P. Horvart & J. M. Forte (Eds.), *Critical Thinking.* New York: Nova Science Publishers.

Dwyer, C. P., Hogan, M. J., & Stewart, I. (2012). An evaluation of argument mapping as a method of enhancing critical thinking performance in e-learning environments. *Metacognition and Learning, 7,* 219–244.

Dwyer, C. P., Hogan, M. J., & Stewart, I. (2014). An integrated critical thinking framework for the 21st century. *Thinking Skills & Creativity, 12,* 43–52.

Dwyer, C. P., Hogan, M. J., & Stewart, I. (2015). The evaluation of argument mapping-infused critical thinking instruction as a method of enhancing reflective judgment performance. *Thinking Skills & Creativity, 16,* 11–26.

Engelmann, T., Baumeister, A., Dingel, A., & Hesse, F. W. (2010). The added value of communication in a CSCL-scenario compared to just having access to the partners' knowledge and information. In J. Sánchez, A. Cañas, & J. D. Novak (Eds.), *Concept maps making learning meaningful: Proceedings of the 4th international conference on concept mapping, 1,* 377–384. Viña del Mar, Chile: University of Chile.

Engelmann, T. & Hesse, F. W. (2010). How digital concept maps about the collaborators' knowledge and information influence computer-supported collaborative problem solving. *Computer-Supported Collaborative Learning, 5,* 299–319.

Ennis, R. H. (1987). A taxonomy of critical thinking dispositions and abilities. In J. B. Baron, & R. J. Sternberg (Eds.), *Teaching Thinking Skills: Theory and Practice,* 9–26. New York: W.H. Freeman.

Ennis, R. H. (1989). Critical thinking and subject specificity: Clarification and needed research. *Educational Researcher, 18,* 4–10.

Ennis, R. (1991). Critical thinking. *Teaching Philosophy, 14,* 1, 5–24.

Ennis, R. H. (1996). *Critical thinking.* Upper Saddle River, NJ: Prentice- Hall.

Ennis, R. H. (1998). Is critical thinking culturally biased? *Teaching Philosophy, 21,* 1, 15–33.

Ennis, R. (2013). Critical thinking across the curriculum. *Inquiry: Critical Thinking across the Disciplines, 28,* 2, 25–45.

Ennis, R. H., Millman, J., & Tomko, T. N. (1985). *Cornell critical thinking tests.* Pacific Grove, CA: Critical Thinking Co.

Ennis, R. H. & Weir, E. (1985). *The Ennis-Weir critical thinking essay test.* Pacific Grove, CA: Midwest Publications.

Epstein, S., Pacini, R., Denes-Raj, V., & Heier, H. (1996). Individual differences in intuitive-experiential and analytical-rational thinking styles. *Journal of Personality and Social Psychology, 71,* 390–405.

Ericsson, K. A. & Kintsch, W. (1995). Long-term working memory. *Psychological Review, 102,* 211–245.

Facione, P. A. (1990a). *The California critical thinking skills test (CCTST): Forms A and B; The CCTST test manual.* Millbrae, CA: California Academic Press.

Facione, P. A. (1990b). *The Delphi report: Committee on pre-college philosophy.* Millbrae, CA: California Academic Press.

Facione, P. A. (2000). The disposition toward critical thinking: Its character, measurement, and relationship to critical thinking, *Informal Logic, 20,* 1, 61–84.

Facione, P. A. & Facione, N. C. (1992). *The California critical thinking dispositions inventory (CCTDI) and CCTDI Test Manual.* California: California Academic Press.

Facione, P. A., Facione, N. C., Blohm, S. W., & Giancarlo, C. A. (2002). *The California critical thinking skills test: CCTST. Form A, form B, and form 2000. Test manual, 2002 updated edition.* Millbrae, CA: Insight Assessment.

Facione, P. A., Facione, N. C., & Giancarlo, C. A. (1997). *Setting expectations for student learning: New directions for higher education.* Millbrae: California Academic Press.

Facione, N. C., Facione, P. A., & Sanchez, C. A. (1994). Critical thinking disposition as a measure of competent clinical judgment: The development of the California Critical Thinking Disposition Inventory. *Journal of Nursing Education, 33,* 8, 345–350.

Farrand, P., Hussain, F., & Hennessy, E. (2002). The efficacy of the 'mind map' study technique. *Medical Education, 36,* 426–431.

Fischer, C. G. & Grant, G. E. (1983). Intellectual levels in college classrooms. In C. L. Ellner & C. P. Barnes (Eds.), *Studies of College Teaching,* 47–60. Lexington, MA: D.C. Heath.

Fischer, K. W. (1980). A theory of cognitive development: The control and construction of hierarchies of skills. *Psychological Review, 87,* 477–431.

Fischer, K. W. & Bidell, T. R. (2006). Dynamic development of action, thought, and emotion. In W. Damon & R. M. Lerner (Eds.), *Handbook of child psychology: Theoretical models of human development* (6th ed.), *1,* 313–399. New York: Wiley.

Fisher, A. (1988). *The logic of real arguments.* Cambridge: Cambridge University Press.

Flavell, J. (1976). Metacognitive aspects of problem solving. In L. Resnick (Ed.), *The nature of intelligence,* 231–236. Hillsdale, NJ: Erlbaum.

Flavell, J. (1979). Metacognition and cognitive monitoring: A new area of psychological inquiry. *American Psychologist, 34,* 906–911.

Folsom-Kovarik, J. T., Schatz, S., Sukthankar, G., & Nicholson, D. (2010). What information does this question convey?: Leveraging help-seeking behavior for improved modeling in a simulation-based intelligent tutor. Proceedings of the 2010 Spring Simulation Multiconference, Orlando, FL, April 11–15.

Fox, T., Grunst, G., & Quast, K. J. (1994). HyPlan: A context-sensitive hypermedia help system. Report No. 743, GMD, St. Augustin, Germany.

Fuster, J. M. (2000). Prefrontal neurons in networks of executive memory. *Brain Research Bulletin, 52*, 331–336.

Gabbenesch, H. (2006). Critical thinking: What is it good for? (In fact, what is it?). *Skeptical Inquirer, 30*, 2, 36–41.

Gailliot, M. T. & Baumeister, R. F. (2007). Self-regulation and sexual restraint: Dispositionally and temporarily poor self-regulatory abilities contribute to failures at restraining sexual behavior. *Personality and Social Psychology Bulletin, 33*, 173–186.

Gadzella, B. M., Ginther, D. W., & Bryant, G. W. (1996). Teaching and learning critical thinking skills. Paper presented at the *26th International Congress of Psychology*, Montreal, August 19.

Garcia, T., Pintrich, P. R., & Paul, R. (1992). Critical thinking and its relationship to motivation, learning strategies and classroom experience. Paper presented at the *100th Annual Meeting of the American Psychological Association*, Washington, DC, August 14–18.

Gerlach, V. & Sullivan, A. (1967). *Constructing statements of outcomes.* Inglewood, CA: Southwest Regional Laboratory for Educational Research and Development.

Gestsdottir, S. & Lerner, R. M. (2008). Positive development in adolescence: The development and role of intentional self-regulation. *Human Development, 51*, 3, 202–224.

Gilovich, T., Griffin, D., & Kahneman, D. (Eds.). (2002). *Heuristics and biases: The psychology of intuitive judgment.* Cambridge: Cambridge University Press.

Glaser, E. M. (1941). *An experiment in the development of critical thinking.* New York: Teachers College of Columbia University, Bureau of Publications.

Glomb, T. M., Duffy, M. K., Bono, J. E., & Yang, T. (2011). Mindfulness at work. *Research in Personnel and Human Resources Management, 30*, 115–157.

Gobet, F. & Clarkson, G. (2004). Chunks in expert memory: Evidence for the magical number four ... or is it two? *Memory, 12*, 732–747.

Goldberg, M. (1990). A quasi-experiment assessing the effectiveness of TV advertising directed to children. *Journal of Marketing Research, 27*, 445–454.

Good, T. L. & Brophy, J. E. (1986). *Educational Psychology* (3rd ed.). New York: Longman.

Granello, D. H. (2001). Promoting cognitive complexity in graduate written work: Using Bloom's taxonomy as a pedagogical tool to improve literature reviews. *Counselor Education and Supervision, 40*, 4, 292–307.

Guthrie, W. K. C. (1968). *The Greek philosophers from Thales to Aristotle.* London: Routledge.

Hake, R. (1998). Interactive-engagement vs. traditional methods: A six-thousand student survey of mechanics test data for introductory physics courses. *American Journal of Physics, 66*, 1, 64–74.

Halpern, D. F. (2003a). *Thought & knowledge: An introduction to critical thinking* (4th ed.). Mahwah, NJ: Erlbaum.

Halpern, D. F. (2003b). The 'how' and 'why' of critical thinking assessment. In D. Fasko (Ed.), *Critical thinking and reasoning: Current research, theory and practice*. Cresskill, NJ: Hampton Press.

Halpern, D. F. (2006). Is intelligence critical thinking? Why we need a new definition of intelligence. In P. C. Kyllonen, R. D. Roberts, & L. Stankov (Eds.), *Extending intelligence: Enhancement and new constructs*, 293–310. New York: Taylor & Francis Group.

Halpern, D. F. (2010a). *The Halpern critical thinking assessment: Manual*. Vienna: Schuhfried.

Halpern, D. F. (2010b). *Undergraduate education in psychology: A blueprint for the future of the discipline*. Washington, DC: American Psychological Association.

Halpern, D. F. (2014). *Thought & knowledge: An introduction to critical thinking* (5th ed.). UK: Psychology Press.

Hamm, R. M. (1988). Clinical intuition and clinical analysis: expertise and the cognitive continuum. In J. Dowie & A. Elstein (Eds.), *Professional judgment: A reader in clinical decision making*, 78–105. Cambridge: Cambridge University Press.

Hammond, K. R. (1981). *Principles of organization in intuitive and analytical cognition*. Report No. 231, Center for Research on Judgment and Policy, University of Colorado, Boulder, CO.

Hammond, K. R. (1996). Upon reflection. *Thinking & Reasoning*, 2, 2–3, 239–248.

Hammond, K. R. (2000). The cognitive continuum theory of judgment. In K. R. Hammond (Ed.), *Judgments under stress*, 83–110. New York: Oxford University Press.

Hart, R., Ivtzan, I., & Hart, D. (2013). Mind the gap in mindfulness research: A comparative account of the leading schools of thought. *Review of General Psychology*, 17, 4, 453–466.

Hattie, J., Biggs, J., & Purdie, N. (1996). Effects of learning skills interventions on student learning: A meta-analysis. *Review of Educational Research*, 66, 2, 99–136.

Heikkila, A. & Lonka, K. (2006). Studying in higher education: Students' approaches to learning, self-regulation and cognitive strategies. *Studies in Higher Education*, 31, 1, 99–117.

Helmstadter, G. C. (1985). Review of Watson-Glaser critical thinking appraisal. In J. V. Mitchell (Ed.), *Ninth mental measurements yearbook*, 1693–1694. Lincoln, NE: University of Nebraska, Lincoln, Buros Institute of Mental Measurements.

Higgins, E. T. (1989). Knowledge accessibility and activation: Subjectivity and suffering from unconscious sources. *Unintended Thought*, 3, 75–123.

Higher Education Quality Council. (1996). *What are graduates? Clarifying the attributes of 'graduateness'*. London: HEQC.

Hitchcock, D. (2004). The effectiveness of computer-assisted instruction in critical thinking. *Informal Logic*, 24, 3, 183–218.

Hodgkinson, G. P., Langan-Fox, J., & Sadler-Smith, E. (2008). Intuition: A fundamental bridging construct in the behavioural sciences. *British Journal of Psychology*, 99, 1, 1–27.

Hodgkinson, G. P., Sadler-Smith, E., Burke, L. A., Claxton, G., & Sparrow, P. R. (2009). Intuition in organizations: implications for strategic management. *Long Range Planning, 42*, 3, 277–297.

Hofer, B. K. (2004). Epistemological understanding as a metacognitive process: Thinking aloud during online searching. *Educational Psychologist, 39*, 1, 43–55.

Hofmann, S. G., Sawyer, A. T., Witt, A. A., & Oh, D. (2010). The effect of mindfulness-based therapy on anxiety and depression: A meta-analytic review. *Journal of Consulting and Clinical Psychology, 78*, 169–183.

Hofmann, W., Schmeichel, B. J., & Baddeley, A. D. (2012). Executive functions and self-regulation. *Trends in Cognitive Sciences, 16*, 3, 174–180.

Hogan, M. J. (2006). Against didacticism: A psychologist's view. *Educational Research and Reviews, 1*, 7, 206–212.

Hogan, M. J., Dwyer, C. P., Noone, C., Harney, O., & Conway, R. (2014). Metacognitive skill development and applied systems science: A framework of metacognitive skills, self-regulatory functions and real-world applications. In A. Peña-Ayala (Ed.), *Metacognition: fundaments, applications, and trends*, 75–106. Berlin: Springer.

Holas, P. & Jankowski, T. A. (2012). Cognitive perspective on mindfulness. *International Journal of Psychology: Journal International de Psychologie, 48*, 3, 232–243.

Holland, J. H., Holyoak, K. J., Nisbett, R. E., & Thagard, P. R. (1986). *Induction: Processes of inference, learning, and discovery*. Cambridge, MA: MIT Press.

Holmes, J. & Clizbe, E. (1997). Facing the 21st century. *Business Education Forum, 52*, 1, 33–35.

Hopwood, A. (1974). *Accounting and human behaviour*. London: Accountancy Age Books.

Horn, R. E. (1999). *Can computers think?* Bainbridge Island, WA: MacroVU, Inc.

Horn, R. E. (2003). Infrastructure for navigating interdisciplinary debates: Critical decisions for representing argumentation. In P. Kirschner, S. Buckingham-Shum, & C. Carr (Eds.), *Visualizing argumentation: Software tools for collaborative and educational sense-making*, 165–184. London: Springer-Verlag.

Horn, R. E. & Weber, R. P. (2007). *New tools for resolving wicked problems: Mess mapping and resolution mapping processes*. Bainbridge Island, WA: MacroVU, Inc. and Strategy Kinetics, LLC.

Huffaker, D. A. & Calvert, S. L. (2003). The new science of learning: Active learning, metacognition and transfer of knowledge in e-learning applications. *Journal of Educational Computing Research, 29*, 3, 325–334.

Huffman, K., Vernoy, M., Williams, B., & Vernoy, J. (1991). *Psychology in action*. New York: John Wiley and Sons.

Hugenholtz, N. I. R., de Croon, E. M., Smits, P. B., van Dijk, F. J. H., & Nieuwenhuijsen, K. (2008). Effectiveness of e-learning in continuing medical education for occupational physicians. *Occupational Medicine, 58*, 370–372.

Hughes, J. N. (1992). Review of Cornell critical thinking tests. In J. J. Kramer & J. C. Conoley (Eds.), *Eleventh mental measurements yearbook*, 241–243. Lincoln, NE: University of Nebraska, Lincoln, Buros Institute of Mental Measurements.

Huitt, W. (2011). Bloom et al.'s taxonomy of the cognitive domain. *Educational psychology interactive*. Valdosta, GA: Valdosta State University. Retrieved 08 August 2011, from www.edpsycinteractive.org/topics/cognition/bloom .html.

Hunt, E. (1995). *Will we be smart enough? A cognitive analysis of the coming workforce*. New York, NY: Russell Sage Foundation.

Hwang, G. J., Shi, Y. R., & Chu, H. C. (2011). A concept map approach to developing collaborative mindtools for context-aware ubiquitous learning. *British Journal of Educational Technology, 42*, 5, 778–789.

Jacobs, S. S. (1995). Technical characteristics and some correlates of the California Critical Thinking Skills Test Forms A and B. *Higher Education Research, 36*, 89–108.

Jensen, L. L. (1998). *The role of need for cognition in the development of reflective judgment*. Doctoral Thesis, University of Denver, Colorado, USA.

Jiang, Y., Olson, I. R., & Chun, M. M. (2000). Organization of visual short-term memory. *Journal of Experimental Psychology: Learning, Memory and Cognition, 26*, 683–702.

Johnson, C. E., Hurtubise, L. C., Castrop, J., French, G., Groner, J., Ladinsky, M., McLaughlin, D., Plachta, L., & Mahan, J. D. (2004). Learning management systems: Technology to measure the medical knowledge competency of the ACGME. *Medical Education, 38*, 599–608.

Johnson, D. W., Johnson, R. T., & Stanne, M. S. (2000). Cooperative learning methods: A meta-analysis. Retrieved 21 June 2011, from www.cooperation.org/pages/cl-methods.html.

Johnson, R. H. & Blair, J. A. (1987). The current state of informal logic. *Informal Logic, 9*, 2–3, 147–151.

Jonassen, D. & Tessmer, M. (1996). An outcomes based taxonomy for instructional systems design, evaluation and research. *Training Research Journal, 2*, 11–46.

Jukes, I. & McCain, T. (2002). *Minds in play: Computer game design as a context of children's learning*. Hillsdale, NJ: Erlbaum.

Kaempf, G. L., Klein, G., Thordsen, M. L., & Wolf, S. (1996). Decision making in complex naval command-and-control environments. *Human Factors: The Journal of the Human Factors and Ergonomics Society, 38*, 2, 220–231.

Kahneman, D. (2003). Maps of bounded rationality: A perspective on intuitive judgment and choice. In T. Frangsmyr (Ed.), *Les prix nobel: The nobel prizes, 2002*, 4, 449–489. Stockholm: Nobel Foundation.

Kahneman, D. (2011). *Thinking fast and slow*. Penguin: Great Britain.

Kahneman, D. & Frederick, S. (2002). Representativeness revisited: Attribute substitution in intuitive judgment. In T. Gilovich, D. Griffin, & D. Kahneman (Eds.), *Heuristics and biases: The psychology of intuitive judgment*, 49–81. New York: Cambridge University Press.

Kahneman, D. & Ritov, I. (1994). Determinants of stated willingness to pay for public goods: A study in the headline method. *Journal of Risk and Uncertainty, 9*, 1, 5–37.

Kahneman, D., Ritov, I., & Schkade, D. (1999). Economic preferences, or attitude expressions? An analysis of dollar responses to public issues. *Journal of Risk & Uncertainty, 19,* 1–3, 203–235.

Kahneman, D., Slovic, P., & Tversky, A. (Eds.). (1982). *Judgment under uncertainty: Heuristics and biases.* UK: Cambridge University Press.

King, P. M. & Kitchener, K. S. (1994). *Developing reflective judgment: Understanding and promoting intellectual growth and critical thinking in adolescents and adults.* San Francisco: Jossey Bass.

King, P. M. & Kitchener, K. S. (2002). The reflective judgment model: Twenty years of epistemic cognition. In B. K. Hofer & P. R. Pintrich (Eds.), *Personal epistemology: The psychology of beliefs about knowledge and knowing,* 37–61. Mahwah, NJ: Erlbaum.

King, P. M. & Kitchener, K. S. (2004). Reflective judgment: Theory and research on the development of epistemic assumptions through adulthood. *Educational Psychologist, 39,* 1, 5–15.

King, P. M., Wood, P. K., & Mines, R. A. (1990). Critical thinking among college and graduate students. *The Review of Higher Education, 13,* 2, 167–186.

Kitchener, K. S. & Fischer, K. W. (1990). A skill approach to the development of reflective thinking. *Contributions to Human Development, 21,* 48–62.

Kitchener, K. S. & King, P. M. (1981). Reflective judgment: Concepts of justifications and their relation to age and gender. *Journal of Applied Developmental Psychology, 2,* 2, 89–116.

Klein, G. A. (1989). Recognition-primed decisions. In W. Rouse (Ed.), *Advances in man-machine systems research,* 5, 47–92. Greenwich, CT: JAI Press, Inc.

Klein, G. (2008). Naturalistic decision making. *Human Factors: The Journal of the Human Factors and Ergonomics Society, 50,* 3, 456–460.

Klein, G. A., Calderwood, R., & Clinton-Cirocco, A. (1986). Rapid decision making on the fireground. In *Proceedings of the Human Factors and Ergonomics Society 30th Annual Meeting,* 1, 576–580. Norwood, NJ: Ablex.

Knight, P. (2007). Grading, classifying and future learning. In D. Boud & N. Falchikov (Eds.), *Rethinking assessment in higher education: Learning for the longer term,* 72–86. UK: Routledge.

Kotovsky, H. A., Hayes, K., & Simon, J. R. (1985). Why are some problems hard? Evidence from the Tower of Hanoi. *Cognitive Psychology, 17,* 22, 248–294.

Krathwohl, D. R. (2002). A revision of Bloom's taxonomy: An overview. *Theory into Practice, 41,* 4, 212–218.

Kreitzer, A. E. & Madaus, G. F. (1994). Empirical investigations of the hierarchical structure of the taxonomy. In L. W. Anderson & L. A. Sosniak (Eds.), *Bloom's taxonomy: A forty-year retrospective, ninety-third yearbook of the national society for the study of education,* 64–81. Chicago: University of Chicago Press.

Kropp, R. P., Stoker, H. W., & Bashaw, W. L. (1966). The validation of the taxonomy of educational objectives. *Journal of Experimental Education, 34,* 3, 69–76.

Ku, K. Y. L. (2009). Assessing students' critical thinking performance: Urging for measurements using multi-response format. *Thinking Skills and Creativity, 4,* 1, 70–76.

Ku, K. Y. L. & Ho, I. T. (2010a). Dispositional factors predicting Chinese students' critical thinking performance. *Personality and Individual Differences*, *48*, 54–58.

Ku, K. Y. L. & Ho, I. T. (2010b). Metacognitive strategies that enhance critical thinking. *Metacognition & Learning*, *5*, 251–267.

Kuhn, D. (1991). *The skills of argument*. Cambridge: Cambridge University Press.

Kuhn, D. (1999). A developmental model of critical thinking. *Educational Researcher*, *28*, 2, 16–25.

Kuhn, D. (2000). Metacognitive development. *Current Directions in Psychological Science*, *9*, 5, 178–181.

Kuhn, D., Goh, W., Iordanou, K., & Shaenfield, D. (2008). Arguing on the computer: A microgenetic study of developing argument skills in a computer-supported environment. *Child Development*, *79*, 5, 1310–1328.

Kuhn, D., Katz, J. B., & D. Dean, Jr. (2004). Developing reason. *Thinking & Reasoning*, *10*, 2, 197–219.

Kuhn, D. & Weinstock, M. (2002). What is epistemological thinking and why does it matter? In B. K. Hofer & P. R. Pintrich (Eds.), *Personal epistemology: The psychology of beliefs about knowledge and knowing*, 121–144. Mahwah, NJ, US: Erlbaum.

Kuran, T. & Sunstein, C. R. (1999). Availability cascades and risk regulation. *Stanford Law Review*, *51*, 4, 683–768.

Langley, A. (1995). Between 'paralysis by analysis' and 'extinction by instinct'. *Sloan Management Review*, *36*, 63–76.

Laplace, P. S. (1902). *A philosophical essay on probabilities*. New York: Wiley.

Larkin, J. H., McDermott, J., Simon, D. P., & Simon, H. A. (1980). Models of competence in solving physics problems. *Cognitive Science*, *4*, 317–345.

Larkin, J. & Simon, H. (1987). Why a diagram is (sometimes) worth ten thousand words. *Cognitive Science*, *11*, 65–99.

Laws, P., Sokoloff, D., & Thornton, R. (1999). Promoting active learning using the results of physics education research. *UniServe Science News*, *13*, 14–19.

LeBlanc, J. (1998). *Thinking clearly: A guide to critical reasoning*. New York: W.W. Norton.

Leventhal, H. (1984). A perceptual-motor theory of emotion. *Advances in Experimental Social Psychology*, *17*, 117–182.

Lewis, C. I. (1918). *A survey of symbolic logic*. London: Bloomsbury Academic, (2001).

Lieberman, M. D. (2003). Reflexive and reflective judgment processes: A social cognitive neuroscience approach. *Social Judgments: Implicit and Explicit Processes*, *5*, 44–67.

Lloyd, M. & Bahr, N. (2010). Thinking critically about critical thinking in higher education. *International Journal for the Scholarship of Teaching and Learning*, *4*, 2, 1–16.

Logie, R. H. (1995). *Visuo-spatial working memory*. Hove, UK: Erlbaum.

Ma, A. W. W. (2009). Computer supported collaborative learning and higher order thinking skills: A case study of textile studies. *The Interdisciplinary Journal of e-Learning and Learning Objects*, *5*, 145–167.

Malcolm, K. K. (1992). Review of Cornell critical thinking tests. In J. J. Kramer & J. C. Conoley (Eds.), *Eleventh mental measurements yearbook*, 243–244.

Lincoln, NE: University of Nebraska, Lincoln, Buros Institute of Mental Measurements.

Marin, L. M. & Halpern, D. F. (2011). Pedagogy for developing critical thinking in adolescents: Explicit instruction produces greatest gains. *Thinking Skills & Creativity*, 6, 1–13.

Marzano, R. J. (1998). *A theory-based meta-analysis of research on instruction*. Aurora, CO: Mid-Continent Regional Educational Laboratory. Retrieved 26 October 2007, from www.mcrel.org/pdf/instruction/5982rr_instructionmeta_analysis.pdf.

Marzano, R. J. (2001). *Designing a new taxonomy of educational objectives*. Thousand Oaks, CA: Corwin Press.

Mascolo, M. F. (2008). The concept of domain in developmental analyses of hierarchical complexity. *World Futures*, 64, 5–7, 330–347.

Maybery, M. T., Bain, J. D. & Halford, G. S. (1986). Information-processing demands of transitive inference. *Journal of Experimental Psychology: Learning, Memory, and Cognition*, 12, 4, 600–613.

Mayer, R. E. (1989). Systematic thinking fostered by illustrations in scientific text. *Journal of Educational Psychology*, 81, 2, 240–246.

Mayer, R. E. (1997). Multimedia learning: Are we asking the right questions? *Educational Psychologist*, 32, 1, 1–19.

Mayer, R. E. (2003). The promise of multimedia learning: Using the same instructional design methods across different media. *Learning and Instruction*, 13, 125–139.

Mayer, R. E. (2004). Should there be a three-strikes rule against pure discovery learning? The case for guided methods of instruction. *American Psychologist*, 59, 1, 14–19.

Mayer, R. E. (2005). Cognitive theory of multimedia learning. In R. E. Mayer (Ed.), *The Cambridge handbook of multimedia learning*, 31–48. New York: Cambridge University Press.

Mayer, R. E. & Anderson, R. B. (1991). Animations need narrations: An experimental test of a dual-coding hypothesis. *Journal of Educational Psychology*, 83, 484–490.

Mayer, R. E. & Anderson, R. B. (1992). The instructive animation: Helping students build connections between words and pictures in multimedia learning. *Journal of Educational Psychology*, 84, 444–452.

Mayer, R. E. & Gallini, J. K. (1990). When is an illustration worth ten thousand words? *Journal of Educational Psychology*, 82, 715–726.

Mayer, R. E. & Sims, V. K. (1994). For whom is a picture worth a thousand words? Extensions of a dual-coding theory of multimedia learning. *Journal of Educational Psychology*, 86, 289–401.

Mayer, R. E., Steinhoff, K., Bower, G., & Mars, R. (1995). A generative theory of textbook design: Using annotated illustrations to foster meaningful learning of science text. *Educational Technology Research and Development*, 43, 1, 31–44.

Means, M. L. & Voss, J. E. (1996). Who reasons well? Two studies of informal reasoning among children of different grade, ability and knowledge levels. *Cognition & Instruction*, 4, 2, 139–178.

Meltzoff, J. (1998). *Critical thinking about research: Psychology and related fields*. Washington, DC: American Psychological Association.

Meyer, B. J. F., Brandt, D. M., & Bluth, G. J. (1980). Use of top-level structure in text: Key for reading comprehension of ninth-grade students. *Reading Research Quarterly, 16*, 1, 72–103.

Miller, G. A. (1956). The magical number seven, plus or minus two: Some limits on our capacity for processing information. *The Psychological Review, 63*, 814–897.

Miyake, A., Friedman, N. P., Emerson, M. J., Witzki, A. H., Howerter, A., & Wager, T. D. (2000). The unity and diversity of executive functions and their contributions to complex 'frontal lobe' tasks: A latent variable analysis. *Cognitive Psychology, 41*, 1, 49–100.

Modjeski, R. B. & Michael, W. B. (1983). An evaluation by a panel of psychologists of the reliability and validity of two tests of CT. *Educational and Psychological Measurement, 43*, 1187–1197.

Monk, P. (2001). Mapping the future of argument. *Australian Financial Review. 16*, 8–9.

Moore, A. & Malinowski, P. (2009). Meditation, mindfulness and cognitive flexibility. *Consciousness and Cognition, 18*, 1, 176–186.

Moreno, R. & Park, B. (2010). Cognitive load theory: Historical development and relation to other theories. In J. L. Plass, R. Moreno, & R. Brünken (Eds.), *Cognitive load theory*, 29–47. New York: Cambridge University Press.

Moseley, D., Baumfield, V., Elliot, J., Gregson, M., Higgins, S., Miller, J., & Newton, D. (2005). *Frameworks for thinking: A handbook for teaching and learning.* Cambridge: Cambridge University Press.

Munch, J. M., Boller, G. W., & Swasy, J. L. (1993). The effects of argument structure and affective tagging on product attitude formation. *Journal of Consumer Research, 20*, 2, 294–302.

Muraven, M., Tice, D. M., & Baumeister, R. F. (1998). Self-control as limited resource: Regulatory depletion patterns. *Journal of Personality and Social Psychology, 74*, 774–789.

Murray, D. J. (1968). Repeated recall in short-term memory. *Journal of Verbal Learning and Verbal Behavior, 7*, 2, 358–365.

Myers, J. L. (1974). *Memory for prose material.* Amherst, MA: University of Massachusetts.

National Academy of Sciences, National Academy of Engineering, Institute of Medicine. (2005). Rising above the gathering storm: Energising and employing America for a brighter economic future. *Committee on Prospering in the Global Economy for the Twenty-First Century*, Washington, DC.

Neisser, U. (1976). *Cognition and reality: Principles and implications of cognitive psychology.* New York: W.H. Freeman.

Newbern, D., Dansereau, D. F., Patterson, M. E., & Wallace, D. S. (1994). Toward a science of cooperation. Paper presented at the *Annual meeting of the American Educational Research Association*, New Orleans, April.

Newell, A. & Simon, H. A. (1972). *Human problem solving*, 104, 9. Englewood Cliffs, NJ: Prentice-Hall.

Newman, D. R., Johnson, C., Cochrane, A. C., & Webb, B. R. (1996). An experiment in group learning technology: Evaluating critical thinking in face-to-face and computer-supported seminars. *Interpersonal Computing & Technology, 4*, 1, 57–74.

Norman, D. A. & Shallice, T. (1986). *Attention to action.* New York: Springer.

Norman, D. A. & Shallice, T. (2000). Attention to action: Willed and automatic control of behaviour. In M. Gazzaniga (Ed.), *Cognitive neuroscience: A reader.* Oxford, UK: Blackwell.

Norris, S. P. (Ed.). (1992). *The generalizability of critical thinking: Multiple perspectives on an educational ideal.* New York: Teachers College Press.

Norris, S. P. (1994). The meaning of critical thinking test performance: The effects of abilities and dispositions on scores. In D. Fasko (Ed.), *Critical thinking: Current research, theory, and practice.* Dordrecht, The Netherlands: Kluwer.

Oliver, K. (2009). An investigation of concept mapping to improve the reading comprehension of science texts. *Journal of Science Education and Technology, 18,* 5, 402–414.

Ong, W. J. (1958). *Ramus, method, and the decay of dialogue: From the art of discourse to the art of reason.* Chicago, IL: University of Chicago Press.

Osman, M. E. & Hannafin, M. J. (1992). Metacognition research and theory: Analysis and implications for instructional design. *Educational Technology Research and Development, 40,* 2, 83–99.

Ostafin, B. D. & Kassman, K. T. (2012). Stepping out of history: Mindfulness improves insight problem solving. *Consciousness and Cognition, 21,* 2, 1031–1036.

Paas, F., Renkl, A., & Sweller, J. (2003). Cognitive load theory and instructional design: Recent developments. *Educational Psychologist, 38,* 1, 1–4.

Paivio, A. (1971). *Imagery and verbal processes.* Hillsdale, NJ: Erlbaum.

Paivio, A. (1986). *Mental representations: A dual-coding approach.* New York: Oxford University Press.

Pascarella, E. T. & Terenzini, P. T. (1991). *How college affects students: Findings and insights from twenty years of research.* San Francisco: Jossey-Bass.

Paul, R. (1987). Dialogical thinking: Critical thought essential to the acquisition of rational knowledge and passions. In J. Baron & R. J. Sternberg (Eds.), *Teaching Thinking Skills: Theory and Practice,* 127–148. New York: W.H. Freeman.

Paul, R. (1993). *Critical thinking: What every person needs to survive in a rapidly changing world.* Rohnert Park, CA: Foundation for Critical Thinking.

Paul, R. & Elder, L. (2008). *Critical thinking.* California: The Foundation for Critical Thinking.

Paul, R., Elder, L., & Bartell, T. (1997). *California teacher preparation for instruction in critical thinking: Research findings and policy recommendations.* Sacramento, CA: State of California Commission on Teacher Credentialing.

Perkins, D. N., Jay, E., & Tishman, S. (1993). Beyond abilities: A dispositional theory of thinking. *Merrill-Palmer Quarterly, 39,* 1–1.

Perkins, D. N. & Ritchhart, R. (2004). When is good thinking? In D. Y. Dai & R. J. Sternberg (Eds.), *Motivation, emotion, and cognition: Integrative perspectives on intellectual functioning and development,* 351–384. Mahwah, NJ: Erlbaum.

Perry, N. W., Huss, M. T., McAuliff, B. D., & Galas, J. M. (1996). An active-learning approach to teaching the undergraduate psychology and law course. *Teaching of Psychology, 23,* 2, 76–81.

Phan, H. P. (2010). Critical thinking as a self-regulatory process component in teaching and learning. *Psicothema, 22,* 2, 284–292.

Phillips, L. M., Norris, S. P., & Macnab, J. S. (2010). Visualization and mathematics. In L. M. Phillips, S. P. Norris, & J. S. Macnab (Eds.), *Visualization in mathematics, reading and science education*, 5. Dordrecht: Springer Science & Business Media.

Piaget, J. (1952). *The origins of intelligence in children*. New York: W.W. Norton & Co.

Pintrich, P. R. (2000). The role of goal orientation in self-regulated learning. In M. Boekaerts, P. R. Pintrich, & M. Zeidner (Eds.), *Handbook of self-regulation*, 451–502. San Diego, CA: Academic Press.

Pintrich, P. R., Smith, D. A. F., Garcia, T., & McKeachie, W. J. (1991). *A manual for the use of the motivated strategies for learning questionnaire (MSLQ)*. Ann Arbour, MI: The University of Michigan, National Center for Research to Improve Post-secondary Teaching and Learning.

Pollio, H. (1984). What students think about and do in college lecture classes. *Teaching Learning Issues*, 53. Knoxville, TN: University of Tennessee Learning Research Center.

Pollock, E., Chandler, P., & Sweller, J. (2002). Assimilating complex information. *Learning & Instruction*, 12, 61–86.

Popper, K. R. (1934/1959). *The logic of scientific discovery*. London: Routledge.

Popper, K. R. (1999). *All life is problem solving*. UK: Psychology Press.

Profeto-McGrath, J. (2003). The relationship of critical thinking skills and critical thinking dispositions of baccalaureate nursing students. *Journal of Advanced Nursing*, 43, 6, 569–577.

Redish, E., Saul, J., & Steinberg, R. (1997). On the effectiveness of active-engagement microcomputer-based laboratories. *American Journal of Physics*, 65, 1, 45.

Reed, C., Walton, D., & Macagno, F. (2007). Argument diagramming in logic, law and artificial intelligence. *The Knowledge Engineering Review*, 22, 1, 87–109.

Reed, J. H. & Kromrey, J. D. (2001). Teaching critical thinking in a community college history course: Empirical evidence from infusing Paul's model. *College Student Journal*, 35, 2, 201–215.

Reeves, M. F. (1990). An application of Bloom's taxonomy to the teaching of business ethics. *Journal of Business Ethics*, 9, 7, 609–616.

Richeson, J. A. & Shelton, J. N. (2003). When prejudice does not pay effects of interracial contact on executive function. *Psychological Science*, 14, 3, 287–290.

Rimiene, V. (2002). Assessing and developing students' critical thinking. *Psychology Learning & Teaching*, 2, 1, 17–22.

Robbins, S. & Judge, T. A. (2007). *Organizational behavior* (12th ed.). Upper Saddle River, NJ: Pearson Prentice Hall.

Robbins, S., Lauver, K., Le, H., Davis, D., Langley, R., & Carlstrom, A. (2004). Do psychosocial and study skill factors predict college outcomes? A meta-analysis. *Psychological Bulletin*, 130, 2, 261–288.

Robinson, D. H. & Kiewra, K. A. (1995). Visual argument: Graphic organizers are superior to outlines in improving learning from text. *Journal of Educational Psychology*, 87, 3, 455–467.

Rogoff, B. (1998). Cognition as a collaborative process. In W. Damon (Ed.), *Handbook of child psychology* (5th ed.). New York: John Wylie.

Romiszowski, A. J. (1981). *Designing instructional systems*. New York: Nichols.

Runco, M. A. & Jaeger, G. J. (2012). The standard definition of creativity. *Creativity Research Journal, 24,* 1, 92–96.

Saddler-Smith, E. & Shefy, E. (2004). The intuitive executive: Understanding and applying 'gut-feel' in decision making. *Academy of Management Executive, 18,* 76–91.

Sanders, J. A., Wiseman, R. L., & Gass, R. H. (1994). Does teaching argumentation facilitate critical thinking? *Communication Reports, 7,* 1, 27–35.

Salas, E., Rosen, M. A., & DiazGranados, D. (2010). Expertise-based intuition and decision making in organizations. *Journal of Management,* doi: 10.1177/0149206309350084.

Sartre, J. P. (1943). Being & Nothingness. Paris, France: Éditions Gallimard.

Scheuer, O., McLaren, B. M., Weinberger, A., & Nieburhr, S. (2012). Scaffolding students for more elaborative and critical discussions. Paper presented at the *11th International Conference on Intelligent Tutoring Systems,* Chania, Crete, June 14–18.

Schmeichel, B. J., Vohs, K. D., & Baumeister, R. F. (2003). Ego depletion and intelligent performance: Role of the self in logical reasoning and other information processing. *Journal of Personality and Social Psychology, 85,* 33–46.

Schwarz, N., Strack, F., Bless, H., Klumpp, G., Rittenauer-Schatka, H., & Simons, A. (1991). Ease of retrieval as information: Another look at the availability heuristic. *Journal of Personality and Social Psychology, 61,* 2, 195–202.

Scott, T. (2003). Bloom's taxonomy applied to testing in computer science classes. *Journal of Computing Sciences in Colleges, 19,* 1, 267–274.

Scriven, M. (1976). *Reasoning.* Point Reyes, CA: Edgepress.

Shapiro, S. L., Jazaieri, H., & Goldin, P. R. (2012). Mindfulness-based stress reduction effects on moral reasoning and decision making. *The Journal of Positive Psychology, 7,* 6, 504–515.

Shin, S.-J. (2002). *The iconic logic of Peirce's graphs.* Cambridge, MA: MIT Press.

Siegel, H. (1999). What (good) are thinking dispositions? *Educational Theory, 49,* 2, 207–221.

Simon, H. A. (1957). *Models of man.* New York: Wiley.

Simon, H. A. (1987). Making management decisions: The role of intuition and emotion. *The Academy of Management Executive (1987–1989),* 57–64.

Simon, H. A. (1992). What is an 'explanation' of behavior? *Psychological Science, 3,* 3, 150–161.

Slavin, R. E. (1995). Research on cooperative learning and achievement: What we know, what we need to know. *Contemporary Educational Psychology, 21,* 43.

Slovic, P., Finucane, M., Peters, E., & MacGregor, D. G. (2002). Rational actors or rational fools: Implications of the affect heuristic for behavioral economics. *The Journal of Socio-Economics, 31,* 4, 329–342.

Slovic, P., Fischhoff, B., & Lichtenstein, S. (1977). Behavioral decision theory. *Annual Review of Psychology, 28,* 1–39.

Slovic, P. & Peters, E. (2006). Risk perception and affect. *Current Directions in Psychological Science, 15,* 6, 322–325.

Smith, D. G. (1983). Instruction and outcomes in undergraduate settings. In C. L. Ellner & C. P. Barnes (Eds.), *Studies of college teaching,* 3–116. Lexington, MA: D.C. Heath.

Solon, T. (2007). Generic critical thinking infusion and course content learning in Introductory Psychology. *Journal of Instructional Psychology, 34,* 2, 95–109.

Stanovich, K. E. (2008). *The psychology of rational thought: What intelligence tests miss.* New Haven, CT: Yale University Press.

Stanovich, K. E. & West, R. F. (2000). Individual differences in reasoning: Implications for the rationality debate? *Behavioral and Brain Sciences, 23,* 5, 645–665.

Sternberg, R. J. (1985). *Beyond IQ: A triarchic theory of human intelligence.* Cambridge: Cambridge University Press.

Sternberg, R. J. (2002). Raising the achievement of all students: Teaching for successful intelligence. *Educational Psychology Review, 14,* 4, 383–393.

Sternberg, R. J. (2003). The development of creativity as a decision-making process. *Creativity and Development,* 91–138.

Sternberg, R. J. (2005). The theory of successful intelligence. *Revista Interamericana de Psicología/Interamerican Journal of Psychology, 39,* 2, 189–202.

Sternberg, R. J. (2006). The nature of creativity. *Creativity Research Journal, 18,* 1, 87–98.

Sternberg, R. J. (2010). The dark side of creativity and how to combat it. In D. H. Cropley et al. (Eds.), *The dark side of creativity,* 316–328. UK: Cambridge University Press.

Sternberg, R. J. & Lubart, T. L. (1999). The concept of creativity. In R. J. Sternberg (Ed.), *Handbook of Creativity.* Cambridge: Cambridge University Press.

Stewart, T. R., Heideman, K. F., Moninger, W. R., & Reagan-Cirincione, P. (1992). Effects of improved information on the components of skill in weather forecasting. *Organizational Behavior and Human Decision Processes, 53,* 2, 107–134.

Strack, F. & Deutsch, R. (2004). Reflective and impulsive determinants of social behavior. *Personality and Social Psychology Review, 8,* 3, 220–247.

Strack, F., Martin, L. L., & Schwarz, N. (1988). Priming and communication: Social determinants of information use in judgments of life satisfaction. *European Journal of Social Psychology, 18,* 5, 429–442.

Sweller, J. (1994). Cognitive load theory, learning difficulty, and instructional design. *Learning and Instruction, 4,* 295–312.

Sweller, J. (1999). *Instructional design in technical areas.* Australian Education Review No. 43. Victoria: Acer Press.

Sweller, J. (2005). The redundancy principle. In R. E. Mayer (Ed.), *The Cambridge handbook of multimedia learning,* 159–167. New York: Cambridge University Press.

Sweller, J. (2010). Cognitive load theory: Recent theoretical advances. In J. L. Plass, R. Moreno, & R. Brünken (Eds.), *Cognitive Load Theory,* 29–47. New York: Cambridge University Press.

Sweller, J. & Chandler, P. (1991). Evidence for cognitive load theory. *Cognition & Instruction, 8,* 4, 351–362.

Sweller, J., Chandler, P., Tierney, P., & Cooper, M. (1990).Cognitive load as a factor in the structuring of technical material. *Journal of Experimental Psychology: General, 119,* 2, 76–192.

Taube, K. T. (1997). Critical thinking ability and disposition as factors of performance on a written critical thinking test. *Journal of General Education, 46,* 129–164.

Taylor, B. M. (1982). Text structure and children's comprehension and memory for expository material. *Journal of Educational Psychology, 74,* 323–340.

Taylor, B. M. & Beach, R. W. (1984). The effects of text structure instruction on middle-grade students' comprehension and production of expository text. *Reading Research Quarterly, 19,* 134–146.

Terenzini, P. T., Springer, L., Pascarella, E. T., & Nora, A. (1995). Influences affecting the development of students' critical thinking skills. *Research in Higher Education, 36,* 1, 23–39.

Teper, R. & Inzlicht, M. (2013). Meditation, mindfulness and executive control: The importance of emotional acceptance and brain-based performance monitoring. *Social Cognitive and Affective Neuroscience, 8,* 1, 85–92.

Teper, R., Segal, Z. V., & Inzlicht, M. (2013). Inside the mindful mind: How mindfulness enhances emotion regulation through improvements in executive control. *Current Directions in Psychological Science, 22,* 6, 449–454.

Tindall-Ford, S., Chandler, P., & Sweller, J. (1997). When two sensory modes are better than one. *Journal of Experimental Psychology: Applied, 3,* 4, 257–287.

Toplak, M. E. & Stanovich, K. E. (2002). The domain specificity and generality of disjunctive reasoning: Searching for a generalizable critical thinking skill. *Journal of Educational Psychology, 94,* 1, 197–209.

Toulmin, S. (1958). *The uses of argument.* Cambridge: Cambridge University Press.

Trout, J. (2005, December 5). Differentiate or die. *Forbes.* Retrieved 17 December 2006, from www.forbes.com/opinions/2005/12/02/ ibm-nordstrom-cocacola-cx_jt_1205trout.html.

Tsui, L. (1999). Courses and instruction affecting critical thinking. *Research in Higher Education, 40,* 2, 185–200.

Tsui, L. (2002). Fostering critical thinking through effective pedagogy. *Journal of Higher Education, 73,* 6, 740–763.

Tulving, E. (1984). Precis of elements of episodic memory. *Behavioral and Brain Sciences, 7,* 223–268.

Tulving, E. & Thompson, D. M. (1973). Encoding specificity and retrieval processes in episodic memory. *Psychological Review, 80,* 352–373.

Tversky, A. & Kahneman, D. (1974). Judgment under uncertainty: Heuristics and biases. *Science, 185,* 4157, 1124–1131.

Tversky, A. & Kahneman, D. (1982). Evidential impact of base rates. In D. Kahneman, P. Slovic, & A. Tversky (Eds.), *Judgment under uncertainty: Heuristics and biases.* UK: Cambridge University Press.

Tversky, A. & Kahneman, D. (1983). Extensional versus intuitive reasoning: The conjunction fallacy in probability judgment. *Psychological Review, 90,* 4, 293.

Twardy, C. R. (2004). Argument maps improve critical thinking. *Teaching Philosophy, 27,* 2, 95–116.

US National Research Council. (2002). *Technology and assessment: Thinking ahead.* Washington, DC: Board on Testing and Assessment Center for Education.

University of Western Australia. (2007). ACE and NSSE. Retrieved 28 August 2010, from www.catl.uwa.edu.au/CATLyst/archive/2007/1/ace_and_nsse.

Valenzuela, J., Nieto, A. M., & Saiz, C. (2011). Critical thinking motivational scale: A contribution to the study of relationship between critical thinking and motivation. *Journal of Research in Educational Psychology, 9,* 2, 823–848.

Van Eemeren, F. H. (2009). The study of argumentation. In A. A. Lunsford, K. H. Wilson, & R. A. Eberly (Eds.), *The SAGE handbook of rhetorical studies,* 109–124.

Van Eemeren, F. H., Grootendorst, R., Henkemans, F. S., Blair, J. A., Johnson, R. H., Krabbe, E. C. W., Planitin, C., Walton, D. N., Willard, C. A., Woods, J., & Zarefsky, D. (1996). *Fundamentals of argumentation theory: A handbook of historical backgrounds and contemporary developments.* Mahwah, NJ: Erlbaum.

Van Gelder, T. J. (2000). Learning to reason: A Reason!Able approach. In C. Davis, T. J. van Gelder, & R. Wales (Eds.), *Cognitive science in Australia, 2000: Proceedings of the fifth Australasian cognitive science society conference.* Adelaide: Causal.

Van Gelder, T. J. (2001). How to improve critical thinking using educational technology. In G. Kennedy, M. Keppell, C. McNaught, & T. Petrovic (Eds.), *Meeting at the crossroads: Proceedings of the 18th annual conference of the Australian society for computers in learning in tertiary education,* 539–548. Melbourne: Biomedical Multimedia Unit, University of Melbourne.

Van Gelder, T. J. (2002). Argument mapping with Reason!Able. *APA Newsletter: Philosophy & Computers, 2,* 1, 85–90.

Van Gelder, T. J. (2007). The rationale for Rationale™. *Law, Probability & Risk, 6,* 23–42.

Van Gelder, T. J., Bissett, M., & Cumming, G. (2004). Enhancing expertise in informal reasoning. *Canadian Journal of Experimental Psychology, 58,* 142–152.

Van Merriënboer, J. J. G. & Ayres, P. (2005). Research on cognitive load theory and its design implications for e-learning, educational technology, research and development. *Educational Technology Research and Development, 53,* 3, 5–13.

Van Merriënboer, J. J. G., Kirschner, P. A., & Kester, L. (2003). Taking the load off a learner's mind: Instructional design for complex learning. *Educational Psychology, 38,* 5–13.

Varian, H. & Lyman, P. (2003). *How much information?* Berkeley, CA: School of Information Management & Systems, UC Berkeley.

Venn, J. (1881). *Symbolic logic.* London: Macmillan and Company.

Vohs, K. D., Baumeister, R. F., & Ciarocco, N. J. (2005). Self-regulation and self-presentation: Regulatory resource depletion impairs impression management and effortful self-presentation depletes regulatory resources. *Journal of Personality and Social Psychology, 88,* 4, 632.

Vohs, K. D., Baumeister, R. F., Schmeichel, B. J., Twenge, J. M., Nelson, N. M., & Tice, D. M. (2014). Making choices impairs subsequent self-control: A limited-resource account of decision making, self-regulation, and active initiative. *Personality Processes and Individual Differences, 94,* 5, 883–898.

Vohs, K. D. & Faber, R. J. (2007). Spent resources: Self-regulatory resource availability affects impulse buying. *Journal of Consumer Research, 33,* 4, 537–547.

Vohs, K. D. & Heatherton, T. F. (2000). Self-regulatory failure: A resource-depletion approach. *Psychological Science, 11,* 249–254.

Vygotsky, L. S. (1978). *Mind and society: The development of higher psychological processes.* Cambridge, MA: Harvard University Press.

Walton, D. N. (2006). *Fundamentals of critical argumentation.* Cambridge: Cambridge University Press.

Wankat, P. (2002). *The effective, efficient professor: Teaching, scholarship and service.* Boston: Allyn and Bacon.

Watson, G. & Glaser, E. M. (1980). *Watson-Glaser critical thinking appraisal.* New York: Psychological Corporation.

Watson, G. & Glaser, E. M. (1994). *Watson-Glaser critical thinking appraisal: Form S manual.* San Antonio, TX: Psychological Corporation.

Weber, E. U. & Johnson, E. J. (2009). Mindful judgment and decision making. *Annual Review of Psychology, 60,* 53–85.

Wegerif, R. (2002). *Literature review in thinking skills, technology and learning: Report 2.* Bristol: NESTA Futurelab.

Wegerif, R. & Dawes, L. (2004). *Thinking and learning with ICT: Raising achievement in the primary classroom.* London: Routledge.

Weinberger, J. & McClelland, D. C. (1991). Cognitive versus traditional motivational models: Irreconcilable or complementary? In E. T. Higgins & R. M. Sorrentino (Eds.), *Handbook of motivation and cognition, 2,* 562–597. New York: Guilford Press.

Weinert, F. E. (1987). Introduction and overview: Metacognition and motivation as determinants of effective learning and understanding. In F. E. Weinert & R. H. Kluwe (Eds.), *Metacognition, motivation and understanding, 1–18.* Hillsdale, NJ: Erlbaum.

West, R. F., Toplak, M. E., & Stanovich, K. E. (2008). Heuristics and biases as measures of critical thinking: Associations with cognitive ability and thinking dispositions. *Journal of Educational Psychology, 100,* 4, 930–941.

Whately, R. (1826). *Elements of Logic.* London: Fellowes.

Wheeler, L. & Collins, S. (2003). The influence of concept mapping on critical thinking skills in baccalaureate nursing students. *Journal of Professional Nursing, 19,* 6, 339–346.

Willingham, D. T. (2007). Critical thinking: Why is it so hard to teach? *American Educator, 31,* 3, 8–19.

Wilson, B. A. & Baddeley, A. D. (1988). Semantic, episodic and autobiographical memory in a post-meningitic amnesic patient. *Brain Cognition, 8,* 31–46.

Wittrock, M. C. (1986). Students' thought processes. In M. C. Wittrock (Ed.), *Handbook of research on teaching* (3rd ed.). New York: Macmillan.

Wood, D. J., Bruner, J. S., & Ross, G. (1976). The role of tutoring in problem solving. *Journal of Child Psychology and Psychiatry, 17,* 89–100.

Wood, P. K. (1993). *Context and development of reflective thinking: A secondary analysis of the structure of individual differences.* Unpublished manuscript. Missouri: University of Missouri at Columbia.

Wood, R. (1977). Multiple choice: A state of the art report. *Evaluation in Education, 1,* 191–280.

Woodman, G. F., Vecera, S. P., & Luck, S. J. (2003). Perceptual organization influences visual working memory. *Psychonomic Bulletin & Review, 10,* 1, 80–87.

Yang, Y.-T. C. (2002). *Use of structured web-based bulletin board discussions with Socratic questioning to enhance students' critical thinking skills in distance education.* Unpublished Doctoral Thesis. Purdue University, West Lafayette.

Zimmerman, B. J. (1989). Models of self-regulated learning and academic achievement. In B. J. Zimmerman & D. H. Schunk (Eds.), *Self-regulated learning and academic achievement: Theory research and practice,* 1–25. New York: Springer-Verlag.

INDEX

Made in United States
North Haven, CT
24 November 2023

44491676R00168